Fror

D0201230

Spanish PhraseFinder & Dictionary

2nd Edition

WILEY
Wiley Publishing, Inc.

Published by:

Wiley Publishing, Inc.

111 River St.
Hoboken, NJ 07030-5774

ISBN-13: 978-0-470-93650-4

Spanish Editor: Neil Schlecht
Series Editor: Jessica Langan-Peck
Photo Editor: Richard H. Fox
Cover design by Paul Dinovo

Translation, Copyediting, Proofreading, Production, and Layout by:
Lingo Systems, 15115 SW Sequoia Pkwy, Ste. 200
Portland, OR 97224

For information on our other products and services or to obtain technical support, please
contact our Customer Care Department within the U.S. at 800/762-2974, outside the U.S. at
317/572-3993 or fax 317/572-4002.

Wiley also publishes its books in a variety of electronic formats. Some content that appears
in print may not be available in electronic formats.

Manufactured in the United States of America

5 4 3 2 1

Contents

An Invitation to the Reader

In researching this book, we discovered many wonderful sayings and terms useful to travelers in Spain or Latin America. We're sure you'll find others. Please tell us about them, so we can share the information with your fellow travelers in upcoming editions. If you were disappointed with an aspect of this book, we'd like to know that, too. Please write to:

Frommer's Spanish PhraseFinder & Dictionary, 2nd Edition
Wiley Publishing, Inc.
111 River St. • Hoboken, NJ 07030-5774

An Additional Note

The packager, editors, and publisher cannot be held responsible for the experiences of readers while traveling. Your safety is important to us, however, so we encourage you to stay alert and be aware of your surroundings. Keep a close eye on cameras, purses, and wallets, all favorite targets of thieves and pickpockets.

Frommers.com

Now that you have the language for a great trip, visit our website at **www.frommers.com** for travel information on more than 3,000 destinations. With features updated regularly, we give you instant access to the most current trip-planning information available. At Frommers.com, you'll also find the best prices on airfares, accommodations, and car rentals—and you can even book travel online through our travel booking partners. At Frommers.com, you'll also find:

- Online updates to our most popular guidebooks

- Vacation sweepstakes and contest giveaways

- Newsletter highlighting the hottest travel trends

- Online travel message boards with featured travel
  discussions

INTRODUCTION: HOW TO USE THIS BOOK

As a Romance language, Spanish is closely related to Latin, French, Italian, Portuguese, and Romanian. But not one of these European tongues is used with half the frequency of Spanish—with more than 332 million speakers, including more than 23 million in the United States. Variations spoken by Mexicans, Spaniards, Ecuadorians, Puerto Ricans, and other Latino ethnic groups are considerable. For simplicity's sake, we have used a universal form of Latin American Spanish throughout this book. But a native Spaniard has reviewed our translations, noting where they're radically different from what is spoken in Spain.

Our intention is not to teach you Spanish; we figure you'll find an audio program for that. Our aim is to provide a portable travel tool that's easy to use. With most phrasebooks, you practically have to memorize the contents before you know where to look for a term on the spot. This phrasebook is designed for fingertip referencing, to help you find the language you need fast.

Part of this book organizes terms by chapters, as in a Frommer's guide—getting a room, getting a good meal, etc. Within those sections, we tried to organize phrases according to how frequently readers are likely to use them. But let's say you're in a cab and received the wrong change, and don't know where to look in the money chapter. With Frommer's PhraseFinder, you can quickly look up "change" in the dictionary, and learn how to say "Sorry, but this isn't the right change." Then you can follow the cross reference for numbers, and specify how much you're missing.

What will make this book most practical? What will make it easiest to use? These are the questions we asked ourselves as we assembled these travel terms.

Our immediate goal was to create a phrasebook as indispensable as your passport. Our far-ranging goal, of course, is to enrich your experience of travel. And with that we offer the following wish: *¡Que tenga un buen viaje!*

CHAPTER ONE

SURVIVAL SPANISH

If you tire of toting around this phrasebook, tear out this chapter. You should be able to navigate your destination with only the terms found in the next 35 pages.

BASIC GREETINGS

For a full list of greetings, see p111.

Hello.	**Hola.**
	OH-lah
How are you?	**¿Cómo está?**
	KOH-moh ehs-TAH
I'm fine, thanks.	**Estoy bien, gracias.**
	ehs-TOY BYEHN, GRAH-syahs
And you?	**¿Y usted?**
	ee oos-TEHD
My name is ____.	**Me llamo ____.**
	meh YAH-mo
And yours?	**¿Y usted?**
	ee oos-TEHD
It's a pleasure to meet you.	**Es un placer conocerle.**
	EHS oon plah-SEHR koh-noh-SEHR-leh
Please.	**Por favor.**
	pohr fah-VOHR
Thank you.	**Gracias.**
	GRAH-syahs
Yes.	**Sí.**
	see
No.	**No.**
	noh

1

Okay.	**De acuerdo.**
	deh ah-KWEHR-doh
	Okay.
	OH-keh
No problem.	**No hay problema.**
	noh aye proh-BLEH-mah
I'm sorry, I don't understand.	**Lo siento, no entiendo.**
	loh SYEHN-toh no ehn-TYEHN-doh
Would you speak slower please?	**¿Puede hablar un poco más lento?**
	PWEH-deh ah-BLAHR oon POH-koh mahs LEHN-to
Would you speak louder please?	**¿Puede hablar un poco más alto?**
	PWEH-deh ah-BLAHR oon POH-koh mahs AHL-toh
Do you speak English?	**¿Usted habla inglés?**
	oos-TEHD AH-blah eeng-GLEHS
Do you speak any other languages?	**¿Usted habla otro idioma?**
	oos-TEHD AH-blah OH-troh ee-DYOH-ma
I speak ____ better than Spanish.	**Yo hablo ____ mejor que español.**
	yoh AH-bloh ____ meh-HOHR keh ehs-pah-NYOL
Would you spell that?	**¿Puede deletrear eso?**
	PWEH-de deh-leh-treh-AHR EH-so
Would you please repeat that?	**¿Puede repetir, por favor?**
	PWEH-deh rreh-peh-TEER pohr fah-VOHR
Would you point that out in this dictionary?	**¿Puede señalarlo en este diccionario?**
	PWEH-deh seh-nyah-LAHR-loh ehn EHS-deh deek-syoh-NAHR-yoh

THE KEY QUESTIONS

With the right hand gestures, you can get a lot of mileage from the following list of single-word questions and answers.

Who?	**¿Quién? ¿Quiénes?**
	KYEHN? KYEH-nehs?
What?	**¿Qué?**
	KEH
When?	**¿Cuándo?**
	KWAHN-doh
Where?	**¿Dónde?**
	DOHN-deh
To where?	**¿Adónde?**
	ah-DOHN-deh
Why?	**¿Por qué?**
	pohr-KEH
How?	**¿Cómo?**
	KOH-moh
Which?	**¿Cuál?**
	KWAHL
How many? / How much?	**¿Cuánto? ¿Cuántos?**
	KWAHN-toh, KWAHN-tohs

THE ANSWERS: WHO

For full coverage of pronouns, see p21.

I	**yo**
	yoh
you	**usted / tú**
	oos-TEHD, too
him	**él**
	ehl
her	**ella**
	EH-yah
us	**nosotros**
	noh-SOH-trohs
them	**ellos / ellas**
	EH-yohs, EH-yahs

THE ANSWERS: WHEN

For full coverage of time, see p12.

now	**ahora** *ah-OH-rah*
later	**después** *dehs-PWEHS*
afterwards	**después** *dehs-PWEHS*
earlier	**antes** *AN-tehs*
in a minute	**en un minuto** *ehn oon mee-NOO-toh*
today	**hoy** *oy*
tomorrow	**mañana** *mah-NYAH-nah*
yesterday	**ayer** *ah-YEHR*
in a week	**en una semana** *ehn oo-nah seh-MAH-nah*
next week	**la próxima semana** *lah PROHK-see-mah seh-MAH-nah*
last week	**la semana pasada** *lah seh-MAH-nah pah-SAH-dah*
next month	**el próximo mes** *ehl PROHK-see-moh MEHS*
At _____	**A las _____** *ah lahs*
ten o'clock this morning.	**diez en punto esta mañana.** *DYEHS ehn POON-toh EHS-tah mah-NYAH-nah*
two o'clock this afternoon.	**dos en punto esta tarde.** *dohs ehn POON-toh EHS-tah TAHR-deh*
seven o'clock this evening.	**siete en punto esta noche.** *SYEH-teh ehn POON-toh EHS-tah NOH-cheh*

For full coverage of numbers, see p7.

THE ANSWERS: WHERE

here	**aquí / acá**
	ah-KEE, ah-KAH
there	**allá / allí**
	ah-YAH, ah-YEE
near	**cerca**
	SEHR-kah
closer	**más cerca**
	mahs SEHR-kah
closest	**lo más cerca**
	loh MAHS SEHR-kah
far	**lejos**
	LEH-hohs
farther	**más lejos**
	mahs LEH-hohs
farthest	**lo más lejos**
	loh MAHS LEH-hohs
across from	**enfrente de**
	ehn-FREHN-teh deh
next to	**al lado de**
	ahl LAH-doh deh
behind	**detrás de**
	deh-TRAHS deh
straight ahead	**adelante / todo recto**
	ah-deh-LAHN-teh / TOH-doh REK-toh
left	**la izquierda**
	lah ees-KYEHR-dah
right	**la derecha**
	lah deh-REH-chah
up	**arriba**
	ah-RREE-bah
down	**abajo**
	ah-BAH-hoh
lower	**más abajo**
	mahs ah-BAH-hoh
higher	**más arriba**
	mahs ah-RREE-bah

forward	**hacia delante**
	AH-syah deh-LAHN-teh
back	**hacia atrás**
	AH-syah ah-TRAHS
around	**alrededor**
	ahl-reh-deh-DOHR
across the street	**al cruzar la calle**
	ahl kroo-SAHR lah KAH-yeh
down the street	**calle abajo**
	KAH-yeh ah-BAH-hoh
on the corner	**en la esquina**
	ehn lah ehs-KEE-nah
kitty-corner	**la esquina diagonal**
	lah ehs-KEE-nah dee-ah-goh-NAHL
____ blocks from here	**a ____ cuadras de aquí**
	ah ____ KWAH-drahs deh ah-KEE

For a full list of numbers, see the next page

THE ANSWERS: WHICH

this one	**éste / ésta**
	EH-steh, EH-stah
that (that one, close by)	**ese / esa**
	EH-seh, EH-sah
(that one, in the distance)	**aquel / aquella**
	ah-KEHL, ah-KEH-yah
these	**estos / estas**
	EHS-tohs, EHS-tahs
those (those there, close by)	**esos / esas**
	EH-sohs, EH-sahs

HELP / EMERGENCIES

Can you help me?	**¿Me puede ayudar?**
	Meh PWEH-deh a-YOO-dahr?
I'm lost.	**Estoy perdido -a.**
	ehs-TOY per-DEE-doh / per-DEE-dah
Help!	**¡Ayuda!**
	A YOO DAH!

Call the police!	**¡Llame a la policía!**
	YAH-meh ah lah poh-lee-SEE-ah [in Spain, use *poh-lee-THEE-ah*]
I need a doctor.	**Necesito un médico.**
	Neh-seh-SEE-toh oon MEH-dee-koh
Thief!	**¡Ladrón!**
	lah-DROHN!
My child is missing.	**Mi hijo / hija se ha perdido.**
	Mee EE-hoh / EE-hah seh ah per-DEE-doh
Call an ambulance.	**Llame a una ambulancia.**
	Yah-meh ah oo-nah am-boo-LAN-see-ah

NUMBERS & COUNTING

one	**uno**	thirteen	**trece**
	OO-noh		*TREH-seh*
two	**dos**	fourteen	**catorce**
	dohs		*kah-TOHR-seh*
three	**tres**	fifteen	**quince**
	trehs		*KEEN-seh*
four	**cuatro**	sixteen	**dieciséis**
	KWAH-troh		*dyeh-see-*
five	**cinco**		*SEH-ees*
	SEENG-koh	seventeen	**diecisiete**
six	**seis**		*dyeh-see-*
	SEH-ees		*SYEH-teh*
seven	**siete**	eighteen	**dieciocho**
	SYEH-teh		*dyeh-SYOH-*
eight	**ocho**		*choh*
	OH-cho	nineteen	**diecinueve**
nine	**nueve**		*dyeh-see-*
	NWEH-veh		*NWEH-veh*
ten	**diez**	twenty	**veinte**
	dyehs		*VEH-een-teh*
eleven	**once**	twenty-one	**veintiuno**
	OHN-seh		*veh-een-*
twelve	**doce**		*tee-OO-noh*
	DOH-seh		

thirty	**treinta**	eighty	**ochenta**
	TREH-een-tah		*o-CHEHN-tah*
forty	**cuarenta**	ninety	**noventa**
	kwah-REN-tah		*noh-VEHN-tah*
fifty	**cincuenta**	one hundred	**cien**
	seen-KWEHN-tah		*syehn*
sixty	**sesenta**	two hundred	**doscientos**
	seh-SEHN-tah		*dohs-SYEHN tohs*
seventy	**setenta**	one thousand	**mil**
	seh-TEHN-tah		*meel*

FRACTIONS & DECIMALS

one eighth	**un octavo**
	oon ohk-TAH-voh
one quarter	**un cuarto**
	oon KWAHR-toh
one third	**un tercio**
	oon TEHR-syoh
one half	**medio**
	MEH-dyoh
two thirds	**dos tercios**
	dohs TEHR-syohs
three quarters	**tres cuartos**
	trehs KWAHR-tohs
double	**doble**
	DOH-bleh
triple	**triple**
	TREE-pleh
one tenth	**un décimo**
	oon DEH-see-moh
one hundredth	**un centésimo**
	oon sehn-TEH-see-moh
one thousandth	**un milésimo**
	oon mee-LEH-see-moh

MATH

addition	**suma**
	SOO-mah
2 +1	**dos más uno**
	dohs mahs OO-noh
subtraction	**resta**
	RREHS-tah
2 - 1	**dos menos uno**
	dohs MEH-nohs OO-noh
multiplication	**multiplicación**
	mool-tee-plee-kah-SYOHN
2 x 3	**dos por tres**
	dohs pohr trehs
division	**división**
	dee-vee-SYOHN
6 ÷ 3	**Seis dividido tres**
	SEH-ees dee-vee-DEE-doh TREHS

ORDINAL NUMBERS

first	**primero -a**
	pree-MEH-roh / pree-MEH-rah
second	**segundo -a**
	seh-GOON-doh / seh-GOON-dah
third	**tercero -a**
	tehr-SEH-roh / tehr-SEH-rah
fourth	**cuarto -a**
	KWAHR-toh / KWAHR-tah
fifth	**quinto -a**
	KEEN-toh / KEEN-tah
sixth	**sexto -a**
	SEHK-sto / SEHK-stah
seventh	**séptimo -a**
	SEHP-tee-moh / SEHP-tee-mah
eighth	**octavo -a**
	ohk-TAH-voh / ohk-TAH-vah

ninth	**noveno -a** *noh-VEH-noh / noh-VEH-nah*
tenth	**décimo -a** *DEH-see-moh / DEH-see-mah*
last	**último -a** *OOL-tee-mo / OOL-tee-mah*

MEASUREMENTS

Measurements will usually be metric, though you may need a few American measurement terms.

inch	**pulgada** *pool-GAH-dah*
foot	**pie** *PYEH*
mile	**milla** *MEE-yah*
millimeter	**milímetro** *mee-LEE-meh-troh*
centimeter	**centímetro** *sehn-TEE-meh-troh*
meter	**metro** *MEH-troh*
kilometer	**kilómetro** *kee-LOH-meh-troh*
hectare	**hectárea** *hehk-TAH-reh-ahs*
squared	**cuadrado -a** *kwah-DRAH-doh / kwah-DRAH-dah*
short	**corto -a** *KOHR-toh / KOHR-tah*
long	**largo -a** *LAHR-goh / LAHR-gah*

VOLUME

milliliters	**mililitros** *mee-lee-LEE-trohs*
liter	**litro** *LEE-troh*

kilo	**kilo**
	KEE-loh
gram	**gramo**
	GRAH-moh
cup	**taza**
	TAH-sah
pint	**pinta**
	PEEN-tah
quart	**cuarto (de galón)**
	KWAHR-toh deh gah-LOHN
gallon	**galón**
	gah-LOHN

QUANTITY

some	**algún -a / algunos -as**
	ahl-GOON / ahl-GOO-nah /
	ahl-GOO-nohs / ahl-GOO-nahs
none	**nada / ninguno -a / ningunos -as**
	NAH-dah / neeng-GOO-noh /
	neeng-GOO-nah / neeng-GOO-
	nohs / neeng-GOO-nahs
all	**todo -a / todos -as**
	TOH-doh / TOH-dah / TOH-dohs /
	TOH-dahs
many / much	**mucho -a / muchos -as**
	MOO-cho / MOO-cha / MOO-chohs
	/ MOO-chas
a little bit (can be used for	**un poco**
quantity or for time)	*oon POH-koh*
dozen	**docena**
	doh-SEH-na

SIZE

small	**pequeño -a**
	peh-KEH-nyoh / peh-KEH-nyah
the smallest (literally "the	**el / la / lo más pequeño -a**
most small")	*ehl / lah / loh mahs peh-KEH-*
	nyoh / peh-KEH-nyah

medium	**mediano -a**
	meh-DYAH-no / meh-DYAH-na
big	**grande**
	GRAHN-deh
fat	**gordo -a**
	GOHR-doh / GOHR-dah
wide	**ancho -a**
	AHN-cho / AHN-cha
narrow	**angosto -a / estrecho -a**
	ahng-GOH-stoh / ahng-GOH-stah
	ehs-TREH-choh / ehs-TREH-chah

TIME

Time in Spanish is referred to, literally, by the hour. What time is it? translates literally as "What hour is it? / What hours are they?"
For full coverage of number terms, see p7.

HOURS OF THE DAY

What time is it?	**¿Qué hora es?**
	KEH OH-ra ehs
At what time?	**¿A qué hora?**
	ah KEH OH-rah
For how long?	**¿Por cuánto tiempo?**
	pohr KWAHN-toh TYEHM-poh
It's one o'clock.	**Es la una en punto.**
	ehs lah oo-nah ehn POON-toh
It's two o'clock.	**Son las dos en punto.**
	sohn lahs DOHS ehn POON-toh

A little tip

By adding a diminutive suffix -ito / -ita, -ico / -ica, or a combination of the two, you can make anything smaller or shorter. These endings replace the original -o and -a.

advice, tip	**consejo** (*kohn-SEH-hoh*)
a little tip	**consejito** (*kohn-seh-HEE-toh*)

It's two thirty.	**Son las dos y media.** *sohn lahs DOHS ee MEH-dyah*
It's two fifteen.	**Son las dos y cuarto.** *sohn lahs DOHS ee KWAHR-toh*
It's a quarter to three.	**Son las tres menos cuarto.** *sohn las TREHS MEH-nohs* *KWAHR-toh* **Falta un cuarto para las tres.** *FAHL-tah oon KWAHR-toh pah-rah* *lahs trehs*
It's noon.	**Es mediodía.** *ehs MEH-dyoh DEE-ah*
It's midnight.	**Es medianoche.** *ehs meh-dyah-NOH-cheh*
It's early.	**Es temprano.** *ehs tehm-PRAH-noh*
It's late.	**Es tarde.** *ehs TAHR-deh*
in the morning	**de la mañana** *deh lah mah-NYAH-nah*
in the afternoon	**de la tarde** *deh lah TAHR-deh*
at night	**de la noche** *deh lah NOH-cheh*
dawn	**la madrugada** *lah mah-droo-GAH-dah*

DAYS OF THE WEEK

Sunday	**domingo** *doh-MEENG-go*
Monday	**lunes** *LOO-nehs*
Tuesday	**martes** *MAHR-tehs*
Wednesday	**miércoles** *MYEHR-koh-lehs*

Thursday	**jueves**
	HWEH-vehs
Friday	**viernes**
	VYEHR-nehs
Saturday	**sábado**
	SAH-bah-doh
today	**hoy**
	oy
tomorrow	**mañana**
	mah-NYAH-nah
yesterday	**ayer**
	ah-YEHR
the day before yesterday	**anteayer**
	ahn-teh-ah-YEHR
one week	**una semana**
	oo-nah seh-MAH-nah
next week	**la próxima semana**
	lah PROHK-see-mah seh-MAH-nah
last week	**la semana pasada**
	lah seh-MAH-nah pah-SAH-dah

MONTHS OF THE YEAR

January	**enero**
	eh-NEH-roh
February	**febrero**
	feh-BREH-roh
March	**marzo**
	MAHR-soh
April	**abril**
	ah-BREEL
May	**mayo**
	MAH-yoh
June	**junio**
	HOO-nee-oh
July	**julio**
	HOO-lee-oh

August	**agosto**
	ah-GOHS-toh
September	**septiembre**
	sehp-TYEHM-breh
October	**octubre**
	ohk-TOO-breh
November	**noviembre**
	noh-VYEHM-breh
December	**diciembre**
	dee-SYEHM-breh
next month	**el mes entrante**
	ehl MEHS ehn-TRAHN-teh
	el próximo mes
	ehl PROHK-see-moh MEHS
last month	**el mes pasado**
	ehl MEHS pah-SAH-doh

SEASONS OF THE YEAR

spring	**la primavera**
	lah pree-mah-VEH-rah
summer	**el verano**
	ehl veh-RAH-noh
autumn	**el otoño**
	ehl oh-TOH-nyoh
winter	**el invierno**
	ehl een-VYEHR-noh

WEATHER

What's the weather like?	**¿Qué tiempo hace?**
	KEH TYEHM-poh AH-seh?
What's the temperature?	**¿Qué temperatura hace?**
	KEH tem-peh-rah-TOO-rah
	AH-seh?
What's the forecast?	**¿Cómo viene el tiempo?**
	KOH-moh bee-EH-neh ehl tee-
	EM-poh?

Falsos amigos

If you try winging it with Spanglish, beware of false cognates, known as falsos amigos, "false friends"—Spanish words that sound like English ones, but with different meanings. Here are some of the most commonly confused terms.

suburbio	slum
barrio	suburb
bomba	pump / tank / bomb
explosivo	bomb
arma	weapon
brazo	arm
constipado -a	congested
estreñido -a	constipated
embarazada	pregnant
avergonzado -a	embarrassed
injuria	insult
herida	injury
parientes	relatives
padres	parents
largo	long
grande	large
actual	now, current
verdadero -a	actual
asistir	to attend
ayudar	to assist
sopa	soup
jabón	soap
ropa	clothing
ropa vieja (lit. old clothes)	delicious Cuban dish of stewed, shredded beef
cuerda	rope

SPANISH GRAMMAR BASICS

Classified as a Romance language, descended from the Latin spoken when Spain was part of the Roman Empire, Spanish is a linguistic amalgamation closely related to Latin, French, Italian, Portuguese, and Romanian. Spanish was strongly influenced by the Arabic of Spain's Moorish conquerors, who occupied the country from A.D. 711 to 1492. When Spain conquered what is today Latin America, it imposed its language on millions of Native Americans, from the Caribbean to Tierra del Fuego. But the indigenous languages they spoke, in turn, affected the local spoken Spanish, accounting for some of the rich diversity of the language.

THE ALPHABET

Spanish is a straightforward language with a simple alphabet. If foreign letters (k and w) are counted, the alphabet has 27 letters (ñ, in addition to the English alphabet).

Spanish also has two double letters: ll (elle), pronounced like y in English "yes," and rr (erre), pronounced like an English r trilled by vibrating the end of the tongue against the hard palate, just above the upper teeth. There is also ch, as in chipmunk.

Letter	Name	Pronunciation of Letter Name
a	a	*ah*
b	be	*beh*
c	ce	*seh*
d	de	*deh*
e	e	*eh*
f	efe	*EH-feh*
g	ge	*heh*
h	hache	*AH-cheh*
i	i	*ee*
j	jota	*HOH-tah*
k	ka	*kah*
l	ele	*EH-leh*
m	eme	*EH-meh*
n	ene	*EH-neh*

Letter	Name	Pronunciation of Letter Name
ñ	eñe	*EH-nyeh*
o	o	*oh*
p	pe	*peh*
q	cu	*koo*
r	ere	*EH-reh*
s	ese	*EH-seh*
t	te	*teh*
u	u	*oo*
v	ve, uve	*veh*
w	doble u, ve doble	*DOH-bleh oo, veh DOH-bleh*
x	equis	*EH-kees*
y	i griega	*ee GRYEH-gah*
z	seta	*SEH-tah*

PRONUNCIATION GUIDE

Vowels

a	ah as the a in father: abajo *(ah BAH hoh)*
au	ow as in cow: automático *(ow-to-MAH-tee-koh)*
ay	aye as in "All in favor, say aye": hay *(aye)*
e	eh to rhyme with the e in nestle: espera *(ehs PEH rah)*
i	ee as in feed: pasillo *(pah SEE yoh)*
o	oh as in boat: modismo *(moh DEES moh)*
oy	oy as in boy: hoy *(oy)*
u	oo as in the word coo: buscar *(boos KAHR)*

Consonants

b	as in bean, but softer with less explosion than in English: buscar *(boos-KAHR)*
c	before e and i as English initial s; ce is pronounced as seh: necesito *(neh seh SEE toh)*; ci is pronounced as see: cinco *(SEENG-koh)*; before a, o, u as English k, but softer with less explosion: caballero *(kah bah YEH roh)*; consejo *(kohn SEH hoh)*; Cuba *(KOO bah)*

cu	in combination with a, e, i, o pronounced like the qu in quick: cuándo *(KWAHN doh)*; cuestión *(kwehs TYOHN)*
d	as the d in day, but softer with less explosion than in English. Some final ds can be pronounced as the d in the: usted *(oo-STEHTH)*. If you pronounce Spanish d like the English d, you will be understood: ciudad *(see-oo-DAHD)*; de *(deh)*
f	as in fox: favor *(fah-VOHR)*
g	before e and i as English h; ge is pronounced like he in hen: emergencia *(eh-mehr-HEHN-syah)*; gi is pronounced like English he: puerta giratoria *(PWEHR-tah hee-rah-TOHR-yah)*
	before a, o, u as initial hard g in English as in gate: llegar *(yeh GAHR)*; tengo *(TEHN-goh)*; seguridad *(seh-goo-ree-DAHD)*
h	silent; hizo *(EE-soh)*, hasta *(AHS-tah)*; hi before a vowel is pronounced like English y: hielo *(YEH-loh)*
j	as English h in hot: equipaje *(eh-kee-PAH-heh)*
k	as in English: kilómetro *(kee-LOH-meh-troh)*
l	as in English: ala *(AH-lah)*
ll	as the initial y in yeah: llegada *(yeh-GAH-dah)*
m	as in English: mesa *(MEH-sah)*
n	as in English: negocios *(neh-GOH-syohs)*
ñ	as ny in canyon: cañón *(kah-NYOHN)*
p	as in English but softer: pasaporte *(pah-sah-POHR-teh)*
q	qu is pronounced as k: máquina *(MAH-kee-nah)*
r	as in English but more clipped: puerta *(PWEHR-tah)*
rr	as a trilled r sound, vibrating the end of the tongue against the area just above the top teeth: perro *(PEH-rroh)*. A single r that starts a word is pronounced like the double r: rayos X *(RRAH-yohs EH-kees)*
s	as in English: salida *(sah-LEE-dah)*

t	as in English but softer: tranvía *(trahn-VEE-ah)*
v	as in English: vuelo *(VWEH-loh)*
w	as in English: waflera *(wah-FLEH-rah)*
x	like English x: próximo *(PROHK-see-moh)*; in some old names and some names of Native American origin, like h: Don Quixote *(dohn kee HOH teh)*, México *(MEH-hee-koh)* spelled with j in Spain; before a consonant, like s: Taxco *(TAHS-koh)*
y	as in English: yo *(yoh)*; by itself, as the ee sound in bead: y *(ee)*
z	like English s: aterrizaje *(ah-teh-rree-SAH-heh)*

WORD PRONUNCIATION

Syllables in words are also accented in a standard pattern. Generally, the last syllable is stressed except when a word ends in a vowel, n, or s; then the stress falls on the second to last syllable. If a word varies from this pattern, an accent mark is shown.

Examples:

Ending in r

comer   *koh-MEHR*

Ending in a

comida   *koh-MEE-dah*

Ending in s

comemos   *koh-MEH-mohs*

Ending in n but with an accent mark

comilón   *koh-mee-LOHN*

GENDER, ADJECTIVES, MODIFIERS

Each noun takes a masculine or feminine gender, most often accompanied by a masculine or feminine definite article (el or la). Definite articles ("the"), indefinite articles ("a," "an"), and related adjectives must also be masculine or feminine, singular or plural, depending on the noun they're modifying.

The Definite Article ("The")

	Masculine	Feminine
Singular	el **perro** (the dog)	la **mesa** (the table)
Plural	los **perros** (the dogs)	las **mesas** (the tables)

The Indefinite Article ("A" or "An")

	Masculine	Feminine
Singular	un **perro** (a dog)	una **mesa** (a table)
Plural	unos **perros** (some dogs)	unas **mesas** (some tables)

PERSONAL PRONOUNS

AMAR: "To Love"		
I love.	Yo amo.	**AH-moh**
You (singular familiar) **love.**	Tú amas.	**AH-mahs**
He / She loves. You (singular, formal) **love.**	Él / Ella / Ud. ama.	**AH-mah**
We love.	Nosotros -as amamos.	**ah-MAH-mohs**
You (plural, familiar) **love.**	Vosotros -as amáis.	**ah-MAH-ees**
They / You (plural, formal) **love.**	Ellos / Ellas / Uds. aman.	**AH-mahn**

Hey, You!

Spanish has two words for "you"—tú, spoken among friends and familiars, and Usted (abbreviated Ud. or Vd.), used among strangers or as a sign of respect toward elders and authority figures. When speaking with a stranger, expect to use Usted, unless you are invited to do otherwise. The second-person familiar plural form (vosotros) is rarely used, and then only in Spain and Chile. Ustedes (abbreviated Uds. or Vds.) is used instead, even among friends, especially in Latin America.

REGULAR VERB CONJUGATIONS

Spanish verb infinitives end in AR (hablar, to speak), ER (comer, to eat), or IR (asistir, to attend). Most verbs (known as "regular verbs") are conjugated according to those endings. To conjugate the present tense of regular verbs, simply drop the AR, ER, or IR and add the following endings:

Present Tense

AR Verbs

	HABLAR "To Speak"	
I speak.	Yo hablo.	AH-bloh
You (singular familiar) speak.	Tú hablas.	AH-blahs
He / She speaks. You (singular formal) speak.	Él / Ella / Ud. habla.	AH-blah
We speak.	Nosotros -as hablamos.	ah-BLAH-mohs
You (plural familiar) speak.	Vosotros -as habláis.	ah-BLAH-ees
They / You (plural formal) speak.	Ellos / Ellas / Uds. hablan.	AH-blahn

ER Verbs — COMER "To Eat"

ER Verbs	COMER "To Eat"	
I eat.	Yo como.	KOH-moh
You (singular familiar) eat.	Tú comes.	KOH-mehs
He / She eats. You (singular formal) eat.	Él / Ella / Ud. come.	KOH-meh
We eat.	Nosotros -as comemos.	koh-MEH-mohs
You (plural familiar) eat.	Vosotros -as coméis.	koh-MEH-ees
They / You (plural formal) eat.	Ellos / Ellas / Uds. comen.	KOH-mehn

IR Verbs — ASISTIR "To Attend"

IR Verbs	ASISTIR "To Attend"	
I attend.	Yo asisto.	ah-SEES-toh
You (singular familiar) attend.	Tú asistes.	ah-SEES-tehs
He / She attends. You (singular formal) attend.	Él / Ella / Ud. asiste.	ah-SEES-teh
We attend.	Nosotros -as asistimos.	ah-sees-TEE-mohs
You (plural familiar) attend.	Vosotros -as asistís.	ah-sees-TEES
They / You (plural formal) attend.	Ellos / Ellas / Uds. asisten.	ah-SEES-tehn

Simple Past Tense

These are the simple past tense conjugations for regular verbs.

AR Verbs	HABLAR "To Speak"	
I spoke.	Yo hablé.	ah-BLEH
You (singular familiar) spoke.	Tú hablaste.	ah-BLAHS-teh
He / She/ You (singular formal) spoke.	Él / Ella / Ud. habló.	ah-BLOH
We spoke.	Nosotros -as hablamos.	ah-BLAH-mohs
You (plural familiar) spoke.	Vosotros -as hablasteis.	ah-BLAHS-teh-ees
They / You (plural formal) spoke.	Ellos / Ellas / Uds. hablaron.	ah-BLAH-rohn

ER Verbs	COMER "To Eat"	
I ate.	Yo comí.	koh-MEE
You (singular familiar) ate.	Tú comiste.	koh-MEES-teh
He / She / You singular formal) ate.	Él / Ella / Ud. comió.	koh-mee-OH
We ate.	Nosotros -as comimos.	koh-MEE-mohs
You (plural familiar) ate.	Vosotros -as comisteis.	koh-MEES-teh-ees
They / You (plural formal) ate.	Ellos / Ellas / Uds. comieron.	koh-MYEH-rohn

IR Verbs	ASISTIR "To Attend"	
I attended.	Yo asistí.	ah-sees-TEE
You (singular familiar) attended.	Tú asististe.	ah-sees-TEES-teh
He / She / You (singular formal) attended.	Él / Ella / Ud. asistió.	ah-sees-TYOH
We attended.	Nosotros -as asistimos.	ah-sees-TEE-mohs
You plural familiar) attended.	Vosotros -as asististeis.	ah-sees-TEES-teh-ees
They / You (plural formal) attended.	Ellos / Ellas / Uds. asistieron.	ah-sees-TYEH-rohn

The Future

For novice Spanish speakers, the easiest way to express the future is to conjugate the irregular verb IR (to go) + a + any infinitive ("I am going to speak," "you are going to speak," etc.).

I am going to speak.	Yo voy a hablar.	voy ah ah-BLAHR
You (singular familiar) are going to speak.	Tú vas a hablar.	vahs ah ah-BLAHR
He / She is going to speak. You (singular formal) are going to speak.	Él / Ella / Ud. va a hablar.	vah ah ah-BLAHR
We are going to speak.	Nosotros -as vamos a hablar.	VAH-mohs ah ah-BLAHR

You (plural familiar) are going to speak.	Vosotros -as vais a hablar.	VAH-ees ah ah-BLAHR
They / You (plural formal) are going to speak.	Ellos / Ellas / Uds. van a hablar.	vahn ah ah-BLAHR

TO BE OR NOT TO BE (ESTAR & SER)

There are two forms of "being" in Spanish. One is for physical location or temporary conditions (estar), and the other is for fixed qualities or conditions (ser).

I am here.
(temporary, estar)

Yo estoy aquí.

I am from the United States.
(fixed, ser)

Yo soy de los Estados Unidos.

Norman is bored.
(temporary, estar)

Norman está aburrido.

Norman is boring.
(quality, ser)

Norman es aburrido.

The TV is old.
(quality, ser)

La televisión es vieja.

The TV is broken.
(condition, estar)

La televisión está rota.

Present Tense

Estar "To Be" (conditional)

I am.	Yo estoy.	ehs-TOY
You (singular, familiar) are.	Tú estás.	ehs-TAHS
He / She is. You (singular formal) are.	Él / Ella / Ud. está.	ehs-TAH
We are.	Nosotros -as estamos.	ehs-TAH-mohs
You (plural familiar) are.	Vosotros -as estáis.	ehs-TAH-ees
They / You (plural formal) are.	Ellos / Ellas / Uds. están.	ehs-TAHN

Simple Past Tense

Estar "To Be" (conditional)

I was.	Yo estuve.	ehs-TOO-veh
You were.	Tú estuviste.	ehs-too-VEES-teh
He / She was. You (formal) were.	Él / Ella / Ud. estuvo.	ehs-TOO-voh
We were.	Nosotros -as estuvimos.	ehs-too-VEE-mohs
You were.	Vosotros -as estuvisteis.	ehs-too-VEES-teh-ees
They / You (plural formal) were.	Ellos / Ellas / Uds. estuvieron.	ehs-too-VYEH-rohn

Present Tense

	Ser "To be" (permanent)	
I am.	Yo soy.	soy
You (singular familiar) are.	Tú eres.	EH-rehs
He/ She is. You (singular formal) are.	Él / Ella / Ud. es.	ehs
We are.	Nosotros -as somos.	SOH-mohs
You (plural familiar) are.	Vosotros -as sois.	SOH-ees
They / You (plural formal) are.	Ellos / Ellas / Uds. son.	sohn

Simple Past Tense

	Ser "To be" (permanent)	
I was.	Yo fui.	foo-EE
You (singular familiar) were.	Tú fuiste.	foo-EES-teh
He/ She was. You (singular formal) were.	Él / Ella / Ud. fue.	foo-EH
We were.	Nosotros -as fuimos.	foo-EE-mohs
You (plural) familiar) were.	Vosotros -as fuisteis.	foo-EES-teh-ees
They / You (plural formal) were.	Ellos / Ellas / Uds. fueron	foo-EH-rohn

IRREGULAR VERBS

Spanish has numerous irregular verbs that stray from the standard AR, ER, and IR conjugations. Rather than bog you down with too much grammar, we're providing the present tense conjugations for the most commonly used irregular verbs.

TENER "To Have" (possess)

I have.	Yo **t**engo.	TEHNG-goh
You (singular familiar) **have.**	Tú **t**ienes.	TYEH-nehs
He / She has. **You** (singular formal) **have.**	Él / Ella / Ud. **t**iene.	TYEH-neh
We have.	Nosotros -as **t**enemos.	TYEH-neh
You (plural familiar) **have.**	Vosotros -as **t**enéis.	teh-NEH-mohs
They / You (plural formal) **have.**	Ellos / Ellas / Uds. **t**ienen.	TYEH-nehn

Tener

Tener means "to have," but it's also used to describe conditions such as hunger, body pain, and age. For example:
Tengo hambre. I'm hungry.
(Literally: I have hunger.)
Tengo dolor de cabeza. I have a headache.
Tengo diez años. I am ten years old.
(Literally: I have ten years.)

HACER "To Do, To Make"

I make.	Yo hago.	AH-goh
You (singular familiar) make.	Tú haces.	AH-sehs
He / She makes. You (singular formal) make.	Él / Ella / Ud. hace.	AH-seh
We make.	Nosotros -as hacemos.	ah-SEH-mohs
You (plural familiar) make.	Vosotros -as hacéis.	ah-SEH-ees
They / You (plural formal) make.	Ellos / Ellas / Uds. hacen.	AH-sehn

Hacer

The verb *hacer* means "to make" or "to do," but it's also used to describe the weather and the passage of time. For example:

Hace calor. It's hot.
(Literally: It makes hot.)
Hace frío. It's cold.
(Literally: It makes cold.)
    OR
Hace tres años que visité España. Three years ago, I visited Spain.
(Literally: It makes three years since I visited Spain.)

QUERER "To Want"

I want.	Yo quiero.	KYEH-roh
You (singular familiar) want.	Tú quieres.	KYEH-rehs
He / She wants. You (singular formal) want.	Él / Ella / Ud. quiere.	KYEH-reh
We want.	Nosotros -as queremos	keh-REH-mohs
You (plural familiar) want.	Vosotros -as queréis.	keh-REH-ees
They / You plural formal) want.	Ellos / Ellas / Uds. quieren.	KYEH-rehn

PODER "To Be Able"

I can. (I)	Yo puedo.	PWEH-doh
You (singular familiar) can.	Tú puedes.	PWEH-dehs
He / She can. You singular formal) can.	Él / Ella / Ud. puede.	PWEH-deh
We can.	Nosotros -as podemos.	poh-DEH-mohs
You (plural familiar) can.	Vosotros -as podéis.	poh-DEH-ees
They / You (plural formal) can.	Ellos / Ellas / Uds. pueden.	PWEH-dehn

HABER "To Have..." (with past participle)

I have.	Yo he...	eh
You (singular familiar) **have**.	Tú has...	ahs
He / She has. You (singular formal) **have**.	Él / Ella / Ud. ha...	ah
We have.	Nosotros -as hemos...	EH-mohs
You (plural familiar) **have**.	Vosotros -as habéis...	ah-BEH-ees
They / You plural formal) **have**.	Ellos / Ellas / Uds. han...	ahn

PEDIR "To Ask"

I ask.	Yo pido.	PEE-doh
You (singular familiar) **ask**.	Tú pides.	PEE-dehs
He / She asks. You (singular formal) **ask**.	Él / Ella / Ud. pide.	PEE-deh
We ask.	Nosotros -as pedimos.	peh-DEE-mohs
You (plural familiar) **ask**.	Vosotros -as pedís.	PEH-dees
They / You (plural formal) **ask**.	Ellos / Ellas / Uds. piden.	PEE-dehn

Note: Verbs that end in **-cer** such as **conocer** change the **c** to **zc** before an ending that begins with **o** or **a**.

	CONOCER "To Know" (someone)	
I know.	Yo conozco.	koh-NOHS-koh
You (singular familiar) **know.**	Tú conoces.	koh-NOH-sehs
He / She knows. You (singular formal) **know.**	Él / Ella / Ud. conoce.	koh-NOH-seh
We know.	Nosotros -as conocemos.	koh-noh-SEH-mohs
You (plural familiar) **know.**	Vosotros -as conocéis.	koh-noh-SEH-ees
They / You (plural formal) **know.**	Ellos / Ellas / Uds. conocen.	koh-NOH-sehn

	SABER "to Know" (something)	
I know.	Yo sé.	SEH
You (singular familiar) **know.**	Tú sabes.	SAH-behs
He/ She knows. You (singular formal) know.	Él / Ella / Ud. sabe.	SAH-beh
We know.	Nosotros -as sabemos.	sah-BEH-mohs
You (plural familiar) know.	Vosotros -as sabéis.	sah-BEH-ees
They / You (plural formal) **know.**	Ellos / Ellas / Uds. saben.	SAH-behn

Gustar

Spanish doesn't have a verb that literally means "to like." Instead, they use *gustar*, which means to please. So rather than say I like chocolate, you say:

Me gusta el chocolate. I like chocolate.
(Literally: Chocolate is pleasing to me.)

When what is liked is plural, the verb is plural:

Me gustan las tortillas. I like tortillas.
(Literally: Tortillas are pleasing to me.)

The person doing the liking is represented by an indirect object pronoun placed in front of the verb, as illustrated below.

	GUSTAR "To Like"
I like the tortilla.	Me **gusta la tortilla.**
You (informal singular) **like the tortilla.**	Te **gusta la tortilla.**
He / She likes the tortilla. **You** (formal singular) **like the tortilla.**	Le **gusta la tortilla.**
We like the tortilla.	Nos **gusta la tortilla.**
You (informal plural) **like the tortilla.**	Os **gusta la tortilla.**
They / You (formal plural) **like the tortilla.**	Les **gusta la tortilla.**

REFLEXIVE VERBS

Spanish has many reflexive verbs (when its subject and object both refer to the same person or thing). The following common verbs are used reflexively: vestirse (to get dressed, literally to dress oneself), quedarse (to stay, literally to stay oneself), bañarse (to bathe oneself), and levantarse (to wake up, literally to raise oneself).

VESTIRSE "To Dress"

I get dressed.	Yo me visto.	meh VEES-toh
You (singular familiar) get dressed.	Tú te vistes.	teh VEES-tehs
He / She gets dressed. You (singular formal) get dressed.	Él / Ella / Ud. se viste.	seh VEES-teh
We get dressed.	Nosotros -as nos vestimos.	nohs vehs-TEE-mohs
You (plural familiar) get dressed	Vosotros -as os vestis	ohs vehs-TEES
They / You (plural formal) get dressed.	Ellos / Ellas / Uds. se visten.	seh VEES-tehn

CHAPTER TWO

GETTING THERE & GETTING AROUND

This section deals with every form of transportation. Whether you've just reached your destination by plane or you're renting a car to tour the countryside, you'll find the phrases you need in the next 30 pages.

AT THE AIRPORT

I am looking for _____	**Estoy buscando _____**
	ehs-TOY boos-KAHN-doh
a porter.	**un portero.**
	oon pohr-TEH-roh
a bus/train to city center.	**un autobús / tren al centro.**
	oon ow-toh-BOOS / TREHN ahl SEHN-troh
the check-in counter.	**el check-in / mostrador de facturación.**
	ehl CHECK-in / mohs-trah-DOHR deh fak-too-rah-see-ON
the ticket counter.	**el mostrador de venta de pasajes.**
	ehl mohs-trah-DOHR deh VEN-ta deh pah-SAH-hehs
security.	**control de seguridad.**
	kohn-TROLL deh seh-gooh-reeh-DAD
inmigration.	**control de pasaportes.**
	kohn-TROLL deh pah-sah-POHR-tehs
customs.	**aduana.**
	ah-DWAH-nah
arrivals.	**las llegadas.**
	lahs yeh-GAH-dahs
departures.	**las salidas.**
	lahs sah-LEE-dahs
gate number _____.	**la puerta de salida _____.**
	lah PWEHR-tah de sah-LEE-dah

For full coverage of numbers, see p7.

the waiting area.	**el área de espera.** *ehl AH-reh-ah deh ehs-PEH-rah*
the men's restroom.	**el baño para caballeros.** *ehl BAH-nyoh PAH-rah kah-bah-* *YEH-rohs*
the women's restroom.	**el baño para damas.** *ehl BAH-nyoh PAH-rah DAH-mahs*
the police station.	**la estación de policías.** *lah ehs-tah-SYOHN deh poh-* *lee-SEE-ahs*
a security guard.	**un guardia de seguridad.** *oon GWAHR-dyah deh seh-goo-* *ree-DAD*
the smoking area.	**el área de fumar.** *ehl AH-reh-ah deh foo-MAHR*
the information booth.	**el puesto de información.** *ehl PWEHS-toh deh een-for-* *mah-SYOHN*
a public telephone.	**un teléfono público.** *oon teh-LEH-foh-noh POO-* *blee-koh*
an ATM.	**un cajero automático.** *oon kah-HEH-roh ow-toh-MAH-* *tee-koh*
baggage claim.	**el reclamo de equipaje.** *ehl rreh-KLAH-moh de eh-kee-* *PAH-heh*
a luggage cart.	**un carrito para equipaje.** *oon kah-RREE-toh PAH-rah eh-* *kee-PAH-heh*
a currency exchange.	**un lugar de cambio de moneda.** *oon loo-GAHR deh KAHM-byoh* *deh moh-NEH-dah*
a café.	**un café.** *oon kah-FEH*
a restaurant.	**un restaurante.** *oon rrehst-ow-RAHN-teh*

a bar.	**un bar.**
	oon bar
a bookstore or newsstand.	**una librería o kiosco.**
	oo-nah lee-breh-REE-ah oh kee-OHS-koh
a duty-free shop.	**una tienda duty free.**
	oo-nah tee-EHN-dah duty free
Is there Wi-Fi?	**¿Hay Wi-Fi?**
	aye wee fee
I'd like to page someone.	**Quisiera mandar a llamar a alguien.**
	kee-SYEH-rah mahn-DAHR ah yah-MAHR ah AHL-gee-ehn
Do you accept credit cards?	**¿Aceptan tarjetas de crédito?**
	ah-SEHP-tahn tahr-HEH-tahs deh KREH-dee-toh

CHECKING IN

I would like a one-way ticket to _____.	**Me gustaría un boleto de ida para _____.**
	meh goos-tah-REE-ah oon boh-LEH-toh deh EE-dah PAH-rah
I would like a round trip ticket to _____.	**Me gustaría un boleto de ida y vuelta para _____.**
	meh goos-tah-REE-ah oon boh-LEH-toh de EE-dah ee VWEHL-tah PAH-rah
How much are the tickets?	**¿Cuánto cuestan los boletos?**
	KWAHN-toh KWEHS-tahn lohs boh-LEH-tohs
Do you have anything less expensive?	**¿Tiene algo más económico?**
	TYEH-neh AHL-goh mahs eh-koh-NOH-mee-koh
How long is the flight?	**¿Cuánto dura el vuelo?**
	KWAHN-toh DOOH-rah ehl VWEH-loh

Common Airport Signs

Llegadas	Arrivals
Salidas	Departures
Terminal	Terminal
Vuelos nacionales	Domestic flights
Vuelos internacionales	International flights
Puerto de salida	Gate
Boletería	Ticketing
Aduana	Customs
Reclamo de equipaje	Baggage Claim
Empuje	Push
Tire / Jale	Pull
No fumar / Prohibido fumar	No Smoking
Entrada	Entrance
Salida	Exit
Caballeros	Men's
Damas	Women's
Autobuses de transporte	Shuttle Buse
Taxis	Taxis

For full coverage of number terms, see p7.
For full coverage of time, see p12.

What time does flight _____ leave?	**¿A qué hora sale el vuelo _____?** *ah KEH OH-rah SAH-leh ehl VWEH-loh*
What time does flight _____ arrive?	**¿A qué hora llega el vuelo _____?** *ah KEH OH-rah YEH-gah ehl VWEH-loh*
Do I have a connecting flight?	**¿Tengo un vuelo de conexión?** *TEHNG-goh oon VWEH-loh deh koh-nehk-SYOHN*
Do I need to change planes?	**¿Necesito cambiar aviones?** *neh-seh-SEE-toh kahm-BYAHR ah-VYOH-nehs*
My flight leaves at __:__.	**Mi vuelo sale a las ___:___.** *mee VWEH-loh SAH-leh ah lahs*

GETTING THERE

For full coverage of numbers, see p7.

What time will the flight arrive?	**¿A qué hora llega el vuelo?** *ah KEH OH-rah YEH-gah ehl VWEH-loh*
Is the flight on time?	**¿El vuelo está a tiempo?** *ehl VWEH-loh ehs-TAH ah TYEHM-poh*
Is the flight delayed?	**¿El vuelo está retrasado?** *ehl VWEH-loh ehs-TAH reh-trah-SAH-doh*
From which terminal is flight ____ leaving?	**¿De cuál terminal sale el vuelo ____?** *deh kwahl tehr-mee-NAHL SAH-leh ehl VWEH-loh*
From which gate is flight ____ leaving?	**¿De cuál puerta de salida sale el vuelo ____?** *deh kwahl PWEHR-tah deh sah-LEE-dah SAH-leh ehl VWEH-loh*
How much time do I need for check-in?	**¿Cuánto tiempo necesito para registrarme?** *KWAHN-toh TYEHM-poh neh-seh-SEE-toh PAH-rah reh-hees-TRAHR-me*
Is there an express check-in line?	**¿Hay una fila para check-in exprés?** *aye oo-nah FEE-lah PAH-rah check-in ehks-PREHS*
Is online check-in available?	**¿Hay facturación / check-in electrónico?** *aye fak-too-rah-see-ON / check-in eh-lehk-TROH-nee-koh*

Questions you may be asked

Su pasaporte, por favor
soo pah-sah-POHR-teh, pohr fah-VOHR

Your passport, please

¿Cuál es el propósito de su viaje?
kwahl ehs ehl proh-POH-see-toh deh soo vee-ah-HEH?

What is the purpose of your visit?

¿Cuánto tiempo se va a quedar?
KWAN-toh tee-EHM-poh seh vah ah keh-DAHR?

How long will you be staying?

¿Dónde se va a alojar?
DOHN-deh seh vah ah ah-loh-HAHR?

Where are you staying?

¿Tiene algo que declarar?
tee-EH-neh AHL-goh keh deh-clah-RAHR?

Do you have anything to declare?

Abra esta bolsa (maleta), por favor
AH-brah EHS-tah BOHL-sah (mah-LEH-tah), pohr fah-VOHR

Open this bag, please

Seat Preferences

I would like ____ ticket(s) in ____

Quisiera ____ boleto(s) en ____
kee-SYEH-rah ____ boh-LEH-toh(s) ehn

   first class.

   primera clase.
   pree-MEH-rah KLAH-seh

   business class.

   la clase de negocios.
   lah KLAH-seh deh neh-GOH-syohs

   economy class.

   la clase económica.
   lah KLAH-seh eh-koh-NOH-mee-kah

I would like ____

Me gustaría ____
meh goos-tah-REE-ah

Please don't give me ____

Por favor no me dé ____
pohr fah-VOHR noh meh deh

   a window seat.

   un asiento de ventana.
   oon ah-SYEHN-toh deh vehn-TAH-nah

   an aisle seat.

   un asiento de pasillo.
   oon ah-SYEHN-toh deh pah-SEE-yoh

an emergency exit row seat.	**un asiento en la fila de emergencia.** *oon ah-SYEHN-toh ehn lah FEE-lah deh eh-mehr-HEHN-syah*
a bulkhead seat.	**un asiento detrás del tabique.** *oon ah-SYEHN-toh deh-TRAHS dehl tah-BEE-keh*
a seat by the restroom.	**un asiento cerca de los baños.** *oon ah-SYEHN-toh SEHR-kah deh lohs BAH-nyohs*
a seat near the front.	**un asiento cerca del frente.** *oon ah-SYEHN-toh SEHR-kah dehl FREHN-teh*
a seat near the middle.	**un asiento cerca del centro.** *oon ah-SYEHN-toh SEHR-kah dehl SEHN-troh*
a seat near the back.	**un asiento cerca de atrás.** *oon ah-SYEHN-toh SEHR-kah deh ah-TRAHS*
Is there a meal on the flight?	**¿Sirven comida en este vuelo?** *SEER-vehn koh-MEE-dah ehn EHS-teh VWEH-loh*
I'd like to order ____	**Quisiera ordenar ____** *kee-SYEH-rah ohr-deh-NAHR*
a vegetarian meal.	**una comida vegetariana.** *oo-nah koh-MEE-dah veh-heh-tah-RYAH-nah*
a gluten-free meal.	**una comida sin gluten.** *oo-nah ko-MEE-dah seen GLUE-ten*
a kosher meal.	**una comida kósher.** *oo-nah koh-MEE-dah KOH-shehr*
a diabetic meal.	**una comida para diabéticos.** *oo-nah koh-MEE-dah PAH-rah dyah-BEH-tee-kohs*
I am traveling to ____.	**Estoy viajando hacia ____.** *ehs-TOY vyah-HAHN-doh HAH-syah*

I am coming from ____.

Estoy regresando de ____.
ehs-TOY reh-greh-SAHN-doh de

I arrived from ____.

Llegué de ____.
yeh-GEH deh

For full coverage of country terms, see English / Spanish dictionary.

I'd like to change / cancel / confirm my reservation.

Quisiera cambiar / cancelar / confirmar mi reservación.
kee-SYEH-rah kahm-BYAHR / kahn-seh-LAHR / kohn-feer-MAHR mee rreh-sehr-vah-SYOHN

I have ____ bags to check.

Tengo ____ bolsas que registrar.
TEHN-goh ____ BOHL-sahs keh reh-hees-TRAHR

For full coverage of numbers, see p7.

Passengers with Special Needs

Is that wheelchair accessible?

¿Eso es accesible para personas con impedimentos?
EH-soh ehs ahk-seh-SEE-bleh PAH-rah pehr-SOH-nahs kohn eem-peh-dee-MEHN-tohs

May I have a wheelchair / walker please?

¿Me puede dar una silla de ruedas / un andador, por favor?
meh PWEH-deh dahr oo-nah SEE-yah deh RWEH-dahs / oon ahn-dah-DOHR pohr fah-VOHR

I need some assistance boarding.

Necesito un poco de ayuda al abordar.
neh-seh-SEE-toh oon POH-koh deh ah-YOO-dah ahl ah-bohr-DAHR

I need to bring my service dog.

Necesito traer a mi perro de servicio.
neh-seh-SEE-toh trah-EHR ah mee PEH-rroh deh sehr-VEE-syoh

Do you have services for the hearing impaired?

¿Tienen servicios para las personas con impedimentos auditivos?
TYEH-nehn sehr-VEE-syohs PAH-rah lahs pehr-SOH-nahs kohn eem-peh-dee-MEHN-tohs ow-dee-TEE-vohs

GETTING THERE

Do you have services for the visually impaired?	**¿Tienen servicios para las personas con impedimentos visuales?** *TYEH-nehn sehr-VEE-syohs pah-rah pehr-SOH-nahs kohn eem-peh-dee-MEHN-tohs vee-soo-AH-lehs*

Trouble at Check-In

How long is the delay?	**¿Cuánto retraso hay?** *KWAN-toh reh-TRAH-soh aye*
My flight was late.	**Mi vuelo vino con retraso.** *Me VWEH-loh VEE-noh kohn reh-TRAH-soh*
I missed my flight.	**Perdí mi vuelo.** *pehr-DEE mee VWEH-loh*
When is the next flight?	**¿Cuándo es el próximo vuelo?** *KWAHN-doh ehs ehl PROHK-see-moh VWEH-loh*
May I have a meal voucher?	**¿Me puede dar un vale para comida?** *meh PWEH-deh dahr oon VAH-leh pah-rah koh-MEE-dah*
May I have a room voucher?	**¿Me puede dar un vale para hospedaje?** *meh PWEH-deh dahr oon VAH-leh pah-rah ohs-peh-DAH-heh*

AT CUSTOMS / SECURITY CHECKPOINTS

I'm traveling with a group.	**Estoy viajando con un grupo.** *ehs-TOY vyah-HAHN-doh kohn oon GROO-poh*
I'm on my own.	**Estoy viajando solo / sola.** *ehs-TOY vyah-HAHN-doh SOH-loh / SOH-lah*
I'm traveling on business.	**Estoy viajando por negocios.** *ehs-TOY vyah-HAHN-doh pohr neh-GOH-syohs*
I'm on vacation.	**Estoy de vacaciones.** *ehs-TOY deh vah-kah-SYOH-nehs*

I have nothing to declare.

No tengo nada que declarar.
noh TEHNG-goh NAH-dah keh deh-klah-RAHR

I would like to declare _____.

Quisiera declarar _____.
kee-SYEH-rah deh-klah-RAHR

I have some liquor.

Tengo un poco de licor.
TEHNG-goh oon POH-koh deh lee-KOHR

I have some cigars.

Tengo unos cigarros.
TEHNG-goh oo-nohs see-GAH-rrohs

They are gifts.

Son regalos.
sohn reh-GAH-lohs

They are for personal use.

Son para uso personal.
sohn PAH-rah OO-soh pehr-soh-NAHL

That is my medicine.

Esa es mi medicina.
EH-sah ehs mee meh-dee-SEE-nah

I have my prescription.

Tengo mi receta.
TEHNG-goh mee rreh-SEH-tah

I'd like a male / female officer to conduct the search.

Quisiera que un oficial varón / mujer haga el registro.
kee-SYEH-rah keh oon oh-fees-YAHL vah-ROHN / moo-HEHR AH-gah ehl rreh-HEES-tro

Trouble at Security
Help me. I've lost _____

Ayúdeme. Perdí _____
ah-YOO-deh-meh pehr-DEE

my passport.

mi pasaporte.
mee pah-sah-POHR-teh

my boarding pass.

mi tarjeta de embarque.
mee tahr-HEH-tah deh em-BAR-keh

my identification.

mi identificación.
mee ee-dehn-tee-fee-kah-SYOHN

my wallet.

mi cartera / billetera.
me kahr-TEH-rah / bee-jeh-TEH-rah

my purse.

mi bolso.
mee BOHL-soh

GETTING THERE

Listen Up: Security Lingo

Por favor, quítese los zapatos.
*pohr fah-VOHR, KEE-teh-seh
lohs sah-PAH-tohs*

Please remove your shoes.

Quítese la chaqueta / el suéter.
*KEE-teh-seh lah chah-KEH-tah /
ehl SWET-ehr*

Remove your jacket / sweater.

Quítese las joyas.
KEE-teh-seh lahs HOH-yas

Remove your jewelry.

**Coloque su equipaje sobre
la cinta transportadora.**
*ko-LOH-keh soo e-kee-PAH-heh
SOH-breh lah SEEN-tah trans-pohr-
tah-DOH-ra*

Place your bags on the conveyor belt.

Por favor hágase a un lado.
*pohr fah-VOHR AH-gah-seh
ah oon LAH-doh*

Step to the side.

**Debemos realizar una
inspección manual.**
*de-BEH-mohs reh-ah-lee-SAHR
OO-nah ins-pek-SYON ma-nooh-AHL*

We have to do a hand search.

Someone stole
my purse / wallet!

**¡Alguien me robó mi bolso /
cartera!**
*AHL-gee-ehn meh roh-BOH mee
BOHL-soh / kahr-TEH-rah*

IN-FLIGHT

It's unlikely you'll need much Spanish on the plane, but these phrases
will help if a bilingual flight attendant is unavailable or if you need to
talk to a Spanish-speaking neighbor.

I think that's my seat.

Creo que ese es mi asiento.
*KREH-oh keh EH-seh ehs mee
ah-SYEHN-toh*

May I have _____

¿Me puede dar _____
meh PWEH-deh dahr

water?	**agua sin gas?**
	AH-wah seen gas
sparkling water?	**agua con gas?**
	AH-wah kohn gas
orange juice?	**jugo de naranja?**
	HOO-goh deh nah-RAHN-hah
soda?	**soda / refresco / gaseosa?**
	SOH-dah / reh-FREHS-koh / gah-seh-OH-sah
diet soda?	**soda / refresco / gaseosa dietética?**
	SOH-dah / reh-FREHS-koh / gah-seh-OH-sah dee-eh-TEH-tee-kah
a beer?	**una cerveza?**
	oo-nah sehr-VEH-sah
wine?	**vino?**
	VEE-noh

For a complete list of drinks, see p88.

a pillow?	**una almohada?**
	oo-nah ahl-moh-AH-dah
a blanket?	**una manta / frazada?**
	oo-nah MAHN-tah / fra-SAH-dah
a hand wipe?	**una toallita húmeda?**
	oo-nah toh-ah-YEE-tah OO-meh-dah
headphones?	**audífonos / auriculares?**
	ow-DEE-foh-nohs / ow-ree-kooh-LAH-rehs
a magazine or newspaper?	**una revista o un periódico?**
	oo-nah rreh-VEES-tah oh oon pehr-YOH-dee-koh
When will the meal be served?	**¿Cuándo servirán la comida?**
	KWAHN-doh sehr-vee-RAHN lah koh-MEE-dah
How long until we land?	**¿Cuánto falta para llegar?**
	KWAHN-toh FAHL-tah pah-rah yeh-GAHR

GETTING THERE

May I move to another seat?	**¿Me puedo mover a otro asiento?** *meh PWEH-doh moh-VEHR ah OH-troh ah-SYEHN-toh*
How do I turn the light on / off?	**¿Cómo apago / enciendo la luz?** *KOH-moh ah-PAH-go / ehn-SYEHN-doh lah loos*

Trouble In-Flight

These headphones are broken.	**Estos audífonos están rotos.** *EHS-tohs ow-DEE-foh-nohs ehs-TAHN ROH-tohs*
I spilled.	**Se volcó / se me cayó.** *seh vohl-KOH / seh meh kah-YOH*
My child spilled.	**Mi niño / niña tuvo un derrame.** *mee NEE-nyoh / NEE-nyah TOO-voh oon deh-RRAH-me*
My child is sick.	**Mi niño / niña está enfermo / enferma.** *mee NEE-nyoh / NEE-nyah ehs-TAH ehn-FEHR-moh / ehn-FEHR-mah*
I need an airsickness bag.	**Necesito una bolsa para casos de mareos.** *neh-seh-SEE-toh oo-nah BOHL-sah pah-rah KAH-sos deh mah-REH-ohs*
I smell something strange.	**Huelo algo extraño.** *WEH-loh AHL-goh ehks-TRAH-nyoh*
That passenger is behaving suspiciously.	**Ese pasajero se está comportando sospechosamente.** *EH-seh pah-sah-HEH-roh seh ehs-TAH kohm-pohr-TAHN-doh sohs-peh-choh-sah-MEHN-teh*

BAGGAGE CLAIM

Where is baggage claim for flight ____?	**¿Dónde está el reclamo de equipaje para el vuelo ____?** *DOHN-deh ehs-TAH ehl rreh-KLAH-moh deh eh-kee-PAH-heh pah-rah ehl VWEH-loh*

Would you please help with my bags?	**¿Me puede ayudar con mis bolsas?** *meh PWEH-deh ah-yoo-DAHR kohn mees BOHL-sahs*
I am missing ____ bags.	**Me faltan ____ bolsas.** *meh FAHL-tahn ____ BOHL-sahs*

For full coverage of numbers, see p7.

My bag is ____	**Mi bolsa ____** *mee BOHL-sah*
lost.	**está perdida.** *ehs-TAH pehr-DEE-dah*
damaged.	**está dañada.** *ehs-TAH dah-NYAH-dah*
stolen.	**fue robada.** *fweh roh-BAH-dah*
a suitcase.	**es una maleta.** *ehs oo-nah mah-LEH-ta*
a briefcase.	**es un maletín.** *ehs oon mah-leh-TEEN*
a carry-on.	**es una maleta de mano.** *ehs oo-nah mah-LEH-tah deh MAH-noh*
a suit bag.	**es una bolsa para trajes.** *ehs oo-nah BOHL-sah PAH-rah TRAH-hehs*
a trunk.	**es un baúl.** *ehs oon bah-OOL*
golf clubs.	**son palos de golf.** *sohn PAH-lohs deh gohlf*

For full coverage of color terms, see English / Spanish Dictionary.

hard.	**es dura.** *ehs DOO-rah*
made out of ____	**está hecha de ____** *ehs-TAH EH-chah deh ____*
canvas.	**lona.** *LOH-nah*

GETTING THERE

vinyl.	**vinilo.** *vee-NEE-loh*
leather.	**cuero.** *KWEH-roh*
hard plastic.	**plástico duro.** *PLAH-stee-koh DOO-roh*
aluminum.	**aluminio.** *ah-loo-MEE-nyoh*

RENTING A VEHICLE

Is there a car rental agency in the airport?	**¿Hay una agencia de alquiler de autos en el aeropuerto?** *aye oo-nah ah-HEN-syah deh ahl-kee-LEHR deh OW-tohs ehn ehl ah-eh-roh-PWEHR-toh*
I have a reservation.	**Tengo una reservación.** *TEHNG-goh oo-nah rreh-sehr-vah-SYOHN*

Vehicle Preferences

I would like to rent _____	**Quisiera alquilar _____** *kee-SYEH-rah ahl-kee-LAHR*
an economy car.	**un auto económico.** *oon OW-toh eh-koh-NOH-mee-koh*
a midsize car.	**un auto mediano.** *oon OW-toh meh-DYAH-noh*
a convertible.	**un convertible.** *oon kohn-vehr-TEE-bleh*
a van.	**una furgoneta.** *oo-nah foor-goh-NEH-tah*
a sports car.	**un auto deportivo.** *oon OW-toh deh-pohr-TEE-voh*
a 4-wheel-drive vehicle.	**un 4 x 4.** *oon KWA-troh pohr KWA-troh*
a motorcycle.	**una motocicleta.** *oo-nah moh-toh-see-KLEH-tah*

a scooter.

una motoneta.
oo-nah mo-toh-NEH-tah

Do you have one with ____

¿Tiene uno con ____
TYEH-neh oo-noh kohn

air conditioning?

aire acondicionado?
AYE-reh ah-kohn-dee-syoh-NAH-doh

a sunroof?

techo corredizo?
TEH-choh koh-rreh-DEE-soh

a CD player?

un lector de discos compactos?
oon lehk-TOHR deh DEES-kohs kohm-PAHK-tohs

an iPod connection?

conexión para iPod?
koh-nex-ee-ON PAH-rah iPod

a GPS system?

sistema GPS?
sees-TEH-mah HEH PEH EH-seh

a DVD player?

un lector de DVD?
oon lehk-TOHR deh deh-veh-DEH

child seats?

asientos infantiles?
ah-SYEHN-tohs een-fahn-TEE-lehs

Do you have a ____

¿Tiene un auto ____
TYEH-neh oon OW-toh

smaller car?

más pequeño?
mahs peh-KEH-nyoh

bigger car?

más grande?
mahs GRAHN-deh

cheaper car?

más barato?
mahs bah-RAH-toh

Do you have a non-smoking car?

¿Tiene un auto de no fumar?
TYEH-neh oon OW-toh deh noh foo-MAHR

I need an automatic transmission.

Necesito una transmisión automática.
neh-seh-SEE-toh oo-nah trahns-mee-SYOHN ow-toh-MAH-tee-kah

GETTING THERE

A standard transmission is okay.	**Una transmisión manual está bien.** *oo-nah trahns-mee-SYOHN mah-NWAHL eh-STAH BYEHN*
May I have an upgrade?	**¿Puedo recibir una mejora de categoría?** *PWEH-doh reh-see-BEER oo-nah meh-HO-rah deh kah-teh-goh-REE-ah*

Money Matters

What's the daily / weekly / monthly rate?	**¿Cuál es la tarifa diaria / semanal / mensual?** *KWAHL ehs lah tah-REE-fah DYAHR-yah / seh-mah-NAHL / mehn-SWAHL*
What is the mileage rate?	**¿Cuál es la tarifa por milla / kilómetro?** *KWAHL ehs lah tah-REE-fah pohr MEE-yah / kee-LOH-meh-troh*
How much is insurance?	**¿Cuánto cuesta el seguro?** *KWAHN-toh KWEHS-tah ehl seh-GOO-roh*
Are there other fees?	**¿Hay otros honorarios?** *aye OH-trohs oh-noh-RAHR-yohs*
Is there a weekend rate?	**¿Hay una tarifa de fin de semana?** *aye oo-nah tah-REE-fah deh feen deh seh-MAH-nah*

Technical Questions

What kind of fuel does it take?	**¿Qué tipo de combustible usa?** *KEH TEE-poh deh kohm-boos-TEE-bleh OO-sah*
Do you have the manual in English?	**¿Tiene el manual en inglés?** *TYEH-neh ehl mah-NWAHL ehn eeng-GLEHS*
Do you have a booklet in English with the local traffic laws?	**¿Tiene un folleto en inglés con las leyes de tráfico locales?** *TYEH-neh oon foh-YEH-toh ehn eeng-GLEHS kohn lahs LEH-yehs deh TRAH-fee-koh loh-KAH-lehs*

Car Troubles

The _____ doesn't work.	_____ no funciona.
	noh foon-SYOH-nah

See diagram on p54 for car parts.

It is already dented.	**Ya está abollado.**
	YAH ehs-TAH ah-boh-YAH-doh
It is scratched.	**Está rayado.**
	ehs-TAH rah-YAH-doh
The windshield is cracked.	**El parabrisas está agrietado.**
	ehl pah-rah-BREE-sahs ehs-TAH ah-gree-eh-TAH-doh
The tires look low.	**Las llantas / ruedas parecen algo vacías.**
	lahs YAHN-tahs / rooh-EH-dahs pah-REH-sehn oon POH-koh vah-SEE-yahs
It has a flat tire.	**Tiene una llanta / rueda vacía.**
	TYEH-neh oo-nah YAHN-ta / rooh-EH-dah vah-SEE-yah
Whom do I call for service?	**¿A quién llamo para servicio?**
	ah KYEHN YAH-moh pah-rah sehr-VEE-syoh
It won't start.	**No enciende / arranca.**
	noh ehn-SYEHN-deh / ah-RAHN-kah
It's out of gas.	**No tiene combustible.**
	noh TYEH-neh kohm-boos-TEE-bleh
The Check Engine light is on.	**La luz de examinar el motor está encendida.**
	lah loos dee ehk-sah-mee-NAHR ehl moh-TOHR ehs-TAH ehn-sehn-DEE-dah
The oil light is on.	**La luz del aceite está encendida.**
	lah loos dehl ah-SEH-ee-teh ehs-TAH ehn-sehn-DEE-dah

GETTING THERE

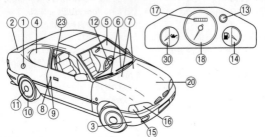

1. la tapa del tanque
   del combustible
2. el baúl
3. los parachoques
4. la ventana
5. el parabrisas
6. el limpiaparabrisas
7. el lavador
   de parabrisas
8. el seguro
9. los seguros
   automáticos
10. las llantas
11. las ruedas
12. la ignición
13. la luz de advertencia
14. el indicador del combustible
15. las luces de giro
16. los focos delanteros

17. el odómetro
18. el velocímetro
19. el silenciador
20. el capó
21. el volante
22. el espejo
23. el cinturón de seguridad
24. el motor
25. el acelerador
26. el embrague
27. los frenos
28. el freno de mano
29. el acumulador
30. el indicador de aceite
31. el radiador
32. la manguera del ventilador

The brake light is on.	**La luz del freno está encendida.**
	lah loos dehl FREH-noh ehs-TAH ehn-sehn-DEE-dah
It runs rough.	**Tiene un andar brusco.**
	TYEH-neh oon ANH-dahr BROOS-koh
The car is over-heating.	**El auto se sobrecalienta.**
	ehl OW-toh seh soh-breh-kah-LYEHN-tah
Asking for Directions	
Excuse me, please.	**Perdóneme.**
	pehr-DOH-neh-meh
How do I get to ____?	**¿Cómo llego a ____?**
	KOH-moh YEH-goh ah
Go straight.	**Siga directo.**
	SEE-gah dee-REHK-toh
Turn left / right.	**Gire a la izquierda / derecha.**
	HEE-reh ah lah ees-KYEHR-dah / deh-REH-chah
Continue right.	**Continúe a mano derecha.**
	kohn-tee-NOO-eh ah MAH-noh deh-REH-chah
It's on the right.	**Está a mano derecha.**
	ehs-TAH ah MAH-noh deh-REH-chah
Can you show me on the map?	**¿Puede mostrarme en el mapa?**
	PWEH-deh mohs-TRAHR-meh ehn ehl MAH-pah
What are the GPS coordinates?	**¿Cuáles son las coordenadas GPS?**
	KWAH-lehs son lahs koh-or-deh-NAH-dahs HEH PEH EH-seh
How far is it from here?	**¿A cuánto está de aquí?**
	ah KWAHN-toh ehs-TAH deh ah-KEEH

Is this the right road for ____?	**¿Es ésta la carretera correcta para ____?**
	ehs EHS-tah lah kah-rreh-TEH-rah koh-RREHK-tah PAH-rah
I've lost my way.	**Estoy perdido -a.**
	ehs-TOY pehr-DEE-doh -dah
Would you repeat that?	**¿Puede repetir eso?**
	PWEH-deh reh-peh-TEER EH-so
Thanks for your help.	**Gracias por su ayuda.**
	GRAH-syahs pohr soo ah-YOO-dah

For full coverage of direction-related terms, see p5.

Sorry, Officer

What is the speed limit?	**¿Cuál es el límite de velocidad?**
	KWAHL ehs ehl LEE-mee-teh deh veh-loh-see-DAD
I wasn't going that fast.	**Yo no iba tan rápido.**
	yoh noh EE-bah tahn RRAH-pee-doh
How much is the fine?	**¿De cuánto es la multa?**
	deh KWAHN-toh ehs lah MOOL-tah
Where do I pay the fine?	**¿Dónde pago la multa?**
	DOHN-deh PAH-goh lah MOOL-tah

Road Signs

Límite de velocidad	Speed Limit
Pare	Stop
Ceda el paso	Yield
Peligro	Danger
Sin salida	No Exit
Una mano / Dirección única	One Way
No entre	Do Not Enter
Carretera cerrada	Road Closed
Peaje	Toll
Efectivo solamente	Cash Only
No estacione	No Parking
Tarifa de estacionamiento	Parking Fee
Estacionamiento	Parking Garage

Do I have to go to court?	¿Tengo que ir a corte?
	TEHNG-goh keh eer ah KOHR-teh
I had an accident.	**Tuve un accidente.**
	TOO-veh oon ahk-see-DEHN-teh
The other driver hit me.	**El otro conductor me chocó.**
	ehl OH-troh kon-dook-TOR meh choh-KOH
I'm at fault.	**Es mi culpa.**
	ehs mee KOOL-pah

BY TAXI

Where is the taxi stand?	¿Dónde está la parada de taxis?
	DOHN-deh ehs-TAH lah pah-RAH-dah deh TAX-ees
Is there a limo / bus / van for my hotel?	¿Hay una limusina / un autobús / una furgoneta para mi hotel?
	aye oo-nah lee-moh-SEE-nah / oon ow-toh-BOOS / oo-nah foor-goh-NEH-tah PAH-rah mee oh-TEHL
I need to get to ___.	**Necesito ir a ___.**
	neh-seh-SEE-toh eer ah
How much will that cost?	¿Cuánto costará eso?
	KWAHN-toh kohs-tah-RAH EH-soh

GETTING THERE

Listen Up: Taxi Lingo

¡Súbanse!	Get in!
SOO-bahn-seh	
Deje su equipaje. Lo tengo.	Leave your luggage. I got it.
DEH-heh soo eh-kee-PAH-heh loh TENG-goh	
Sale 100 pesos por cada maleta.	It's 100 pesos for each bag.
SAH-le SYEN PEH-sohs pohr KAH-dah mah-LEH-tah	
¿Cuántos pasajeros?	How many passengers?
KWAN-tohs pah-sah-HEH-rohs?	
¿Tiene prisa?	Are you in a hurry?
TYEH-neh PREE-sah?	

How long will it take?	**¿Cuánto tomará?** *KWAHN-toh toh-mah-RAH*
Can you take me / us to the train / bus station?	**¿Puede llevarme / llevarnos a la estación del tren / autobús?** *PWEH-deh yeh-VAHR-meh / yeh-VAHR-nohs ah lah ehs-tah-SYOHN dehl trehn / ow-toh-BOOS*
I am in a hurry.	**Tengo prisa.** *TEHNG-goh PREE-sah*
Slow down.	**Reduzca la velocidad.** *rreh-DOOS-kah lah veh-loh-see-DAHD*
Am I close enough to walk?	**¿Estoy suficientemente cerca como para caminar?** *ehs-TOY soo-fee-syehn-teh-MEHN-teh SEHR-kah koh-moh pah-rah kah-mee-NAHR*
Let me out here.	**Déjeme salir de aquí.** *DEH-heh-meh sah-LEER deh ah-KEE*
That's not the correct change.	**Ese no es el cambio correcto.** *EH-seh noh ehs ehl KAM-byoh koh-REHK-toh*

BY TRAIN

How do I get to the train station?	**¿Cómo llego a la estación del tren?** *KOH-moh YEH-goh ah lah ehs-tah-SYOHN dehl trehn*
Would you take me to the train station?	**¿Puede llevarme a la estación del tren?** *PWEH-deh yeh-VAHR-meh ah lah ehs-tah-SYOHN dehl trehn*
How long is the trip to _____?	**¿Cuánto tarda el viaje a _____?** *KWAN-toh TAHR-dah ehl VYAH-heh ah*

When is the next train?	**¿Cuándo sale el próximo tren?** *KWAHN-doh SAH-leh ehl PROHK-see-moh trehn*
Do you have a schedule / timetable?	**¿Tiene un horario?** *TYEH-neh oon oh-RAH-ryoh*
Do I have to change trains?	**¿Tengo que cambiar trenes?** *TEHNG-goh keh kahm-BYAHR TREH-nehs*
a one-way ticket	**un boleto de ida** *oon boh-LEH-toh deh EE-dah*
a round-trip ticket	**un boleto de ida y vuelta** *oon boh-LEH-toh deh EE-dah ee VWEHL-tah*
Which platform does it leave from?	**¿De qué plataforma / andén sale?** *deh KEH plah-tah-FOHR-mah / an-DEHN SAH-le*
Is there a bar car?	**¿Hay un vagón cantina?** *aye oon vah-GOHN kahn-TEE-nah*
Is there a dining car?	**¿Hay un vagón para cenar?** *aye oon vah-GOHN pah-rah seh-NAHR*
Which car is my seat in?	**¿En cuál vagón está mi asiento?** *ehn kwahl vah-GOHN ehs-TAH mee ah-SYEHN-toh*
Is this seat taken?	**¿Este asiento está ocupado?** *EHS-teh ah-SYEHN-toh ehs-TAH oh-koo-PAH-doh*
Where is the next stop?	**¿Dónde es la próxima parada?** *DOHN-deh ehs lah PROHK-see-mah pah-RAH-dah*
How many stops to _____?	**¿Cuántas paradas hasta _____?** *KWAHN-tahs pah-RAH-dahs AHS-tah*

What's the train number and destination?	**¿Cuál es el número del tren y su destino?** *KWAHL ehs ehl NOO-meh-roh dehl trehn ee soo dehs-TEE-noh*

BY BUS

How do I get to the bus station?	**¿Cómo llego a la estación de autobuses?** *KOH-moh YEH-go ah lah ehs-tah-SYOHN deh ow-toh-BOO-sehs*
Would you take me to the bus station?	**¿Me puede llevar a la estación de autobuses?** *meh PWEH-deh yeh-VAHR ah lah ehs-tah-SYOHN deh ow-toh-BOO-sehs*
May I have a bus schedule?	**¿Me puede dar un itinerario?** *meh PWEH-deh dahr oon ee-tee-neh-RAH-ryoh*
Which bus goes to ____?	**¿Cuál autobús va para ____?** *KWAHL ow-toh-BOOS vah pah-rah*
Where does it leave from?	**¿De dónde sale?** *deh DOHN-deh SAH-leh*
How long does the bus take?	**¿Cuánto se tarda el autobús?** *KWAHN-toh seh TAHR-dah ehl ow-toh-BOOS*
How much is it?	**¿Cuánto cuesta?** *KWAHN-to KWEH-stah*
Is there an express bus?	**¿Hay un autobús exprés?** *aye oon ow-toh-BOOS ehks-PREHS*
Does it make local stops?	**¿Hace paradas locales?** *AH-seh pah-RAH-dahs loh-KAH-lehs*

Does it run at night?	**¿El autobús anda de noche?** *ehl ow-toh-BOOS AN-dah deh NOH-che*
When does the next bus leave?	**¿Cuándo parte el próximo autobús?** *KWAHN-doh PAHR-teh ehl PROHK-see-moh ow-toh-BOOS*
a one-way ticket	**un boleto de ida** *oon boh-LEH-toh deh EE-dah*
a round-trip ticket	**un boleto de ida y vuelta** *oon boh-LEH-toh deh EE-dah ee VWEHL-tah*
How long will the bus be stopped?	**¿Por cuánto tiempo estará detenido el autobús?** *pohr KWAHN-toh TYEHM-poh ehs-tah-RAH deh-teh-NEE-doh ehl ow-toh-BOOS*
Is there an air conditioned bus?	**¿Hay un autobús con aire acondicionado?** *aye oon ow-toh-BOOS kohn AYE-reh ah-kohn-dee-syoh-NAH-doh*
Is this seat taken?	**¿Este asiento está ocupado?** *EHS-teh ah-SYEHN-toh ehs-TAH oh-koo-PAH-doh*
Where is the next stop?	**¿Dónde es la próxima parada?** *DOHN-deh ehs lah PROHK-see-mah pah-RAH-dah*

GETTING THERE

Humping the Bus?!

Be very careful with the verb *coger*. In Spain, it means to catch or grab—as in, I'm going to catch the bus. But in much of Latin America, coger is an obscenity—the equivalent of "fuck" in English. If all you want to do is *ride* the bus (in the literal sense), it's best to say **Voy a tomar el autobús** in Latin America.

Please tell me when we reach ____.	**Por favor dígame cuando lleguemos a ____.** *pohr fah-VOHR DEE-gah-meh KWAHN-doh yeh-GEH-mohs ah*
Let me off here.	**Déjeme aquí.** *DEH-heh-meh ah-KEE*

BY BOAT OR SHIP

Would you take me to the port?	**¿Me puede llevar al puerto?** *meh PWEH-deh yeh-VAHR ahl PWEHR-toh*
When does the ship sail?	**¿Cuándo zarpa el barco?** *KWAHN-doh SAHR-pah ehl BAHR-koh*
How long is the trip?	**¿Cuán largo es el viaje?** *kwahn LAHR-goh ehs ehl VYAH-heh*
Where are the life preservers?	**¿Dónde están los salvavidas?** *DOHN-deh ehs-TAHN lohs sahl-vah-VEE-dahs*
I would like a private cabin.	**Quisiera un camarote privado.** *kee-SYEH-rah oon kah-mah-ROH-teh pree-VAH-doh*
Is the trip rough?	**¿El viaje es brusco?** *ehl VYAH-heh ehs BROOS-koh*
I feel seasick.	**Me siento mareado -a.** *meh SYEHN-toh mah-reh-AH-doh / mah-reh-AH-dah*
I need some seasick pills.	**Necesito unas píldoras para los mareos.** *neh-seh-SEE-toh oo-nahs peel-DOH-rahs pah-rah lohs mah-REH-ohs*
Where is the bathroom?	**¿Dónde está el baño?** *DOHN-deh ehs-TAH ehl BAH-nyoh*

Does the ship have a casino?

¿El barco tiene un casino?
ehl BAHR-koh TYEH-neh oon kah-SEE-noh

Will the ship stop at ports along the way?

¿El barco se detendrá en puertos a lo largo del camino?
ehl BAHR-koh seh deh-tehn-DRAH ehn PWEHR-tohs ah loh LAHR-goh dehl kah-MEE-noh

BY SUBWAY

Where's the subway station?

¿Dónde está la estación de metro?
DOHN-deh ehs-TAH lah ehs-tah-SYOHN deh MEH-troh

Where can I buy a ticket?

¿Dónde puedo comprar un boleto?
DOHN-deh PWEH-doh kohm-PRAHR oon boh-LEH-toh

SUBWAY TICKETS

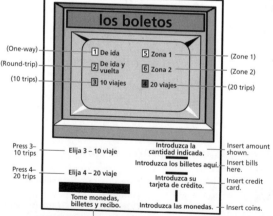

los boletos

(One-way) — 1 De ida
(Round-trip) — 2 De ida y vuelta
(10 trips) — 3 10 viajes
5 Zona 1 — (Zone 1)
6 Zona 2 — (Zone 2)
4 20 viajes — (20 trips)

Press 3– 10 trips — Elija 3 – 10 viaje
Press 4– 20 trips — Elija 4 – 20 viaje
Tome monedas, billetes y recibo.

Introduzca la cantidad indicada. — Insert amount shown.
Introduzca los billetes aquí. — Insert bills here.
Introduzca su tarjeta de crédito. — Insert credit card.
Introduzca las monedas. — Insert coins.

(Take change, tickets, receipt)

Could I have a map of the subway?	**¿Puede darme un mapa del metro?** *PWEH-deh DAHR-meh oon MAH-pah dehl MEH-troh*
Which line goes to ___?	**¿Qué línea va para ___?** *KEH LEEH-neh-ah vah pah-rah*
Is this the right line for ___?	**¿Es ésta la línea correcta para ___?** *ehs EHS-tah lah LEE-neh-ah koh-RREHK-tah PAH-rah*
Which stop is it for ___?	**¿Cuál es la parada para ___?** *KWAHL ehs lah pah-RAH-dah PAH-rah*
How many stops is it to ___?	**¿Cuántas paradas faltan para ___?** *KWAHN-tahs pah-RAH-dahs FAHL-tahn PAH-rah*
Do I need to change trains?	**¿Tengo que cambiar de tren?** *TEHN-goh keh kam-bee-AHR deh trehn*
Is the next stop ___?	**¿La próxima parada es ___?** *lah PROHK-see-mah pah-RAH-dah ehs*
Where are we?	**¿Dónde estamos?** *DOHN-deh ehs-TAH-mohs*
Where do I change to ___?	**¿Adónde me cambio para ___?** *ah-DOHN-deh meh KAHM-byoh PAH-rah*
What time is the last train to ___?	**¿A qué hora pasa el último tren para ___?** *ah KEH OH-rah PAH-sah ehl OOL-tee-moh trehn PAH-rah*

CONSIDERATIONS FOR TRAVELERS WITH SPECIAL NEEDS

Do you have wheelchair access?	**¿Tienen acceso para sillas de ruedas?** *TYEH-nehn ahk-SEH-soh PAH-rah SEE-yahs deh RWEH-dahs*

Do you have elevators?
Where?

¿Tienen elevadores? ¿Dónde?
TYEH-nehn eh-leh-vah-DOH-rehs DOHN-deh

Do you have ramps?
Where?

¿Tienen rampas? ¿Dónde?
TYEH-nehn RRAHM-pahs DOHN-deh

Are the restrooms
wheelchair accessible?

¿Los baños son accesibles para sillas de ruedas?
lohs BAH-nyohs sohn ahk-seh-SEE-blehs pah-rah SEE-yahs deh RWEH-dahs

Do you have audio
assistance for the hearing
impaired?

¿Ustedes tienen asistencia auditiva para las personas con impedimentos auditivos?
oos-TEH-dehs TYEH-nehn ah-sees-TEHN-syah ow-dee-TEE-vah PAH-rah lahs pehr-SOH-nahs kohn eem-peh-dee-MEHN-tohs ow-dee-TEE-vohs

I am deaf.

Yo tengo impedimentos auditivos.
yoh TEHN-goh eem-peh-dee-MEHN-tohs ow-dee-TEE-vohs

May I bring my service dog?

¿Puedo traer a mi perro de servicio?
PWEH-doh trah-EHR ah mee PEH-rroh deh sehr-VEE-syoh

I am blind.

Yo tengo impedimentos visuales.
yoh TEHN-goh eem-peh-dee-MEHN-tohs vee-SWAH-lehs

I need to charge my
power chair.

Necesito recargar mi silla de ruedas eléctrica.
neh-seh-SEE-toh reh-kahr-GAHR mee SEE-yah deh RWEH-dahs eh-LEHK-tree-kah

CHAPTER THREE

LODGING

This chapter will help you find the right accommodations, at the right price, and the amenities you might need during your stay.

ROOM PREFERENCES

Please recommend ____
Por favor recomiende ____
pohr fah-VOHR reh-koh-MYEHN-deh

a clean hostel.
una hospedería limpia.
oo-nah ohs-peh-deh-REE-ah LEEM-pyah

a moderately priced hotel.
un hotel de precio módico.
oon oh-TEHL deh PREH-syoh MOH-dee-koh

a moderately priced B&B.
una hospedería con cama y desayuno de precio módico.
oo-nah ohs-peh-deh-REE-ah kohn KAH-mah ee deh-sah-YOO-noh deh PREH-syoh MOH-dee-ko

a good hotel / motel.
un buen hotel / motel.
oon bwehn oh-TEHL / moh-TEHL

Does the hotel have ____
¿El hotel tiene ____
ehl oh-TEHL TYEH-neh

an indoor / outdoor pool?
una piscina en exteriores / cubierta?
oo-na pees-SEE-nah ehn ehx-te ree-OH-rehs / kuh-bee-EHR-tah

a casino?
un casino?
oon kah-SEE-noh

suites?
suites?
soo-EETS

a fitness center?
un centro de gimnasia?
oon SEHN-troh deh heem-NAH-syah

66

a spa?	**un balneario?**
	oon bahl-neh-AH-ryoh
a private beach?	**una playa privada?**
	oo-nah PLAH-yah pree-VAH-dah
a tennis court?	**una cancha de tenis?**
	oo-nah KAHN-chah deh TEH-nees
air conditioned rooms?	**habitaciones con aire acondicionado?**
	ah-bee-tah-SYOH-nehs kohn AYE-reh ah-kohn-dee-syoh-NAH-doh
free Wi-Fi?	**Wi-Fi gratis?**
	wee fee GRAH-tees
I would like a room for _____.	**Quisiera una habitación para ___.**
	kee-SYEH-rah oo-nah ah-bee-tah-SYOHN pah-rah

For full coverage of number terms, see p7.

I would like _____	**Quisiera ____**
	kee-SYEH-rah
a king-sized bed.	**una cama king.**
	oo-nah KAH-mah keeng
a double bed.	**una cama doble.**
	oo-nah KAH-mah DOH-bleh
twin beds.	**dos camas individuales.**
	dohs KAH-mahs een-dee-vee-DWAHL-ehs
adjoining rooms.	**habitaciones adjuntas.**
	ah-bee-tah-SYOH-nehs ad-HOON-tahs

Listen Up: Reservations Lingo

No tenemos vacantes.	We have no vacancies.
noh teh-NEH-mohs bah-KAHN-tehs	
¿Cuánto tiempo se queda?	How long will you be staying?
KWAN-toh TYEM-poh seh KEH-dah?	
¿Sección para fumadores o no fumadores?	Smoking or non smoking?
sek-SYON PAH-rah foo-mah-DOH-rehs oh noh foo-mah-DOH-rehs?	

LODGING

a smoking room.	una habitación en la que se pueda fumar.
	oo-nah ah-bee-tah-SYOHN deh foo-MAHR
a non-smoking room.	una habitación de no fumar.
	oo-nah ah-bee-tah-SYOHN deh noh foo-MAHR
a private bathroom.	un baño privado.
	oon BAH-nyoh pree-VAH-doh
a shower.	una ducha.
	oo-nah DOO-cha
a bathtub.	una bañera.
	oo-nah bah-NYEH-rah
air conditioning.	aire acondicionado.
	AYE-reh ah-cohn-dee-syoh-NAH-doh
television.	un televisor.
	oon teh-leh-vee-SOHR
cable.	televisión por cable.
	teh-leh-vee-SYOHN pohr KAH-bleh
satellite TV.	televisión por satélite.
	teh-leh-vee-SYOHN pohr sah-TEH-lee-teh
a telephone.	un teléfono.
	oon teh-LEH-foh-noh
Internet access.	acceso a Internet.
	ahk-SEH-soh ahl een-tehr-NEHT
Wi-Fi.	Wi-Fi / red inalámbrica.
	wee fee / rehd eeh-nah-LAM-breeh-kah
a refrigerator.	un refrigerador.
	oon rreh-free-heh-rah-DOHR
a beach view.	vista a la playa.
	VEES-tah ah lah PLAH-yah

a city view.
vista a la ciudad.
VEES-tah ah lah see-oo-DAD

a kitchenette.
una cocina pequeña.
oo-nah koh-SEE-nah
peh-KEH-nyah

a balcony.
un balcón.
oon bahl-KOHN

a suite.
una suite.
oo-nah soo-EET

a penthouse.
un ático de lujo.
oon AH-tee-koh deh LOO-ho

I would like a room _____
Quisiera una habitación ____
kee-SYEH-rah oo-nah ah-bee-tah-SYOHN

on the ground floor.
en el primer piso.
ehn ehl pree-MEHR PEE-soh

near the elevator.
cerca del elevador.
SEHR-kah dehl eh-leh-vah-DOHR

near the stairs.
cerca de las escaleras.
SEHR-kah deh lahs ehs-kah-LEH-rahs

near the pool.
cerca de la piscina.
SEHR-kah deh lah pees-SEE-nah

away from the street.
lejos de la calle.
LEH-hohs deh lah KAH-yeh

I would like a corner room.
Quisiera una habitación de esquina.
kee-SYEH-rah oo-nah ah-bee-tah-SYOHN deh ehs-KEE-nah

Do you have _____
¿Tiene ____
TYEH-neh

a crib?
una cuna?
oo-nah KOO-nah

a foldout bed?
una cama desplegable?
oo-nah KAH-mah dehs-pleh-GAH-bleh

LODGING

FOR GUESTS WITH SPECIAL NEEDS

I need a room with ____	**Necesito una habitación con ____** *neh-seh-SEE-toh oo-nah ah-bee-tah-SYOHN kohn*
wheelchair access.	**acceso para silla de ruedas.** *ahk-SEH-soh pah-rah SEE-yah deh RWEH-dahs*
services for the visually impaired.	**servicios para las personas con impedimentos visuales.** *sehr-VEE-syohs pah-rah lahs pehr-SOH-nahs kohn eem-peh-dee-MEHN-tohs vee-SWAH-lehs*
services for the hearing impaired.	**servicios para las personas con impedimentos auditivos.** *sehr-VEE-syohs pah-rah lahs pehr-SOH-nahs kohn eem-peh-dee-MEHN-tohs ow-dee-TEE-vohs*
I am traveling with a service dog.	**Estoy viajando con un perro de servicio.** *ehs-TOY vyah-HAHN-doh kohn oon PEH-rroh deh sehr-VEE-syoh*

MONEY MATTERS

I would like to make a reservation.	**Quisiera hacer una reservación.** *kee-SYEH-rah ah-SEHR oo-nah rreh-sehr-vah-SYOHN*
How much per night?	**¿Cuánto cuesta por noche?** *KWAHN-toh KWEHS-tah pohr NOH-cheh*
Do you have a ____	**¿Tiene una tarifa ____?** *TYEH-neh oo-nah tah-REE-fah*
weekly / monthly rate?	**semanal / mensual?** *seh-mah-NAHL / mehn-SWAHL*
a weekend rate?	**una tarifa de fin de semana?** *oo-nah tah-REE-fah deh feen deh seh-MAH-nah*
a special rate?	**una tarifa especial?** *oo-nah tah-REEH-fah ehs-peh-see-AL*

a discount?	**descuento?**
	dehs-KWEHN-toh
We will be staying for ___ days / weeks.	**¿Nos quedaremos por ___ días / semanas.**
	nohs keh-dah-REH-mohs pohr ___ DEE-ahs / seh-MAH-nahs

For full coverage of number terms, see p7.

| When is checkout time? | **¿Cuál es la hora de salida?** |
| | *KWAHL ehs lah OH-rah deh sah-LEE-dah* |

For full coverage of time-related terms, see p12.

Do you accept credit cards?	**¿Aceptan tarjetas de crédito?**
	ah-SEHP-tahn tahr-HEH-tahs deh KREH-dee-toh
May I see a room?	**¿Puedo ver una habitación?**
	PWEH-doh VEHR oo-nah ah-bee-tah-SYOHN

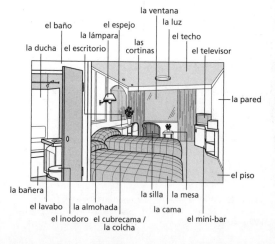

la ventana
el baño   el espejo   la luz
la ducha   la lámpara   el techo
el escritorio   las cortinas   el televisor
    la pared
la bañera
el lavabo   la almohada   la silla   la mesa   el piso
el inodoro   el cubrecama / la colcha   la cama   el mini-bar

LODGING

How much are taxes?	**¿Cuántos son los impuestos?**
	KWAHN-tohs sohn lohs eem-PWEHS-tohs
Is there a service charge?	**¿Hay un cargo por servicio?**
	aye oon KAHR-goh pohr sehr-VEE-syoh
I'd like to speak with the manager.	**Quisiera hablar con el gerente.**
	kee-SYEH-rah ah-BLAHR kohn ehl heh-REHN-teh

IN-ROOM AMENITIES

I'd like _____	**Quisiera _____**
	kee-SYEH-rah
to place an international call.	**hacer una llamada internacional.**
	ah-SEHR oo-nah yah-MAH-dah een-tehr-nah-syoh-NAHL
to place a long-distance call.	**hacer una llamada de larga distancia.**
	ah-SEHR oo-nah yah-MAH-dah deh LAHR-gah dees-TAHN-syah
directory assistance in English.	**asistencia en inglés.**
	ah-sees-TEHN-syah ehn een-GLEHS
room service.	**servicio a las habitaciones.**
	sehr-VEE-syoh ah lahs ah-bee-tah-SYOH-nehs

Instructions for dialing the hotel phone

Para llamar a otra habitación, marque el número de la habitación. *PAH-rah jah-MAHR ah OH-trah ah-bee-tah-SYON, MAHR-keh ehl NOO-meh-roh deh lah ah-bee-tah-SYON*	To call another room, dial the room number.
Para llamadas locales, marque primero el 9. *PAH-rah jah-MA-dahs loh-KAH-lehs, MAHR-keh pree-MEH-roh ehl noo-EH-beh*	To make a local call, first dial 9.
Para la operadora, marque el 0. *PAH-rah lah oh-peh-rah-DOH-rah, MAHR-keh ehl SEH-roh*	To call the operator, dial 0.

maid service.	**servicio de mucama.**
	sehr-VEE-syoh deh moo-KAH-mah
the front desk ATT operator.	**la operadora de ATT de la recepción.**
	lah oh-peh-rah-DOH-rah deh ah teh teh deh lah reh-sehp-SYOHN
Do you have room service?	**¿Tienen servicio a las habitaciones?**
	TYEH-nehn sehr-VEE-syoh ah lahs ah-bee-tah-SYOH-nehs
When is the kitchen open?	**¿Cuándo abre la cocina?**
	KWAHN-doh AH-breh lah koh-SEE-nah
When is breakfast served?	**¿Cuándo se servirá el desayuno?**
	KWAHN-doh seh sehr-vee-RAH ehl deh-sah-YOO-noh

For full coverage of time-related terms, see p12.

Do you offer massages?	**¿Ustedes ofrecen masajes?**
	oos-TEH-dehs oh-FREH-sehn mah-SAH-hehs
Do you have a lounge?	**¿Tienen un salón público?**
	TYEH-nehn oon sah-LOHN POO-blee-koh
Do you have a business center?	**¿Tienen un centro de negocios?**
	TYEH-nehn oon SEHN-troh deh neh-GOH-syohs
Do you serve breakfast?	**¿Sirven desayuno?**
	SEER-vehn deh-sah-YOO-noh
Do you have Wi-Fi in rooms, or in the lobby only?	**¿Tienen Wi-Fi en las habitaciones, o sólo en recepción?**
	TEE-EH-nehn wee fee ehn lahs ah-bee-tah-SYOH-nes, oh SOH-loh ehn reh-sehp-SYON
May I have a newspaper in the morning?	**¿Puedo recibir un periódico en la mañana?**
	PWEH-deh reh-see-BEER oon peh-RYOH-dee-koh ehn lah mah-NYAH-nah

LODGING

Do you offer a tailor service?	**¿Ustedes ofrecen un servicio de sastrería?** *oos-TEH-dehs oh-FREH-sehn oon sehr-VEE-syoh deh sahs-treh-REE-ah*
Do you offer laundry service?	**¿Ustedes ofrecen servicio de lavandería?** *oos-TEH-dehs oh-FREH-sehn sehr-VEE-syoh deh lah-vahn-deh-REE-ah*
Do you offer dry cleaning?	**¿Ustedes ofrecen servicio de limpieza en seco?** *oos-TEH-dehs oh-FREH-sehn sehr-VEE-syoh deh leem-PYEH-sah ehn SEH-koh*
May we have _____	**¿Podemos tener _____** *poh-DEH-mohs teh-NEHR*
clean sheets today?	**sábanas limpias hoy?** *SAH-bah-nahs LEEM-pee-ahs oy*
more towels?	**más toallas?** *mahs toh-AH-yahs*
more toilet paper?	**más papel sanitario?** *mahs pah-PEHL sah-nee-TAH-ryoh*
extra pillows?	**almohadas adicionales?** *ahl-moh-AH-dahs ah-dee-syoh-NAH-lehs*
shampoo?	**champú?** *cham-POO*
toothpaste?	**pasta de dientes?** *PAHS-tah deh dee-EHN-tehs*
a toothbrush?	**cepillo de dientes?** *seh-PEE-yoh deh dee-EHN-tehs*
an adapter?	**un adaptador?** *oon ah-dap-tah-DOHR*
a bottle opener?	**un abridor?** *oon ah-BREE-dohr*

Do you have an ice machine?	**¿Tienen una máquina de hielo?** *TYEH-nehn oo-nah MAH-kee-nah deh YEH-loh*
Did I receive any ____	**¿Recibí ____** *reh-see-BEE*
messages?	**algún mensaje?** *ahl-GOON mehn-SAH-heh*
mail?	**alguna correspondencia?** *ahl-GOO-nah koh-rrehs-pohn-DEHN-syah*
faxes?	**algún fax?** *ahl-GOON fahks*
A spare key, please.	**Una llave adicional, por favor.** *oo-nah YAH-veh ah-dee-syoh-NAHL, pohr fah-VOHR*
More hangers please.	**Más perchas por favor.** *mahs PEHR-chahs pohr fah-VOHR*
I am allergic to down pillows	**Soy alérgico / alérgica a las almohadas de plumas.** *soy ah-LEHR-hee-koh ah-LEHR-hee-kah ah lahs ahl-moh-AH-dahs deh PLOO-mahs*
I'd like a wake up call.	**Quisiera una llamada para despertar.** *kee-SYEH-rah oo-nah yah-MAH-dah pah-rah dehs-pehr-TAHR*

For full coverage of how to tell time, see p12.

Do you have alarm clocks?	**¿Tiene relojes despertadores?** *TYEH-neh reh-LOH-hehs dehs-pehr-tah-DOH-rehs*
Is there a safe in the room?	**¿Hay una caja fuerte en la habitación?** *aye oo-nah KAH-hah FWEHR-teh ehn lah ah-bee-tah-SYOHN*
Does the room have a hair dryer?	**¿La habitación tiene un secador de pelo?** *lah ah-bee-tah-SYOHN TYEH-neh oon seh-kah-DOHR deh PEH-loh*

LODGING

HOTEL ROOM TROUBLE

May I speak with the manager?

¿Puedo hablar con el gerente?
PWEH-doh ah-BLAHR kohn ehl heh-REHN-teh

The ____ does not work.

____ no funciona.
noh foon-SYOH-nah

television

El televisor
ehl teh-leh-vee-SOHR

telephone

El teléfono
ehl teh-LEH-foh-noh

air conditioning

El aire acondicionado
ehl AYE-reh ah-kohn-dee-syoh-NAH-doh

Internet access

El acceso al Internet
ehl ahk-SEH-soh ahl een-tehr-NET

cable TV

El servicio de cable TV
ehl sehr-VEE-syoh deh KAH-bleh teh VEH

There is no hot water.

No hay agua caliente.
noh aye AH-wah kah-LYEHN-teh

The toilet is over-flowing!

¡El inodoro se está desbordando!
ehl ee-noh-DOH-roh seh ehs-TAH dehs-bohr-DAHN-doh

This room is ____
Esta habitación ____
EHS-tah ah-bee-tah-SYOHN

  too noisy.
  es muy ruidosa.
  ehs MOO-ee roo-ee-DOH-sah

  too cold.
  está muy fría.
  ehs-TAH MOO-ee FREE-ah

  too warm.
  está muy cálida.
  ehs-TAH MOO-ee KAH-lee-dah

  dirty.
  está sucia.
  ehs-TAH SOOH-sya

This room has ____
Esta habitación tiene ____
EHS-tah ah-bee-tah-SYOHN TYEH-neh

  bugs.
  insectos.
  een-SEHK-tohs

  mice.
  ratones.
  rah-TOH-nehs

I'd like a different room.
Quisiera una habitación diferente.
kee-SYEH-rah oo-nah ah-bee-tah-SYOHN dee-feh-REHN-teh

Do you have a bigger room?
¿Tiene una habitación más grande?
TYEH-neh oo-nah ah-bee-tah-SYOHN mahs GRAHN-deh

I locked myself out of my room.
Me quedé fuera de mi habitación.
meh keh-DEH FWEH-rah deh mee ah-bee-tah-SYOHN

I lost my keys.
He perdido las llaves.
eh pehr-DEE-doh lahs YAH-vehs

Do you have a fan?
¿Tiene un ventilador?
TYEH-neh oon ven-tee-lah-DOHR

The sheets are not clean.
Las sábanas no están limpias.
lahs SAH-bah-nahs noh ehs-TAHN LEEM-pyahs

The towels are not clean.
Las toallas no están limpias.
lahs to-AH-yahs noh ehs-TAHN LEEM-pyahs

The room is not clean.

La habitación no está limpia.
lah ah-bee-tah-SYOHN noh ehs-TAH LEEM-pyah

The guests next door / above / below are being very loud.

Los huéspedes al lado / arriba / abajo son muy ruidosos.
lohs WEHS-peh-dehs ahl LAH-doh / ah-RREE-bah / ah-BAH-hoh sohn MOO-ee roo-ee-DOH-sohs

CHECKING OUT

May I leave these bags?

¿Puedo dejar este equipaje?
PWEH-doh deh-HAHR EHS-teh eh-keeh-PAH-heh

I'm missing _____.

No encuentro _____.
noh ehn-KWEN-troh

I've lost _____.

He perdido _____.
eh pehr-DEE-doh

I think this charge is a mistake.

Creo que este cargo es un error.
KREH-oh keh EHS-teh KAHR-goh ehs oon eh-RROHR

Please explain this charge to me.

Por favor explíqueme este cargo.
pohr fah-VOHR ehks-PLEE-keh-meh EHS-teh KAHR-goh

Thank you, we enjoyed our stay.

Gracias, disfrutamos nuestra estadía.
GRAH-syahs dees-froo-TAH-mohs NWEHS-trah ehs-tah-DEE-ah

The service was excellent.

El servicio fue excelente.
ehl sehr-VEE-syoh fweh ehk-seh-LEHN-teh

The staff is very professional and courteous.

El personal es muy profesional y cortés.
ehl pehr-soh-NAHL ehs MOO-ee proh-feh-syoh-NAHL ee kohr-TEHS

Please call a cab for me.

Por favor, llame a un taxi para mí.
pohr fah-VOHR YAH-meh ah oon TAX-see PAH-rah mee

Would someone please get my bags?

¿Alguien puede ayudarme con mis bolsas?
AHLG-yehn PWEH-deh ah-yoo-DAHR-meh kohn mees BOHL-sahs

HAPPY CAMPING

I'd like a site for _____

Quisiera un lugar para _____
kee-SYEH-rah oon loo-GAHR pah-rah

a tent.

una carpa.
oo-nah KAHR-pah

a camper.

un carro de acampar / autocaravana.
oon KAY-rroh deh ah-kahm-PAHR / ow-toh-kah-rah-VAH-nah

Are there _____

¿Hay _____
aye

bathrooms?

baños?
BAH-nyohs

showers?

duchas?
DOOH-chahs

Is there running water?

¿Hay agua corriente?
aye AH-wah koh-rree-EHN-teh

Is the water drinkable?

¿El agua es potable?
ehl AH-wah ehs poh-TAH-bleh

Where is the electrical hookup?

¿Dónde está la conexión eléctrica?
DOHN-deh ehs-TAH lah koh-nehk-SYOHN eh-LEHK-tree-kah

CHAPTER FOUR

DINING

This chapter includes a menu reader and the language you need to communicate in a range of dining establishments and food markets.

FINDING A RESTAURANT

Would you recommend a good _____ restaurant?	¿Podría recomendar un buen restaurante _____ *poh-DREE-ah reh-koh-mehn-DAHR oon bwehn rrehst-ow-RAHN-teh*
local	local? *loh-KAHL*
Italian	italiano? *ee-tah-LYAH-noh*
French	francés? *frahn-SEHS*
German	alemán? *ah-leh-MAHN*
Spanish	español? *ehs-pah-NYOHL*
Chinese	chino? *CHEE-noh*
Japanese	japonés? *hah-poh-NEHS*
Asian	asiático? *ah-SYAH-tee-koh*
pizza	de pizza? *deh PEET-sah*
steakhouse	de parrilla? *deh pah-RREE-yah*
family	familiar? *fah-mee-LYAHR*

seafood	**de mariscos?**
	deh mah-REES-kohs
vegetarian	**vegetariano?**
	veh-heh-tah-RYAH-noh
buffet-style	**estilo buffet?**
	ehs-TEE-loh boo-FEH
Greek	**griego?**
	GRYEH-goh
budget	**económico?**
	eh-koh-NOH-mee-koh
Which is the best restaurant in town?	**¿Cuál es el mejor restaurante en el pueblo?**
	kwahl ehs ehl meh-HOHR rrehst-ow-RAHN-teh ehn ehl PWEH-bloh
Is there a late-night restaurant nearby?	**¿Hay un restaurante cercano abierto hasta tarde en la noche?**
	aye oon rrehst-ow-RAHN-teh SEHR-kah-noh ah-BYEHR-toh AHS-tah TAHR-deh ehn lah NOH-cheh
Is there a restaurant that serves breakfast nearby?	**¿Hay un restaurante cercano que sirva desayuno?**
	aye oon rrehst-ow-RAHN-teh SEHR-ka-noh keh SEER-vah deh-sah-YOO-noh
Is it very expensive?	**¿Es muy caro?**
	ehs MOO-ee KAH-roh
Do I need a reservation?	**¿Necesito una reservación?**
	neh-seh-SEE-toh oo-nah rreh-sehr-vah-SYOHN
Do I have to dress up?	**¿Necesito vestirme elegante-mente?**
	neh-seh-SEE-toh vehs-TEER-meh eh-leh-gahn-teh-MEHN-teh

Do they serve lunch?	**¿Sirven almuerzo?** *SEER-vehn ahl-MWEHR-soh*
What time do they open for dinner?	**¿A qué hora abren para la cena?** *ah KEH OH-rah AH-brehn PAH-rah lah SEH-nah*
For lunch?	**¿Para el almuerzo?** *PAH-rah ehl ahl-MWEHR-soh*
What time do they close?	**¿A qué hora cierran?** *ah KEH OH-rah SYEH-rrahn*
Do you have a take out menu?	**¿Tienen un menú de comidas para llevar?** *TYEH-nehn oon meh-NOO deh ko-MEE-dahs PAH-rah yeh-VAHR*
Do you have a bar?	**¿Tienen un bar?** *TYEH-nehn oon bar*
Is there a café nearby?	**¿Hay un café cerca?** *aye oon kah-FEH SEHR-kah*

GETTING SEATED

Are you still serving?	**¿Todavía están sirviendo?** *toh-dah-VEE-ah ehs-TAHN seer-VYEHN-doh*
How long is the wait?	**¿Cuán larga es la espera?** *kwahn LAHR-gah es lah ehs-PEH-rah*
May I see the menu?	**¿Me permite ver la carta?** *meh pehr-MEE-teh vehr lah KAR-ta*
Do you have a no-smoking section?	**¿Tienen una sección de no fumar?** *TYEH-nehn oo-nah sehk-SYOHN deh noh foo-MAHR*
A table for ____, please.	**Una mesa para ____, por favor.** *oo-nah MEH-sah PAH-rah ____, pohr fah-VOHR*

For a full list of numbers, see p7.

Do you have a quiet, table?	**¿Tienen una mesa tranquila?** *TYEH-nehn oo-nah MEH-sah trahn-KEE-lah*
Do you have highchairs?	**¿Tienen sillas para bebes?** *TYEH-nen SEE-yahs PAH-ra beh-BEHS*

Listen Up: Restaurant Lingo

¿Sección de fumar o de no fumar?	Smoking or nonsmoking?
sehk-SYOHN deh foo-MAHR oh deh noh foo-MAHR	
Necesita una corbata y una chaqueta.	You'll need a tie and jacket.
neh-seh-SEE-tah oo-nah kohr-BAH-tah ee oo-na chah-KEH-tah	
Lo siento, no se permite pantalones cortos.	I'm sorry, no shorts are allowed.
loh SYEHN-toh noh seh pehr-MEE-tehn pahn-tah-LOH-nehs KOHR-tohs	
¿Le puedo traer algo de tomar?	May I bring you something to drink?
leh PWEH-doh trah-EHR AHL-goh deh toh-MAHR	
¿Le gustaría ver una lista de vinos?	Would you like to see a wine list?
leh goos-tah-REE-ah vehr oo-nah LEES-tah deh VEE-nohs	
¿Le gustaría saber cuáles son nuestros platos especiales?	Would you like to hear our specials?
leh goos-tah-REE-ah sah-BEHR KWAH-lehs sohn NWEHS-trohs PLAH-tohs ehs-peh-SYAH-lehs	
¿Está listo para ordenar?	Are you ready to order?
ehs-TAH LEES-toh PAH-rah ohr-deh-NAHR	
Lo siento señor. Su tarjeta de crédito ha sido rechazada.	I'm sorry, sir, your credit card was declined.
loh SYEHN-toh seh-NYOHR soo tahr-HEH-tah deh KREH-dee-toh hah SEE-doh reh-chah-SAH-dah	

May we sit outside / inside please?	**¿Podemos sentarnos afuera / adentro por favor?** *poh-DEH-mohs sehn-TAHR-nohs ah-FWEH-rah / ah-DEHN-troh pohr fah-VOHR*
May we sit at the counter?	**¿Podemos sentarnos en el la barra?** *poh-DEH-mohs sehn-TAHR-nohs ehn lah BAH-rrah*
I'd like to order.	**Me gustaría pedir / ordenar.** *meh guhs-tah-REEH-a peh-DEEHR / ohr-deh-NAHR*

ORDERING

Do you have a special tonight?	**¿Tienen un especial esta noche?** *TYEH-nehn oon ehs-peh-SYAHL EHS-tah NOH-cheh*
What do you recommend?	**¿Qué recomienda usted?** *KEH reh-koh-MYEHN-dah oos-TEHD*
May I see a wine list?	**¿Puedo ver una carta de vinos?** *PWEH-doh vehr oo-nah KAR-tah deh VEE-nohs*
Do you serve wine by the glass?	**¿Ustedes sirven vino por copa?** *oos-TEH-dehs SEER-vehn VEE-noh pohr KOH-pah*
May I see a drink list?	**¿Puedo ver una carta de bebidas?** *PWEH-doh vehr oo-nah KAR-tah deh beh-BEE-dahs*
I would like it cooked _____	**Me gustaría _____** *meh goos-tah-REE-ah*
rare.	**vuelta y vuelta.** *vooh-EHL-tah eeh vooh-EHL-tah*
medium rare.	**antes del punto.** *ahn-tehs dehl POON-toh*
medium.	**a punto.** *ah POON-toh*

medium well.	**medio bien cocido.**
	MEH-dyoh BYEHN koh-SEE-doh
well.	**bien cocido.**
	BYEHN koh-SEE-doh
charred.	**achicharrado.**
	ah-chee-chah-RRAH-doh
Do you have a _____ menu?	**¿Tiene un menú _____**
	TYEH-neh oon meh-NOO
diabetic	**para diabéticos?**
	pah-rah dee-ah-BEH-tee-kohs
kosher	**kósher?**
	KOH-shehr
	KOH-shehr
gluten-free	**sin gluten**
	seen GLUE-ten
vegetarian	**vegetariano?**
	veh-heh-tah-REE-AH-noh
children's	**para niños?**
	PAH-rah NEE-nyohs
What is in this dish?	**¿Qué hay en este plato?**
	KEH aye ehn EHS-teh PLAH-toh
How is it prepared?	**¿Cómo está preparado?**
	KOH-moh ehs-TAH preh-PAH-rah-do
What kind of oil is that cooked in?	**¿En qué tipo de aceite está cocido?**
	ehn KEH TEE-poh deh ah-SEH-ee-teh eh-STAH koh-SEE-doh
Do you have any low-salt dishes?	**¿Tiene platos con poca sal?**
	TYEH-neh PLAH-tohs kohn POH-ka sahl
On the side, please.	**Al lado, por favor.**
	ahl LAH-doh pohr fah-VOHR
May I make a substitution?	**¿Puedo hacer una sustitución?**
	PWEH-doh ah-SEHR oo-nah soos-tee-too-SYOHN

I'd like to try that.	**Me gustaría probar eso.** *meh goos-tah-REE-ah proh-BAHR* *EH-soh*
Is that fresh?	**¿Eso es fresco?** *EH-so ehs FREHS-koh*
Waiter!	**¡Mozo! ¡Mesero!** (Colombia) *MOH-soh / meh-SEH-roh*
Extra butter, please.	**Mantequilla adicional, por favor.** *mahn-teh-KEE-yah ah-dee-syoh-* *NAHL pohr fah-VOHR*
No butter, thanks.	**Sin mantequilla, por favor.** *seen mahn-teh-KEE-yah pohr fah-* *VOHR*
No cream, thanks.	**Sin crema, por favor.** *seen KREH-mah pohr fah-VOHR*
Dressing on the side, please.	**El aderezo aparte, por favor.** *ehl ah-deh-REH-soh ah-PAHR-teh,* *pohr fah-VOHR*
No salt, please.	**Sin sal, por favor.** *SEEN sahl pohr fah-VOHR*
May I have some oil, please?	**¿Me puede dar un poco de aceite,** **por favor?** *meh PWEH-deh dahr oon POH-koh* *deh ah-SEH-ee-teh pohr fah-VOHR*
More bread, please.	**Más pan, por favor.** *mahs PAHN pohr fah-VOHR*
I am lactose intolerant.	**Soy intolerante a la lactosa.** *soy een-toh-leh-RAHN-teh ah lah* *lahk-TOH-sah*
Would you recommend something without milk?	**¿Podría recomendar algo sin** **leche?** *poh-DREE-ah reh-koh-mehn-DAHR* *AHL-goh seen LEH-cheh*
I am allergic to _____	**Soy alérgico / alérgica a _____** *soy ah-LEHR-hee-koh / ah-LEHR-* *hee-kah ah*

seafood.	**los mariscos.** *lohs mah-REES-kohs*
shellfish.	**los crustáceos.** *lohs kroos-TAH-seh-ohs*
nuts.	**las nueces.** *lahs-NWEH-sehs*
peanuts.	**los cacahuates, los manís (Puerto Rico, S.Am.)** *lohs kah-kah-WAH-tehs, lohs mah-NEES*
Water ____, please.	**Agua ____, por favor.** *AH-wah ____ pohr fah-VOHR*
with ice	**con hielo** *kohn YEH-loh*
without ice	**sin hielo** *seen YEH-loh*
sparkling water	**con gas** *kohn gas*
still water	**sin gas** *seen gas*
I'm sorry, I don't think this is what I ordered.	**Lo siento, no creo que esto sea lo que ordené.** *loh SYEHN-toh noh KREH-oh keh EHS-toh SEH-ah loh keh ohr-deh-NEH*
My meat is a little over / under cooked.	**Mi carne está un poco recocida / cruda.** *mee KAHR-neh ehs-TAH oon POH-koh reh-koh-SEE-dah / KROO-dah*
My vegetables are a little over / under cooked.	**Mis vegetales están un poco recocidos / crudos.** *mees veh-he-TAH-lehs ehs-TAHN oon POH-koh reh-koh-SEE-dohs / KROO-dohs*
There's a bug in my food!	**¡Hay un insecto en mi comida!** *aye oon een-SEHK-toh ehn mee koh-MEE-dah*

DINING

May I have another?	**¿Me pone otro / otra?**
	meh POH-ne OH-troh / OH-trah
A dessert menu, please.	**Un menú de postres, por favor.**
	oon meh-NOO deh POHS-trehs
	pohr fah-VOHR

DRINKS

alcoholic	**con alcohol**
	kohn ahl-KOHL
cocktail	**un trago / cóctel**
	oon TRAH-goh / KOHK-tehl
neat / straight	**sencillo**
	sehn-SEE-yoh
on the rocks	**con hielo**
	kohn YEH-loh
with (seltzer or soda)	**con agua (seltzer o soda)**
water	*kohn AH-wah (sehlt-SEHR oh*
	SOH-dah)
beer	**cerveza**
	sehr-VEH-sah
wine	**vino**
	VEE-noh
house wine	**vino de la casa**
	VEE-noh deh lah KAH-sah
sweet wine	**vino dulce**
	VEE-noh DOOL-seh
dry white wine	**vino blanco seco**
	VEE-noh BLAHN-koh SEH-koh
rosé	**vino rosado**
	VEE-noh roh-SAH-doh
light-bodied wine	**vino de cuerpo liviano / ligero**
	VEE-noh deh KWEHR-poh
	lee-VEE-ah-noh / LEE-heh-roh
red wine	**vino tinto**
	VEE-noh TEEN-toh

How Do You Take It?

Tomar means to take. But if a bartender asks, ¿*Quiere tomar algo*?, he's not inviting you to steal his fancy corkscrew. He's asking what you'd like to drink.

full-bodied wine	**vino de cuerpo entero**
	VEE-noh deh KWEHR-poh ehn-TEH-roh
sparkling sweet wine	**vino dulce burbujeante**
	VEE-noh DOOL-seh boor-boo-heh-AHN-teh
champagne	**champán**
	cham-PAN
liqueur	**licor**
	lee-KOHR
brandy	**brandy**
	BRAHN-dee
cognac	**coñac**
	koh-NYAHK
gin	**ginebra**
	hee-NEH-brah
vodka	**vodka**
	VOHD-kah
rum	**ron**
	rohn
nonalcoholic	**sin alcohol**
	seen ahl-KOHL
hot chocolate	**chocolate caliente**
	cho-koh-LAH-teh kah-LYEHN-teh
lemonade	**limonada**
	lee-moh-NAH-dah
milkshake	**batido de leche / malteado (Mexico)**
	bah-TEE-doh deh LEH-cheh / mahl-teh-AH-doh

milk	**leche**
	LEH-cheh
tea	**té**
	TEH
coffee	**café**
	kah-FEH
café au lait	**café con leche**
	kah-FEH kohn LEH-cheh
cappuccino	**cappuccino**
	kah-poo-CHEE-noh
espresso	**café expreso**
	kah-FEH ehks-PREH-soh
iced coffee	**café helado**
	kah-FEH heh-LAH-doh
fruit juice	**jugo de fruta**
	HOO-goh deh FROO-tah

For a full list of fruits, see p103.

SETTLING UP

The check, please.	**La cuenta, por favor.**
	lah KWEN-tah pohr fah-VOHR
I'm stuffed.	**Estoy lleno / llena.**
	ehs-TOY YEH-noh / YEH-nah
The meal was excellent.	**La comida estuvo excelente.**
	lah koh-MEE-dah ehs-TOO-voh
	ehk-seh-LEHN-teh
There's a problem with my bill.	**Hay un problema con mi factura.**
	aye oon proh-BLEH-mah kohn mee
	fahk-TOO-rah
Is the tip included?	**¿La propina está incluida?**
	lah proh-PEE-nah ehs-TAH
	een-kloo-EE-dah
My compliments to the chef!	**¡Mis felicitaciones para el chef!**
	mees feh-lee-see-tah-SYOH-nehs
	PAH-rah ehl chef

MENU READER

Latin American cuisine varies broadly from region to region, but we've tried to make our list of classic dishes as encompassing as possible.

APPETIZERS / TAPAS (APERITIVOS / TAPAS)

aceitunas: olives
ah-seh-ee-TOO-nahs

albóndigas: meatballs in sauce
ahl-BOHN-dee-gahs

bacalao: dried salt cod
bah-kah-LAH-oh

conejo: braised rabbit
koh-NEH-ho

croquetas: croquettes
kroh-KEH-tahs

gambas: broiled shrimp with garlic
GAHM-bahs

jamón: ham
hah-MOHN

   jamón de bellota: free-range, acorn-fed ham
   hah-MOHN deh beh-YOH-tah

   jamón ibérico: aged Iberian ham
   hah-MOHN ee-BEH-ree-koh

   jamón serrano: dry-cured serrano ham
   hah-MOHN seh-RRAH-noh

pescado frito: fried fish
pehs-KAH-doh FREE-toh

quesos: cheeses
KEH-sohs

   de leche de cabra: goat's milk
   deh LEH-cheh deh KAH-brah

   mozzarella: mozzarella
   moht-sah-REH-yah

   parmesano: Parmesan
   pahr-meh-SAH-noh

   rallado: grated
   rah-YAH-doh

requesón: cottage
reh-keh-SOHN
suave: mild
soo-AH-veh
tortilla española: omelet with potato
tohr-TEE-yah ehs-pah-NYOH-lah

SALADS (ENSALADAS)

chonta: hearts-of-palm salad
CHOHN-tah
ensalada mixta: mixed salad (ingredients vary by region)
ehn-sah-LAH-dah MEES-tah
ensalada de verduras: green salad
ehn-sah-LAH-dah deh vehr-DOO-rahs
ensalada de espinacas: spinach salad
ehn-sah-LAH-dah deh ehs-pee-NAH-kahs
ensalada de arúgula: arugula salad
ehn-sah-LAH-dah deh ah-ROO-goo-lah
ensalada de tomates: tomato salad
ehn-sah-LAH-dah deh toh-MAH-tehs
ensalada de berro: watercress salad
ehn-sah-LAH-dah deh BEH-rroh
ensalada de lechuga romana: romaine salad
ehn-sah-LAH-dah deh leh-CHOO-gah rroh-MAH-nah
ensalada de palmitos: hearts of palm salad
ehn-sah-LAH-dah deh pahl-MEE-tohs
ensalada de quinoa: quinoa (Andean grain) salad
ehn-sah-LAH-dah deh kee-NOH-ah

SAUCES / SEASONING BASES (SALSAS / ALIÑOS)

adobo: mixture of crushed peppercorns, salt, oregano, garlic, olive oil, and lime juice or vinegar
ah-DOH-boh
mole: sauce of unsweetened chocolate, chiles, and spices
MOH-leh
romesco: tomato / almond sauce with olive oil and garlic
rroh-MEHS-koh
sofrito: mixture of onions, cilantro, garlic, and chiles
soh-FREE-toh

SOUPS AND STEWS (SOPAS Y GUISOS)

asopao: Puerto Rican gumbo made with chicken or shellfish
ah-soh-PAH-oh

buseca: stew with sausages
boo-SEH-kah

caldo gallego: soup with salt pork, white beans, chorizo, ham, and
turnip / collard greens
KAHL-doh gah-YEH-goh

gazpacho: cold vegetable soup
gahs-PAH-cho

locro de papas: creamy potato soup
LOH-kroh deh PAH-pahs

manchamantel: chicken or pork stew with mixed vegetables and fruit
mahn-chah-mahn-TEHL

menudo: all parts (neck, tripe, etc.) of poultry
meh-NOO-doh

mondongo: beef tripe
mohn-DOHN-goh

sancocho, sancochado: thick soup with meats, vegetables, and corn
on the cob, served with rice
sahn-KOH-choh, sahn-koh-CHAH-doh

sancocho de gallina: chicken soup
sahn-KOH-choh deh gah-YEE-nah

sopa de ajo: garlic soup
SOH-pah deh AH-hoh

sopa de chiles poblanos: green chili soup
SOH-pah deh CHEE-lehs poh-BLAH-nohs

sopa negra / frijoles negros: black bean soup
SOH-pah NEH-grah / free-HOH-lehs NEH-grohs

RICE DISHES (PLATOS CON ARROZ)

arroz con gandules: yellow rice with pigeon peas
ah-RROHS kohn gahn-DOO-lehs

arroz con pollo: chicken and rice
ah-RROHS kohn POH-yoh

arroz negro: rice stew with octopus in its own ink
ah-RROHS NEH-groh

paella: festive seafood / meat rice stew with vegetables, seasoned with saffron
pah-EH-yah

SIDE / VEGETABLE DISHES (GUARNICIONES / VERDURAS)

aguacate relleno, palta rellena (S.Am.): stuffed avocado
ah-wah-KAH-teh rreh-YEH-noh

calabacitas en crema: squash in cream sauce
kah-lah-bah-SEE-tahs ehn KREH-mah

chiles rellenos: poblano peppers stuffed with cheese or ground meat, battered and fried
CHEE-lehs rreh-YEH-nohs

choclo: corn
CHOH-cloh

papas fritas: French fries
PAH-pahs FREE-tahs

patacones, chifles (Peru, Ecuador): fried plantains
pah-tah-KOH-nehs, CHEE-flehs

pristinos: pumpkin fritters
prees-TEE-nohs

rocoto relleno: stuffed pepper
rroh-KOH-toh rreh-YEH-noh

tostones: fried breadfruit or plantain slices
tohs-TOH-nehs

yuca frita: fried yucca
YOO-kah FREE-tah

For a full list of vegetables, see p105.

SAUSAGES (CHARCUTERÍA)

butifarra: spiced pork breakfast sausage
boo-tee-FAH-rrah

chorizo: spicy pork sausage
cho-REE-soh

morcilla: black pudding / blood sausage
mohr-SEE-yah

salchichón: Puerto Rican salami-style sausage
sahl-chee-CHOHN

BEEF / CARNE (DE RES / VACA)

bife de lomo: filet mignon
BEE-feh deh LOH-moh

carne en polvo: seasoned ground beef
KAHR-neh ehn POHL-voh

carne mechada: Cuban-style stuffed beef
KAHR-neh meh-CHAH-dah

locro criollo: beef stew with potatoes
LOH-kroh kree-OH-yoh

lomo fino: beef tenderloin in port sauce
LOH-moh FEE-noh

lomo salteado, lomo saltado (S.Am.): beef strips with mixed vegetables and rice
LOH-moh sahl-teh-AH-doh, LOH-moh sahl-TAH-do

olla de carne: beef stew with yucca, squash, and pumpkin
OH-yah deh KAHR-neh

ropa vieja: stewed shredded beef
ROH-pah VEE-EH-hah

ORGAN MEATS (CASQUERÍA)

menudo: all parts (neck, tripe, etc.) of poultry
meh-NOO-doh

mollejas: sweetbread
moh-YEH-hahs

pastelón de menudencias: tripe pie
pahs-teh-LOHN deh meh-noo-DEHN-syahs

riñoncitos al vino: chicken kidneys stewed in a wine sauce.
rree-nyohn-SEE-tohs ahl VEE-noh

guisado de riñones: kidney stew
gee-SAH-doh deh ree-NYOH-nehs

GOAT (CABRITO)

cabrito asado: oven-roasted kid (young goat)
kah-BREE-toh ah-SAH-doh

seco de chivo: goat stew
SEH-koh deh CHEE-voh

PORK (CERDO)

carnitas: slow-cooked pork served with corn tortillas
kahr-NEE-tahs

chicharrón: deep-fried pork skin
chee-chah-RROHN
cochinillo / lechón asado: roast suckling pig
koh-chee-NEE-yoh / leh-CHOHN ah-SAH-doh
costillas: pork or cow ribs
kohs-TEE-yahs
puerco en adobo: pork in chili sauce
PWEHR-koh ehn ah-DOH-boh
seco de chancho: pork stew
SEH-koh deh CHAHN-cho

POULTRY (AVES)

ají de gallina: creamed chicken with green chilis
ah-HEE deh gah-YEE-nah
arroz con pollo: rice with chicken and vegetables
ah-RROHS kohn POH-yoh
chilaquiles: chicken / cheese / tortilla casserole
chee-lah-KEE-lehs
mole poblano: chicken with bitter chocolate / chile sauce
MOH-leh poh-BLAH-noh
pollo a la brasa: spit-roasted chicken
POH-yoh ah lah BRAH-sah
pollo al jerez: chicken in sherry
POH-yoh ahl heh-REHS
pollo frito: fried chicken
POH-yoh FREE-toh
empanadas de pavo: turkey individual meat pies
ehm-pah-NAH-dahs deh PAH-voh
patas de pavo rellenas: stuffed turkey legs
PAH-tahs deh PAH-voh reh-YEH-nahs
sopa de pavo: turkey soup
SOH-pah deh PAH-voh

FISH AND SEAFOOD (PESCADO Y MARISCOS)

ceviche: seafood marinated with lemon or lime, along with cilantro, garlic, red pepper, and onion; served cold
seh-VEE-cheh

sushi / tiraditos: sushi
su-shi / tee-rah-DEE-tohs

escabeche: pickling brine or marinade
ehs-kah-BEH-cheh

zarzuela: mixed fish and seafood soup with tomatoes, saffron, garlic, and wine served over bread
sahr-SWEH-lah

cangrejos / jueyes hervidos: boiled crab
kahn-GREH-hohs / HWEH-yehs ehr-VEE-dohs

camarones en cerveza: shrimp in beer
kah-mah-ROH-nehs ehn sehr-VEH-sah

bacalao guisado: cod marinated in herbs
bah-kah-LAH-oh gee-SAH-doh

camarones al ajillo: garlic shrimp stew
kah-mah-ROH-nehs ahl ah-HEE-yoh

chupín de camarones: spicy shrimp stew
choo-PEEN deh kah-mah-ROH-nehs

salmorejo de jueyes: crab in tomato and garlic sauce
sahl-moh-REH-hoh deh HWEH-ee-ehs

taquitos de pescado: grilled fish in tomato sauce on tacos
tah-KEE-tohs deh pehs-KAH-doh

guiso de róbalo: Cuban style sea bass stew
GEE-soh deh ROH-bah-loh

For a full list of fish, see p102.

DESSERTS (POSTRES)

arroz con leche / arroz con dulce: rice pudding
ah-RROHS kohn LEH-cheh / ah-RROHS kohn DOOL-seh

buñuelos: round, thin fritters dipped in sugar (may also be savory)
boo-nyoo-EH-lohs

dulce de plátano: ripe yellow plantains cooked in wine and spices
DOOL-seh deh PLAH-tah-noh

flan: custard
flahn

helado: ice cream
eh-LAH-doh

panqueques: dessert crepes with caramel and whipped cream
pahn-KEH-kehs

sopapillas: puffed up crisps of a pie crust like dough, drizzled with honey and sprinkled with powdered sugar
soh-pah-PEE-yahs

tembleque: coconut milk custard
tehm-BLEH-keh

pastel tres leches: three-milk cake
pahs-TEHL trehs LEH-chehs

STREET FOOD (COMIDA CALLEJERA)

arepas: savory stuffed cornmeal patties
ah-REH-pahs

caña: raw sugar cane
KAH-nyah

chalupas: corn tortillas filled with meat and cheese
chah-LOO-pahs

chicha: fermented (alcoholic) corn drink
CHEE-chah

chorreados: corn pancakes with sour cream
choh-rreh-AH-dohs

churros: breakfast / dessert fritters
CHOO-rrohs

coco verde: green coconut
KOH-koh VEHR-deh

cuchifrito: deep-fried pork pieces (ears, tail, etc.)
koo-chee-FREE-toh

empanadas: turnovers filled with meat and / or cheese, beans, potatoes
ehm-pah-NAH-dahs

Eating out of Pocket

Street food is usually inexpensive. Keep a supply of small-denomination bills and change on you because street vendors usually won't be able to change large bills.

empanadas chilenas: turnovers filled with meat, boiled onion and raisins, an olive, and part of a hard-boiled egg
ehm-pah-NAH-dahs chee-LEH-nahs

enchiladas: pastries stuffed with cheese, meat, or potatoes
ehn-chee-LAH-dahs

gorditas: thick, fried corn tortillas stuffed with cheese, beans, and / or meat
gohr-DEE-tahs

juanes: rice tamales with chicken or fish
HWAH-nehs

piraguas, raspadillas (Peru): shaved ice with fruit syrup
pee-RAH-wahs, rahs-pad-DEE-yahs

pupusas: corn pancakes with cheese
poo-POO-sahs

quesadillas: tortillas with cheese
keh-sah-DEE-yahs

rellenos: bits of meat or cheese breaded with yucca or potato paste and deep fried
rreh-YEH-nohs

salteñas (aka empanadas chilenas): chicken or beef with onions and raisins wrapped in pastry
sahl-TEH-nyahs

tacos: corn/flour tortillas with beef/chicken/pork
TAH-kohs

tamales: chicken, pork, or potatoes with chiles in cornmeal steamed inside a banana leaf or corn husk
tah-MAH-lehs

tortas: sandwiches with meat and/or cheese, garnished with vegetables (frosted cake in S.Am.)
TOHR-tahs

BUYING GROCERIES

In most Latin American countries, groceries can be bought at open-air "farmers' markets," neighborhood stores, or large supermarkets.

AT THE SUPERMARKET

Which aisle has _____	¿En cuál pasillo se encuentran _____ *ehn kwahl pah-SEE-yoh seh ehn-KWEHN-trahn*
spices?	las especias? *lahs ehs-PEH-syahs*
toiletries?	los artículos de tocador? *lohs ahr-TEE-koo-lohs deh toh-kah-DOHR*
paper plates and napkins?	los platos de papel y las servilletas? *lohs PLAH-tohs deh pah-PEHL ee lahs sehr-vee-YEH-tahs*
canned goods?	los artículos enlatados? *lohs ahr-TEE-koo-lohs ehn-lah-TAH-dohs*
snack food?	los bocadillos? *lohs boh-kah-DEE-yohs*
baby food?	la comida para bebés? *lah koh-MEE-dah pah-rah beh-BEHS*
water?	el agua? *ehl AH-wah*
juice?	el jugo / zumo? *ehl HOO-goh / SOOH-moh*
bread?	el pan? *ehl pahn*
cheese?	el queso? *ehl KEH-soh*
fruit?	las frutas? *lahs FROO-tahs*
cookies?	las galletas? *lahs gah-YEH-tahs*

AT THE BUTCHER SHOP

Do you sell ____	**¿Ustedes venden ____**
	oos-TEH-dehs VEHN-dehn
beef?	**carne de res?**
	KAHR-neh deh rrehs
pork?	**cerdo?**
	SEHR-doh
lamb?	**cordero?**
	kohr-DEH-roh
goat?	**cabra?**
	KAH-brah
I would like a cut of ____	**Quisiera un corte de ____**
	kee-SYEH-rah oon KOHR-teh deh
tenderloin.	**lomo / filete.**
	LOH-moh / fee-LEH-teh
T-bone.	**chuletón.**
	choo-leh-TOHN
brisket.	**falda.**
	FAL-dah
rump roast.	**cuadril / solomillo.**
	kwah-DREEL / soh-loh-MEE-yoh
chops.	**chuletas.**
	choo-LEH-tahs
filet.	**filete.**
	fee-LEH-teh
Thick / Thin cuts please.	**Cortes finos / gruesos por favor.**
	KOHR-tehs FEE-nohs / GRWEH-sohs pohr fah-VOHR
Please trim the fat.	**Por favor, córtele la grasa.**
	pohr fah-VOHR KOHR-teh-leh lah GRAH-sah
Do you have any sausage?	**¿Tiene salchichas?**
	TYEH-neh sahl-CHEE-chas
Is the ____ fresh?	**¿Es fresco / fresca _____?**
	ehs_____ FREHS-koh / FRESH-kah

fish	**el pescado?**
	ehl pehs-KAH-doh
seafood	**los mariscos?**
	lohs mah-REES-kohs
shrimp	**los camarones?**
	lohs kah-mah-ROH-nehs
octopus	**el pulpo?**
	ehl POOL-poh
squid	**el calamar?**
	ehl kah-lah-MAHR
sea bass	**el róbalo / la lubina?**
	ehl RROH-bah-loh / lah loo-BEE-nah
flounder	**la platija?**
	lah plah-TEE-hah
clams	**las almejas?**
	lahs ahl-MEH-hahs
oysters	**las ostras?**
	lahs OHS-trahs
May I smell it?	**¿Puedo olerlo / olerla?**
	PWEH-doh oh-LEHR-loh / oh-LEHR-lah
Would you please _____	**¿Por favor, puede _____**
	pohr fah-VOHR PWEH-deh
filet it?	**cortarlo / cortarla en filetes?**
	kohr-TAHR-loh / kohr-TAHR-lah ehn fee-LEH-tehs
debone it?	**deshuesarlo / deshuesarla?**
	dehs-weh-SAHR-loh / dehs-weh-SAHR-lah
remove the head and tail?	**quitarle la cabeza y la cola?**
	kee-TAHR-leh lah kah-BEH-sah ee lah KOH-lah

AT THE PRODUCE STAND / MARKET

Fruits

banana	**plátano, banana**
	PLAH-tah-noh, bah-NAH-nah
apple	**manzana**
	mahn-ZAH-nah
grapes (green, red)	**uvas (verdes, rojas)**
	OO-vahs (VEHR-dehs, RROH-hahs)
orange	**naranja**
	nah-RAHN-hah
lime	**lima, limoncillo,**
	limón verde (Mexico)
	LEE-mah, lee-mohn-SEE-yoh,
	lee-mohn VEHR-de
lemon	**limón, limón amarillo (Mexico)**
	lee-MOHN, lee-MOHN ah-mah-
	REE-yoh
mango	**mango**
	MAHNG-goh
melon	**melón**
	meh-LOHN
cantaloupe	**cantalupo, melón**
	kahn-tah-LOO-poh, meh-LOHN
watermelon	**sandía, melón de agua**
	sahn-DEE-ah, meh-LOHN deh
	AH-wah
honeydew	**melón**
	meh-LOHN
cranberry	**arándano rojo**
	ah-RAHN-dah-noh ROH-hoh
cherry	**cereza**
	seh-REH-sah
peach	**melocotón, durazno**
	meh-loh-koh-TOHN,
	doo-RAHS-noh

apricot	**albaricoque / damasco** *ahl-bah-ree-KOH-keh / dah-MAHS-koh*
strawberry	**fresa, frutilla (Chile)** *FREH-sah, froo-TEE-yah*
blueberry	**arándano azul, mora azul** *ah-RAHN-dah-noh ah-SOOL,* *MOH-rah ah-SOOL*
kiwi	**kiwi** *KEE-wee*
pineapple	**piña** *PEE-nyah*
blackberries	**zarzamora, mora negra** *sahr-sah-MOH-rah, MOH-rah NEH-grah*
carambola, star fruit	**carambola** *kah-rahm-BOH-lah*
citron	**cidra** *SEE-drah*
coconut	**coco** *KOH-koh*
grapefruit	**toronja / pomelo** *toh-ROHN-hah / poh-MEH-loh*
guava	**guayaba** *wah-YAH-bah*
gooseberry	**grosella** *groh-SEH-yah*
papaya	**papaya** *pah-PAH-yah*
palm fruit	**fruta de palma** *FROO-tah deh PAHL-mah*
breadfruit	**fruta de pan, panapén, pana** *FROO-tah deh pahn, pah-nah-PEHN, PAH-nah*

soursop (spiny, yellow-green fruit with tart pulp)	**guanábana** *wah-NAH-bah-nah*
tamarind	**tamarindo** *tah-mah-REEN-doh*
tangerine	**mandarina** *mahn-dah-REE-nah*
plum	**ciruela** *seer-WEH-lah*
pear	**pera** *PEH-rah*

Vegetables

plantain	**plátano verde, plantaina, llantén** *PLAH-tah-noh VEHR-deh, plahn-tah-EE-nah, yahn-TEHN*
regular	**regular** *reh-goo-LAHR*
ripe	**maduro** *mah-DOO-roh*
lettuce	**lechuga** *leh-CHOO-gah*
spinach	**espinaca** *ehs-pee-NAH-kah*
avocado	**aguacate, palta (S.Am.)** *ah-wah-KAH-teh, PAHL-tah*
artichoke	**alcachofa** *ahl-kah-CHOH-fah*
olives	**aceitunas** *ah-seh-ee-TOO-nahs*
beans	**frijoles** *free-HOH-lehs*
green beans	**frijoles verdes, vainitas (S.Am.)** *free-HOH-lehs VEHR-dehs, vah-ee-NEE-tahs*

tomato	**tomate, jitomate (Mexico)**
	toh-MAH-teh, hee-toh-MAH-teh
potato	**papa, patata**
	PAH-pah, pah-TAH-tah
peppers	**pimiento, chile**
	pee-MYEHN-toh, CHEE-leh
hot	**picante**
	pee-KAHN-teh
mild	**suave**
	soo-AH-veh
poblano	**poblano**
	poh-BLAH-noh
jalapeno	**jalapeño**
	hah-lah-PEH-nyoh
habanero	**habanero, habañero**
	ah-bah-NEH-roh, ah-bah-
	NYEH-roh
chipotle	**chipotle**
	chee-POH-tleh
cayenne	**pimienta de Cayena**
	pee-MYEHN-tah deh
	kah-YEH-nah
cascabeles	**cascabeles**
	kahs-kah-BEH-lehs
onion	**cebolla**
	seh-BOH-yah
celery	**apio**
	AH-pyoh
broccoli	**brócoli**
	BROH-koh-lee
cauliflower	**coliflor**
	koh-lee-FLOHR

carrot	**zanahoria**
	sah-nah-OH-ree-ah
corn	**maíz**
	mah-EES
cucumber	**pepino**
	peh-PEE-noh
bean sprouts	**brotes de soja**
	BROH-tehs deh SOH-ha
okra	**quimbombo**
	keem-BOHM-boh
bamboo shoots	**retoños de bambú**
	reh-TOH-nyohs deh bahm-BOO
breadnut	**panapén**
	pah-nah-PEHN
sweet corn	**maíz dulce**
	mah-EES DOOL-seh
eggplant	**berenjena**
	beh-rehn-HEH-nah
sorrel	**acedera**
	ah-seh-DEH-rah
yam	**batata, camote (S.Am.)**
	bah-TAH-tah, kah-MOH-teh
squash	**zapallo**
	sah-PAH-yoh
white yam	**ñame (batata blanca)**
	NYAH-meh (bah-TAH-tah BLAHN-kah)

Fresh herbs and spices

cilantro	**cilantro** *see-LAHN-troh*
coriander	**culantro** *kooh-LAHN-troh*
black pepper	**pimienta negra** *pee-MYEHN-tah NEH-grah*
salt	**sal** *sahl*
basil	**albahaca** *ahl-BAH-kah*
parsley	**perejil** *peh-reh-HEEL*
oregano	**orégano** *oh-REH-gah-noh*
sage	**salvia** *SAHL-vyah*
thyme	**tomillo** *toh-MEE-yoh*
cumin	**comino** *koh-MEE-noh*
paprika	**paprika** *pah-PREE-kah*
garlic	**ajo** *AH-hoh*
clove	**clavo** *KLAH-voh*
allspice	**pimienta inglesa** *pee-MYEHN-tah eeng-GLEH-sah*
saffron	**azafrán** *ah-sah-FRAHN*
rosemary	**romero** *rroh-MEH-roh*
anise	**anís** *AH-nees*

sugar	**azúcar**
	ah-SOO-kahr
marjoram	**mejorana**
	meh-hoh-RAH-nah
dill	**eneldo**
	eh-NEHL-doh
caraway	**alcaravea**
	ahl-kah-rah-VEH-ah
bay leaf	**hoja de laurel seca**
	OH-hah deh lah-oo-REHL SEH-kah
cacao	**cacao**
	kah-KAH-oh
dried	**seco**
	SEH-koh
fresh	**fresco**
	FREHS-koh
seed	**en semilla**
	ehn seh-MEE-yah

AT THE DELI

What kind of salad is that?	**¿Qué tipo de ensalada es esa?**
	KEH TEE-poh deh ehn-sah-LAH-dah ehs EH-sah
What type of cheese is that?	**¿Qué tipo de queso es ese?**
	KEH TEE-poh deh KEH-soh ehs EH-seh
What type of bread is that?	**¿Qué tipo de pan es ese?**
	KEH TEE-poh deh PAHN ehs EH-seh
Some of that, please.	**Un poco de eso, por favor.**
	oon POH-koh deh EH-soh pohr fah-VOHR
Is the salad fresh?	**¿La ensalada es fresca?**
	lah ehn-sah-LAH-dah ehs FREHS-kah

I'd like _____	**Quisiera** _____
	kee-SYEH-rah
a sandwich.	**un sándwich.**
	oon SAHND-weech
a salad.	**una ensalada.**
	oo-nah ehn-sah-LAH-dah
tuna salad.	**ensalada de atún.**
	ehn-sah-LAH-dah deh ah-TOON
chicken salad.	**ensalada de pollo.**
	ehn-sah-LAH-dah deh POH-yoh
roast beef.	**asado de res.**
	ah-SAH-doh deh REHS
ham.	**jamón.**
	hah-MOHN
that cheese.	**ese queso.**
	EH-seh KEH-soh
cole slaw.	**ensalada de col.**
	ehn-sah-LAH-dah deh KOHL
a package of tofu.	**un paquete de tofu.**
	oon pah-KEH-teh deh TOH-foo
mustard.	**mostaza.**
	mohs-TAH-sah
mayonnaise.	**mayonesa.**
	mah-yoh-NEH-sah
a pickle.	**un pepinillo.**
	oon peh-pee-NEE-yoh
Is that smoked?	**¿Eso es ahumado?**
	EH-soh ehs ah-oo-MAH-doh
gram	**un gramo**
	oon GRAH-moh
kilo	**un kilo**
	oon KEE-loh
half-kilo	**medio kilo**
	MEH-dee-oh KEE-loh
quarter-kilo	**cuarto de kilo**
	KWAR-toh deh KEE-loh

CHAPTER FIVE

SOCIALIZING

Whether you're meeting people in a bar or a park, you'll find the language you need, in this chapter, to make new friends.

GREETINGS

Hello.	**Hola.** *OH-lah*
How are you?	**¿Cómo estás?** *KOH-moh ehs-TAHS*
Fine, thanks.	**Bien, gracias.** *byehn GRAH-syahs*
And you?	**¿Y usted?** *ee oos-TED*
I'm exhausted from the trip.	**Estoy cansado / cansada del viaje.** *ehs-TOY kahn-SAH-doh / kahn-SAH-dah dehl VYAH-heh*
I have a headache.	**Tengo dolor de cabeza.** *TEHNG-goh doh-LOHR deh kah-BEH-sah*
I don't feel well.	**No me encuentro bien.** *noh meh en-KWEN-troh bee-EHN*
I have a cold.	**Tengo un resfriado.** *TEHNG-goh oon rrehs-free-AH-doh*
Good morning.	**Buenos días.** *BWEH-nohs DEE-ahs*
Good evening.	**Buenas noches.** *BWEH-nahs NOH-chehs*
Good afternoon.	**Buenas tardes.** *BWEH-nahs TAHR-dehs*
Good night.	**Buenas noches.** *BWEH-nahs NOH-chehs*

Listen Up: Common Greetings

Es un placer.	It's a pleasure.
ehs oon plah-SEHR	
Mucho gusto.	Delighted.
MOO-choh GOOS-toh	
A la orden.	At your service. / As you wish.
ah lah OHR-dehn	
Encantado / Encantada.	Charmed.
ehn-kahn-TAH-doh /	
ehn-kahn-TAH-dah	
Buenas.	Good day. (shortened)
BWEH-nahs	
Hola.	Hello.
OH-lah	
¿Qué tal?	How's it going?
KEH TAHL	
¿Cómo anda?	How's it going?
KOH-moh AHN-dah	
¿Qué hubo / qué hay?	What's up?
KEH OOH-boh / keh AYE	
¿Qué pasa?	What's going on?
KEH PAH-sah	
¡Venga!	OK! / Perfect! (Spain)
VEHN-gah	
Adiós.	Goodbye.
ah-DYOHS	
Nos vemos.	See you later.
nohs VEH-mohs	

THE LANGUAGE BARRIER

I don't understand.	**No entiendo.**
	noh ehn-TYEHN-doh
Please speak more slowly.	**Por favor hable más lento.**
	pohr fah-VOHR AH-bleh mahs
	LEHN-toh

Please speak louder.	**Por favor hable más alto.** *pohr fah-VOHR AH-bleh mahs AHL-toh*
Do you speak English?	**¿Usted habla inglés?** *oos-TED AH-blah eeng-GLEHS*
I speak ____ better than Spanish.	**Yo hablo ____ mejor que español.** *yoh AH-bloh ____ meh-HOHR keh ehs-pah-NYOHL*

Curse Words

Here are some common curse words, used across Latin America and Spain.

mierda / cagada *MYEHR-dah / kah-GAH-dah*	shit
hijo de puta *EE-hoh deh POO-tah*	son of a bitch (literally, son of a whore)
huevón *weh-VOHN*	jerk
carajo *kah-RAH-hoh*	damn
culón *koo-LOHN*	ass
jodido / jodienda *hoh-DEE-doh / hoh-DYEHN-dah*	screwed up
cabrón *kah-BROHN*	bastard
chingada *cheeng-GAH-dah*	fucked up (Mexican)
follar / coger / joder *foh-YAHR / koh-HEHR / hoh-DEHR*	to fuck

See p22, 23 for conjugation.

Please spell that.	**Por favor deletree eso.** *pohr fah-VOHR deh-leh-TREH-eh* *EH-soh*
Please repeat that?	**¿Por favor repita eso?** *pohr fah-VOHR reh-PEE-tah* *EH-soh*
How do you say ____?	**¿Cómo se dice ____?** *KOH-moh seh DEE-seh*
Would you show me that in this dictionary?	**¿Me puede mostrar eso en este diccionario?** *meh PWEH-deh mohs-TRAHR* *EH-soh ehn EHS-teh deek-syoh-* *NAH-ryoh*

GETTING PERSONAL

People in Latin America are generally friendly, but more formal than Americans or Europeans. Remember to use the *usted* form of address, until given permission to employ the more familiar *tú*.

INTRODUCTIONS

What is your name?	**¿Cómo se llama?** *KOH-moh seh YAH-mah*
My name is ____.	**Me llamo ____.** *meh YAH-moh*
I'm very pleased to meet you.	**Es un placer conocerle.** *ehs oon plah-SEHR koh-noh-SEHR-leh*
May I introduce my ____?	**¿Puedo presentarle a mi ____ ?** *PWEH-doh preh-sehn-TAHR-leh* *ah mee*
How is your ____	**¿Cómo está su / están sus ____** *KOH-moh ehs-TAH soo / ehs-TAHN* *soos*
wife?	**esposa?** *ehs-POH-sah*
husband?	**esposo?** *ehs-POH-soh*
child?	**hijo / hija?** *EE-hoh / EE-hah*

boyfriend / girlfriend?	**novio / novia?**
	NOH-vyoh / NOH-vyah
family?	**familia?**
	fah-MEE-lyah
mother?	**madre?**
	MAH-dreh?
father?	**padre?**
	PAH-dreh
brother / sister?	**hermano / hermana?**
	ehr-MAH-noh / ehr-MAH-nah
friend?	**amigo / amiga?**
	ah-MEE-goh / ah-MEE-gah
neighbor?	**vecino?**
	veh-SEE-noh
boss?	**jefe?**
	HEH-feh
cousin?	**primo / prima?**
	PREE-moh / PREE-mah?
aunt / uncle?	**tía / tío?**
	TEE-ah / TEE-oh
boyfriend / girlfriend?	**novio / novia?**
	NOH-vyoh / NOH-vyah
fiancée / fiancé?	**prometido / prometida?**
	proh-meh-TEE-doh / proh-meh-TEE-dah
partner?	**socio / socia?**
	SOH-syoh / SOH-syah
niece/nephew?	**sobrina / sobrino?**
	soh-BREE-nah / soh-BREE-noh
parents?	**padres?**
	PAH-drehs
grandparents?	**abuelos?**
	ah-BWEH-lohs
grandchildren?	**nietos?**
	nee-EH-tohs

Dos and Don'ts

Don't refer to your parents as *los parientes*, which means relatives. Do call them *los padres* (even though *el padre* means father).

Are you married / single?	**¿Usted es casado(a) /soltero (a)?** *oos-TED ehs kah-SAH-doh -dah / sohl-TEH-roh -rah*
I'm married.	**Estoy casado / casada.** *ehs-TOY kah-SAH-doh / kah-SAH-dah*
I'm single.	**Estoy soltero / soltera.** *ehs-TOY sohl-TEH-roh / sohl-TEH-rah*
I'm divorced.	**Estoy divorciado / divorciada.** *ehs-TOY dee-vohr-SYAH-doh / dee-vohr-SYAH-dah*
I'm a widow / widower.	**Estoy viudo / viuda.** *ehs-TOY VYOO-doh / VYOO-dah*
We're separated.	**Estamos separados.** *ehs-TAH-mohs seh-pah-RAH-dohs*
I live with my boyfriend / girlfriend.	**Vivo con mi novio / novia.** *VEE-voh kohn mee NOH-vyoh / NOH-vyah*
I live with a roommate.	**Vivo con otras personas.** *VEE-voh kohn OH-trahs per-SOH-nahs*
How old are you?	**¿Qué edad tiene?** *KEH eh-DAD TEE-EH-neh*
How old are your children?	**¿Qué edad tienen sus hijos?** *KEH eh-DAD TYEH-nehn soos EE-hos*
Wow! That's very young.	**¡Caramba! ¡muy joven!** *kah-RAHM-bah MOO-ee HOH-vehn*
No you're not! You're much younger.	**¡No lo es! Usted es mucho más joven.** *noh loh ehs oos-TED ehs MOO-choh mahs HOH-vehn*

Your wife / daughter is beautiful.	**Su esposa / hija es bella.** *soo ehs-POH-sah / EE-hah ehs BEH-yah*
Your husband / son is handsome.	**Su esposo / hijo es guapo.** *soo ehs-POH-soh / EE-hoh ehs WAH-poh*
What a beautiful baby!	**¡Que bebé tan lindo!** *keh beh-BEH tahn LEEN-doh*
Are you here on business?	**¿Usted está aquí por negocios?** *oos-TED ehs-TAH ah-KEE pohr neh-GOH-syohs*
I'm traveling with my husband / wife.	**Estoy viajando con mi esposo / esposa.** *ehs-TOY vee-ah-HAN-doh kohn me ehs-POH-soh / ehs POH-sah*
I am vacationing.	**Estoy de vacaciones.** *ehs-TOY deh vah-kah-SYOH-nehs*
I'm attending a conference.	**Estoy asistiendo a una conferencia.** *ehs-TOY ah-sees-TYEHN-doh ah oo-nah kohn-feh-REHN-syah*
How long are you staying?	**¿Por cuánto tiempo se va a quedar?** *pohr KWAHN-toh TYEHM-poh seh vah ah keh-DAHR*
What are you studying?	**¿Qué estudia?** *KEH ehs-TOO-dyah*
I'm a student.	**Soy estudiante.** *soy ehs-too-DEE-AHN-teh*
Where are you from?	**¿De dónde es?** *deh DOHN-deh ehs*

PERSONAL DESCRIPTIONS

blond(e)	**rubio -a** *ROO-byoh -byah*
brunette	**moreno -a** *moh-REH-noh -nah*
redhead	**pelirrojo -a** *peh-lee-RRO-hoh -hah*

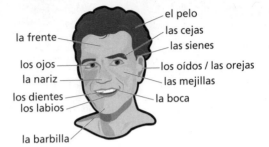

el pelo
las cejas
las sienes
la frente
los ojos
los oídos / las orejas
la nariz
las mejillas
los dientes
la boca
los labios
la barbilla

straight hair	**pelo lacio**	
	PEH-loh LAH-syoh	
curly hair	**pelo rizado / crespo**	
	PEH-loh ree-SAH-doh / KREHS-poh	
kinky hair	**pelo rizado**	
	PEH-loh ree-SAH-doh	
long hair	**pelo largo**	
	PEH-loh LAHR-goh	
short hair	**pelo corto**	
	PEH-loh KOHR-toh	
tanned	**bronceado -a**	
	brohn-seh-AH-doh-dah	
pale	**pálido -a**	
	PAH-lee-doh -dah	
mocha-skinned	**moreno -a**	
	moh-REH-noh -nah	
black	**negro -a**	
	NEH-groh-grah	
white	**blanco -a**	
	BLAHN-koh -kah	
Asian	**Asiático -a**	
	ah-see-AH-tee-koh -kah	

African-American	**afroamericano -a**
	ah-froh-ah-meh-ree-KAH-noh -nah
caucasian	**caucásico -a**
	kow-KAH-see-koh -kah
biracial	**birracial**
	bee-rrah-SYAHL
tall	**alto -a**
	AHL-toh -tah
short	**bajo -a**
	BAH-hoh -hah
thin	**delgado -a**
	dehl-GAH-doh -dah
fat	**gordo -a**
	GOHR-doh -dah
blue eyes	**ojos azules**
	OH-hohs ah-SOO-lehs
brown eyes	**ojos marrones**
	OH-hohs mah-RROH-nehs
green eyes	**ojos verdes**
	OH-hohs VEHR-dehs
hazel eyes	**ojos cafés**
	OH-hohs kah-FEHS
eyebrows	**cejas**
	SEH-hahs
eyelashes	**pestañas**
	pehs-TAH-nyahs
freckles	**pecas**
	PEH-kahs
moles	**lunares**
	looh-NAH-rehs
face	**cara**
	KAH-rah

Listen Up: Nationalities

Soy inglés / inglesa.
soy een-GLEHS / GLEH-sah

I'm English.

Soy americano -a.
soy ah-meh-ree-KAH-noh -nah

I'm American.

Soy Canadiense.
soy kah-nah-DEE-ehn-seh

I'm Canadian.

Soy alemán -a.
soy ah-leh-MAHN -nah

I'm German.

Soy argentino -a.
soy ahr-hehn-TEE-noh -nah

I'm Argentinean.

Soy boliviano -a.
soy boh-lee-VYAH-noh -nah

I'm Bolivian.

Soy brasileño -a.
soy brah-see-LEH-nyoh -nyah

I'm Brazilian.

Soy chino -a.
soy CHEE-noh -nah

I'm Chinese.

Soy colombiano -a.
soy koh-lohm-BYAH-noh -nah

I'm Colombian.

Soy costarricense.
soy kohs-tah-rree-SEHN-seh

I'm Costa Rican.

Soy ecuatoriano -a.
soy eh-kwah-toh-RYAH-noh -nah

I'm Ecuadorian.

Soy español -a.
soy ehs-pah-NYOHL -lah

I'm Spanish.

Soy francés / francesa.
soy frahn-SEHS / SEH-sah

I'm French.

Soy guatemalteco -a.
soy wah-teh-mahl-TEH-koh -kah

I'm Guatemalan.

Soy hindú.
soy een-DOO

I'm Hindu.

Soy hondureño -a.
soy ohn-doo-REH-nyoh -nyah

I'm Honduran

Soy italiano -a.
soy ee-tah-LYAH-noh -nah

I'm Italian.

Soy japonés / japonesa.
soy hah-poh-NEHS -NEH-sah

I'm Japanese.

Soy mexicano -a.
soy meh-hee-KAH-noh -nah

I'm Mexican.

Soy nicaragüense.	I'm Nicaraguan.
soy nee-kah-rah-WEHN-seh	
Soy panameño -a.	I'm Panamanian.
soy pah-nah-MEH-nyoh -nyah	
Soy paraguayo -a.	I'm Paraguayan.
soy pah-rah-WAH-yoh -yah	
Soy peruano -a.	I'm Peruvian.
soy peh-roo-AH-noh -nah	
Soy puertorriqueño -a.	I'm Puerto Rican.
soy pwehr-toh-rree-KEH-nyoh -nyah	
Soy ruso -a.	I'm Russian.
soy ROO-soh -sah	
Soy salvadoreño -a.	I'm Salvadorian.
soy sahl-vah-doh-REH-nyoh -nyah	
Soy uruguayo -a.	I'm Uruguayan.
soy oo-roo-WAH-yoh -yah	
Soy venezolano -a.	I'm Venezuelan.
soy veh-neh-soh-LAH-noh -nah	

For a full list of nationalities, see English / Spanish dictionary..

DISPOSITIONS AND MOODS

sad	**triste**
	TREES-teh
happy	**feliz / alegre**
	feh-LEES / ah-LEH-greh
angry	**enojado -a**
	eh-noh-HAH-doh -dah
tired	**cansado -a**
	kahn-SAH-doh -dah
depressed	**deprimido -a**
	deh-pree-MEE-doh -dah
stressed	**estresado -a**
	ehs-treh-SAH-doh -dah
anxious	**ansioso -a**
	ahn-SYOH-soh -sah
confused	**confundido -a**
	kohn-foon-DEE-doh -dah
enthusiastic	**entusiasmado -a**
	ehn-too-syahs-MAH-doh -dah

PROFESSIONS

What do you do for a living?	**¿En qué trabaja usted?** *ehn KEH trah-BAH-hah oo-STEHD*
Here is my business card.	**Aquí tiene mi tarjeta de presentación.** *ah-KEE TYEH-neh mee tahr-HEH-tah deh preh-sehn-tah-SYOHN*
I am ____	**Soy ____** *soy*
a doctor.	**médico.** *MEH-dee-koh*
an engineer.	**ingeniero -a.** *een-heh-NYEH-roh -rah*
a lawyer.	**abogado -a.** *ah-boh-GAH-doh -dah*
a salesperson.	**vendedor -a.** *vehn-deh-DOHR -DOH-rah*
a writer.	**escritor -a.** *ehs-kree-TOHR -TOH-rah*
an editor.	**editor -a.** *eh-dee-TOHR -TOH-rah*
a designer.	**diseñador -a.** *dee-seh-nyah-DOHR -DOH-rah*
an educator / a teacher.	**educador / profesor.** *eh-doo-kah-DOHR / proh-feh-SOHR*
an artist.	**artista.** *ahr-TEES-tah*
a craftsperson.	**artesano -a.** *ahr-teh-SAH-noh -nah*
a homemaker.	**ama de casa.** *AH-mah deh KAH-sah*
an accountant.	**contable (Spain) / contador -a (Latin America).** *kohn-TAH-bleh / kohn-tah-DOHR -DOH-rah*
a nurse.	**enfermero -a.** *ehn-fehr-MEH-roh -rah*

a musician.	**músico -a.** *MOO-see-koh -kah*
a military professional.	**profesional militar.** *proh-feh-syoh-NAHL mee-lee-TAHR*
a government employee.	**funcionario.** *foon-see-oh-NAH-ryo*
a web designer.	**diseñador Web.** *dee-seh-NYAH-dohr web*
a computer programmer.	**programador informático.** *proh-grah-mah-DOHR in-for-MAH-tee-koh*

DOING BUSINESS

I'd like an appointment.	**Quisiera hacer una cita.** *kee-SYEH-rah ah-SEHR oo-nah SEE-tah*
I'm here to see ____.	**Estoy aquí para ver a ____.** *ehs-TOY ah-KEE pa-rah vehr ah*
May I photocopy this?	**¿Puedo fotocopiar esto?** *PWEH-doh foh-toh-koh-PYAHR EHS-toh*
May I use my laptop here?	**¿Puedo usar mi portátil aquí?** *PWEH-doh ooh-SAR mee pohr-TAH-teel ah-KEEH*
What's the password?	**¿Cuál es la contraseña?** *KWAHL ehs lah kohn-trah-SEH-nyah*
May I access the Internet?	**¿Puedo acceder a Internet?** *PWEH-doh ahk-seh-DEHR ah een-tehr-NEHT*
May I send a fax?	**¿Puedo enviar un fax?** *PWEH-doh ehn-vee-AHR oon fahks*
May I use the phone?	**¿Puedo usar el teléfono?** *PWEH-doh oo-SAHR ehl teh-LEH-foh-noh*
Do you have a Wi-Fi network?	**¿Tiene red Wi-Fi?** *TYEH-neh red wee fee*

PARTING WAYS

Keep in touch.

Manténgase en contacto.
mahn-TEHNG-gah-seh ehn kohn-TAHK-toh

Please write or email.

Por favor escríbame o envíeme un e-mail.
pohr fah-VOHR ehs-KREE-bah-meh oh ehn-VEE-eh-meh oon EE-meh-eel

Here's my phone number.
Call me.

**Aquí tiene mi número de teléfono.
Llámeme.**
ah-KEE TYEH-neh mee NOO-meh-roh deh teh-LEH-foh-noh. YAH-meh-meh

May I have your phone number / e-mail please?

¿Me puede dar su número de teléfono / dirección de e-mail, por favor?
meh PWEH-deh dahr soo NOO-meh-roh deh teh-LEH-foh-noh / dee-rehk-SYOHN deh EE-meh-eel pohr fah-VOHR

May I have your card?

¿Me puede dar su tarjeta?
meh PWEH-deh dahr soo tahr-HEH-tah

Are you on Facebook / Twitter?

¿Tiene cuenta en Facebook / Twitter?
TYEH-neh KWEN-tah ehn face book/twitter

TOPICS OF CONVERSATION

As in the United States or Europe, the weather and current affairs are common conversation topics.

THE WEATHER

It's so ____.

Es tan ____.
Ehs tahn

Is it always so _____ ?

¿Siempre es tan _____ ?
SYEHM-preh ehs tahn

sunny

soleado
soh-leh-AH-doh

rainy

lluvioso
yoo-vee-OH-soh

cloudy

nublado
noo-BLAH-doh

humid

húmedo
OO-meh-doh

warm

caliente
kah-LYEHN-teh

cool

frío
FREE-oh

windy

ventoso
vehn-TOH-soh

Do you know the weather forecast for tomorrow?

¿Usted sabe el pronóstico del tiempo para mañana?
oos-TED SAH-beh ehl proh-NOHS-tee-koh dehl TYEHM-poh PAH-rah mah-NYAH-nah

THE ISSUES

What do you think about _____

¿Qué opina usted de _____
KEH oh-PEE-nah oos-TED deh

the government?

el gobierno?
ehl goh-bee-EHR-noh

democracy?

la democracia?
lah deh-moh-KRAH-syah

socialism?

el socialismo?
ehl soh-syah-LEES-moh

the environment?

el medio ambiente?
ehl MEH-dyoh ahm-bee-EHN-teh

women's rights?

los derechos de las mujeres?
lohs deh-REH-chohs deh lahs moo-HEH-rehs

gay rights?	**los derechos de los homo-sexuales?** *lohs deh-reh-chos deh lohs oh-moh-sehk-SWAH-lehs*
the economy?	**la economía?** *lah eh-koh-noh-MEE-ah*
What political party do you belong to?	**¿A qué partido político usted pertenece?** *ah KEH pahr-TEE-doh poh-LEE-tee-koh oos-TED pehr-teh-NEH-seh*
What did you think of the American election?	**¿Qué opina usted de las elecciones de Estados Unidos?** *keh oh-PEE-nah oos-TED deh lahs eh-lehk-SYOH-nehs deh ehs-TAH-dohs oo-NEE-dohs*
What do you think of the war in ____?	**¿Qué opina usted de la guerra en ____?** *keh oh-PEE-nah oos-TED deh lah GEH-rrah ehn*

RELIGION

Do you go to church / temple / mosque?	**¿Usted asiste a una iglesia / un templo / una mezquita?** *oos-TED ah-SEES-teh ah oo-nah ee-GLEH-syah / oon TEHM-ploh / oo-nah mehs-KEE-tah*
Are you religious?	**¿Usted es religioso?** *oos-TED ehs reh-lee-HYOH-soh*
I'm ____ / I was raised ____	**Soy ____ / Fui criado ____** *soy / foo-EE kree-AH-doh*
Protestant.	**protestante.** *proh-tehs-TAHN-teh*

Catholic.

católico.
kah-TOH-lee-koh

Jewish.

judío.
hoo-DEE-oh

Muslim.

musulmán.
moo-sool-MAHN

Buddhist.

budista.
boo-DEES-tah

Greek Orthodox.

ortodoxo griego.
orh-toh-DOHK-soh GRYEH-goh

Hindu.

hindú.
een-DOO

agnostic.

agnóstico.
ahg-NOHS-tee-koh

atheist.

ateo -a.
ah-TEH-oh -ah

I'm spiritual but I don't attend services.

Soy espiritual pero no asisto a los servicios.
soy ehs-pee-ree-TWAHL peh-roh noh ah-SEES-toh ah lohs sehr-VEE-syohs

I don't believe in that.

Yo no creo en eso.
yoh noh KREH-oh ehn EH-soh

That's against my beliefs.

Eso va en contra de mis creencias.
EH-soh vah ehn KOHN-trah deh mees kreh-EHN-syahs

I'd rather not talk about it.

Preferiría no hablar de ello.
preh-feh-ree-REE-ah noh ah-BLAHR deh EH-yoh

GETTING TO KNOW SOMEONE

Following are some conversation starters.

MUSICAL TASTES

What kind of music do you like?	**¿Qué tipo de música le gusta?** *KEH TEE-poh deh MOO-see-kah leh GOOS-tah*
I like _____	**Me gusta _____** *meh GOOS-tah*
rock 'n' roll.	**el rock and roll.** *ehl rohk-ahn-rohl*
hip hop.	**el hip hop, el jip jop.** *ehl eep ohp, ehl heep HOHP*
techno.	**el techno.** *ehl TEHK-noh*
disco.	**el disco.** *ehl DEES-koh*
classical.	**la música clásica.** *lah MOO-see-kah KLAH-see-kah*
jazz.	**el jazz.** *ehl jahs*
country and western.	**la música country.** *lah MOO-see-kah KOHN-tree*
reggae.	**el reggae.** *ehl RREH-geh*
calypso.	**el calipso.** *ehl kah-LEEP-soh*
opera.	**la ópera.** *lah OH-peh-rah*
show-tunes / musicals.	**los musicales.** *lohs moo-see-KAH-lehs*
New Age.	**la nueva era.** *lah NWEH-vah EH-rah*
pop.	**la música pop.** *lah MOO-see-kah pohp*

HOBBIES

What do you like to do in your spare time?

¿**Qué hace usted en su tiempo libre?**
KEH AH-seh oos-TED ehn soo TYEHM-poh LEE-breh

I like _____

Me gusta _____
meh GOOS-tah

playing guitar.

tocar la guitarra.
toh-KAHR lah gee-TAH-rrah

piano.

el piano.
ehl PYAH-noh

For other instruments, see the English / Spanish dictionary.

painting.

pintar.
peen-TAHR

drawing.

dibujar.
dee-boo-HAHR

dancing.

bailar.
bah-ee-LAHR

reading.

leer.
leh-EHR

watching TV.

ver televisión.
vehr teh-leh-vee-SYOHN

blogging.

escribir en mi blog.
ehs-cree-BYR ehn mee blog

shopping.

ir de compras.
eer deh KOHM-prahs

going to the movies.

ir al cine.
eer ahl SEE-neh

hiking.

caminatas / senderismo.
kah-mee-NAH-tahs / sehn-deh-REES-moh

camping.

acampar.
ah-kahm-PAHR

hanging out.

pasar el rato.
pah-SAHR ehl RRAH-toh

traveling.

viajar.
vyah-HAR

eating out.	**comer afuera.**
	koh-MEHR ah-FWEH-rah
cooking.	**cocinar.**
	koh-see-NAHR
sewing.	**coser.**
	koh-SEHR
sports.	**los deportes.**
	lohs deh-POHR-tehs
Do you like to dance?	**¿A usted le gusta bailar?**
	ah oos-TED leh GOOS-tah bah-ee-LAHR
Would you like to go out?	**¿Le gustaría salir?**
	leh goos-tah-REE-ah sah-LEER
May I buy you dinner sometime?	**¿Le puedo invitar a cenar alguna vez?**
	leh PWEH-doh een-vee-TAHR ah SEH-nahr ahl-GOO-nah vehs
What kind of food do you like?	**¿Qué tipo de comida le gusta?**
	KEH TEE-poh deh koh-MEE-dah leh GOOS-tah

For a full list of food types, see Dining in Chapter 4.

Would you like to go _____	**¿Le gustaría ir _____**
	leh goos-tah-REE-ah eer
to a movie?	**al cine?**
	ahl SEE neh
to a concert?	**a un concierto?**
	ah oon kohn-SYEHR-toh
to the zoo?	**al zoológico?**
	ahl soh-oh-LOH-hee-koh
to the beach?	**a la playa?**
	ah lah PLAH-yah
to a museum?	**al museo?**
	ahl moo-SEH-oh
for a walk in the park?	**a caminar en el parque?**
	ah kah-mee-NAHR ehn ehl PAHR-keh

dancing?	**a bailar?**
	ah bah-ee-LAHR
Would you like to get ____	**¿Le gustaría ir ____**
	leh goos-tah-REE-ah eer
lunch?	**a almorzar?**
	ah ahl-mohr-SAHR
coffee?	**a tomar café?**
	ah toh-MAHR kah-FEH
dinner?	**a cenar?**
	ah seh-NAHR
What kind of books do you like to read?	**¿Qué tipo de libros le gusta leer?**
	KEH TEE-poh deh LEE-brohs leh GOOS-tah leh-EHR
I like ____	**Me gusta / gustan ____**
	meh GOOS-tah / GOOS-tahn
mysteries.	**los misterios.**
	lohs mees-TEH-ryohs
Westerns.	**de vaqueros.**
	deh vah-KEH-rohs
dramas.	**los dramas.**
	lohs DRAH-mahs
novels.	**las novelas.**
	lahs noh-VEH-lahs
biographies.	**las biografías.**
	lahs bee-oh-grah-FEE-ahs
auto-biographies.	**las autobiografías.**
	lahs ow-toh-bee-oh-grah-FEE-ahs
romance.	**los romances.**
	lohs rroh-MAHN-sehs
history.	**la historia.**
	lah ees-TOH-ree-ah

For dating terms, see Nightlife in Chapter 10.

CHAPTER SIX

MONEY & COMMUNICATIONS

This chapter covers money, the mail, phone, Internet service, and other tools you need to connect with the outside world.

MONEY

I need to exchange money.	**Necesito cambiar dinero.** *neh-seh-SEE-toh kam-BYAR dee-NEH-roh*
Do you accept _____	**¿Aceptan _____** *ah-SEHP-tahn*
Visa / MasterCard / Discover / American Express / Diners' Club? credit cards?	**Visa / MasterCard / Discover / American Express / Diners' Club?** *Pronounced as in English* **tarjetas de crédito?** *tahr-HEH-tahs deh KREH-dee-toh*
bills?	**billetes?** *bee-YEH-tehs*
coins?	**monedas?** *moh-NEH-dahs*
checks?	**cheques?** *CHEH-kehs*
money transfer?	**transferencia de dinero?** *trahns-feh-REHN-syah deh dee NEH-roh*
May I wire transfer funds here?	**¿Puedo hacer una transferencia de dinero aquí?** *PWEH-doh ah-SEHR oo-nah trahns-feh-REHN-syah deh dee-NEH-roh ah-KEE*
Would you please tell me where to find _____	**Por favor, ¿puede decirme dónde puedo encontrar _____** *pohr fah-VOHR PWEH-deh deh-SEER-meh DOHN-deh PWEH-doh ehn-kohn-TRAHR*

a bank?	**un banco?** *oon BAHN-koh*
a credit bureau?	**una agencia de crédito?** *oo-nah ah-HEHN-syah deh* *KREH-dee-toh*
an ATM?	**un cajero automático?** *oon kah-HEH-roh ow-toh-MAH-* *tee-koh*
a currency exchange?	**un lugar de cambio de moneda?** *oon loo-HAHR deh KAHM-byoh* *deh moh-NEH-dah*
A receipt, please.	**Un recibo, por favor.** *oon rreh-SEE-boh pohr fah-VOHR*
Would you tell me _____	**Me puede decir _____** *meh PWEH-deh deh-SEER*
the exchange rate for dollars to _____?	**la tasa de cambio de dólares a _____?** *lah TAH-sah deh KAHM-byoh* *deh DOH-lah-rehs ah*
Is there a service charge?	**¿Hay un cargo por servicio?** *aye oon KAHR-goh pohr sehr-* *VEE-syoh*
May I have a cash advance on my credit card?	**¿Puedo obtener un adelanto en efectivo de mi tarjeta de crédito?** *PWEH-doh ohb-teh-NEHR oon ah-* *deh-LAHN-toh ehn eh-fehk-TEE-* *voh deh mee tahr-HEH-tah deh* *KREH-dee-toh*
Will you accept a credit card?	**¿Aceptarían una tarjeta de crédito?** *ah-sehp-tah-REE-ahn oo-nah tahr-* *HEH-tah deh KREH-dee-toh*

Listen Up: Bank Lingo

Por favor, firme aquí. *pohr fah-VOHR FEER-meh ah-KEE*	Please sign here.
Aquí está su recibo. *ah-KEE ehs-TAH soo reh-SEE-boh*	Here is your receipt.
Por favor, ¿puedo ver su identificacion? *pohr fah-VOHR PWEH-doh vehr soo ee-dehn-tee-fee-kah-SYOHN*	May I see your ID, please?
Solo en efectivo. *SOH-loh ehn eh-fehk-TEE-voh*	Cash only.

May I have smaller bills, please.	**Me puede dar billetes más pequeños, por favor.** *meh PWEH-deh dahr bee-YEH-tehs mahs peh-KEH-nyohs pohr fah-VOHR*
Can you make change?	**¿Puede darme cambio?** *PWEH-deh DAHR-meh KAHM-byoh*
I only have bills.	**Sólo tengo billetes.** *SOH-loh TEHN-goh bee-YEH-tehs*
Some coins, please.	**Unas monedas por favor.** *oo-nahs moh-NEH-dahs pohr fah-VOHR*

PHONE SERVICE

Where can I buy or rent a cell phone?	**¿Dónde puedo comprar o alquilar un teléfono celular / móvil?** *DOHN-deh PWEH-doh kohm-PRAHR oh ahl-kee-LAHR oon teh-LEH-foh-noh seh-loo-LAHR / MOH-beel*

ATM Machine

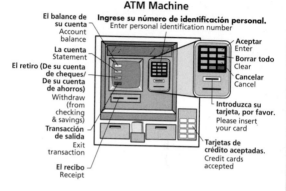

El balance de su cuenta
Account balance

Ingrese su número de identificación personal.
Enter personal identification number

La cuenta
Statement

El retiro (De su cuenta de cheques/ De su cuenta de ahorros)
Withdraw (from checking & savings)

Transacción de salida
Exit transaction

El recibo
Receipt

Aceptar
Enter

Borrar todo
Clear

Cancelar
Cancel

Introduzca su tarjeta, por favor.
Please insert your card

Tarjetas de crédito aceptadas.
Credit cards accepted

What rate plans do you have?	¿Qué planes de tarifas tienen? *KEH PLAH-nehs deh tah-REE-fahs TYEH-nehn*
Is this good throughout the country?	¿Esto sirve en todo el país? *EHS-teh SEER-veh ehn TOH-doh ehl pah-EES*
May I have a prepaid phone?	¿Me puede dar un teléfono pre-pagado? *meh PWEH-deh dahr oon teh-LEH-foh-noh preh-pah-GAH-doh*
Where can I buy a phone card?	¿Dónde puedo comprar una tarjeta telefónica? *DOHN-deh PWEH-doh kohm-PRAHR oo-nah tahr-HEH-tah teh-leh-FOH-nee-kah*
May I add more minutes to my phone card?	¿Puedo añadirle más minutos a mi tarjeta de llamadas? *PWEH-doh ah-nyah-DEER-leh mahs mee-NOO-tohs ah mee tahr-HEH-tah deh yah-MAH-dahs*

MAKING A CALL

May I dial direct?	**¿Puedo marcar directo?**
	PWEH-doh MAHR-kahr dee-REHK-toh
Operator please.	**Operadora, por favor.**
	oh-peh-rah-DOH-rah pohr fah-VOHR
I'd like to make an international call.	**Quisiera hacer una llamada internacional.**
	kee-SYEH-rah ah-SEHR oo-nah yah-MAH-dah een-tehr-nah-syoh-NAHL
I'd like to make a collect call.	**Quisiera hacer una llamada a cobro revertido.**
	kee-SYEH-rah ah-SEHR oo-nah yah-MAH-dah ah KOH-broh reh-vehr-TEE-doh
I'd like to use a calling card.	**Quisiera usar una tarjeta de llamadas.**
	kee-SYEH-rah oo-SAHR oo-nah tahr-HEH-tah deh yah-MAH-dahs

Fuera de Servicio

Before you stick your coins or bills in a vending machine, watch out for the little sign that says *Fuera de servicio* (Out of Service).

Listen Up: Telephone Lingo

¿Diga? / ¿Bueno? / ¿Hola?	Hello?
DEE-gah, BWEH-noh, OH-lah	
¿A qué número?	What number?
ah KEH NOO-meh-roh	
Lo siento, la línea está ocupada.	I'm sorry, the line is busy.
loh SYEHN-toh lah LEE-neh-ah ehs-TAH oh-koo-PAH-dah	
Por favor, cuelgue el teléfono y marque el número de nuevo.	Please, hang up and redial.
pohr fah-VOHR KWEHL-geh ehl teh-LEH-foh-noh ee MAHR-keh ehl NOO-meh-roh deh NWEH-voh	
Lo siento. Nadie responde.	I'm sorry, nobody is answering.
loh SYEHN-toh NAH-dyeh rehs-POHN-deh	
Su tarjeta tiene diez minutos.	Your card has ten minutes left.
soo tahr-HEH-tah TYEH-neh dyehs mee-NOO-tohs	

COMMUNICATIONS

Bill my credit card.

Cargue a mi tarjeta de crédito.
*KAHR-geh ah mee tahr-HEH-tah
deh KREH-dee-toh*

May I bill the charges to
my room?

**¿Puedo cargar los gastos a mi
habitación?**
*PWEH-doh kahr-GAHR lohs GAHS-
tohs ah mee ah-bee-tah-SYOHN*

Information, please.

Información, por favor.
*een-fohr-mah-SYOHN pohr fah-
VOHR*

I'd like the number
for _____.

Quisiera el número para _____.
*kee-SYEH-rah ehl NOO-meh-roh
PAH-rah*

I just got disconnected.

Se me cortó (la línea).
seh-meh-kohr-TOH lah-LEE-neh-ah

The line is busy.

La línea está ocupada.
*lah LEE-neh-ah ehs-TAH oh-koo-
PAH-dah*

I lost the connection.

Perdí la conexión.
pehr-DEE lah koh-nehk-SYOHN

INTERNET ACCESS

Where is an Internet café?

¿Dónde hay un café con acceso a Internet?
DOHN-deh aye oon kah-FEH kohn ahk-SEH-soh ah een-tehr-NET

Is there Wi-Fi?

¿Hay Wi-Fi / red inalámbrica?
aye wee fee / red een-ah-LAM-bree-kah

How much do you charge per minute / hour?

¿Cuánto cobra por minuto / hora?
KWAHN-toh KOH-brah pohr mee-NOO-toh / OH-rah

Can I print here?

¿Puedo imprimir aquí?
PWEH-doh eem-pree-MEER ah-KEE

Can I burn a CD?

¿Puedo quemar un CD?
PWEH-doh keh-MAHR oon seh-DEH

Would you please help me change the language preference to English?

¿Me puede ayudar a cambiar la opción de idioma al inglés?
meh PWEH-deh ah-yoo-DAHR ah kahm-BYAHR lah ohp-SYOHN deh ee-DYOH-mah ahl eeng-GLEHS

May I scan something?	**¿Puedo escanear algo?**
	PWEH-doh ehs-kah-neh-AHR
	AHL-goh
Can I upload photos?	**¿Puedo cargar mis fotos?**
	PWEH-doh kahr-GAHR mees
	FOH-tohs
Do you have a USB port	**¿Tiene un puerto de USB para**
so I can download music?	**poder descargar música?**
	TYEH-neh oon PWEHR-toh deh oo-
	EH-seh-BEH PAH-rah poh-DEHR
	dehs-kahr-GAHR MOO-see-kah
Do you have a Mac?	**¿Tiene una computadora**
	Macintosh?
	TYEH-neh oo-nah kohm-poo-tah-
	DOH-rah ah mah-keen-TOHSH
Do you have a PC?	**¿Tiene una computadora PC?**
	TYEH-neh oo-nah kohm-poo-tah-
	DOH-rah peh-SEH
Do you have a newer	**¿Tiene la versión más nueva de**
version of this software?	**este software?**
	TYEH-neh lah vehr-SYOHN mahs
	NWEH-vah deh EHS-teh SOHFT-
	wehr
Do you have broadband?	**¿Tiene conexión de Internet de**
	alta velocidad?
	TYEH-neh koh-nehk-SYOHN deh
	een-tehr-NEHT deh AHL-tah veh-
	loh-see-DAD
How fast is your	**¿Cuán rápida es su conexión?**
connection speed?	*kwahn RAH-pee-dah ehs soo koh-*
	nehk-SYOHN

GETTING MAIL

Where is the post office?

¿Dónde está el correo?
DOHN-deh ehs-TAH ehl koh-RREH-oh

May I send an international package?

¿Puedo enviar un paquete internacional?
PWEH-doh ehn-vee-AHR oon pah-KEH-teh een-tehr-nah-syoh-NAHL

Do I need a customs form?

¿Necesito un formulario de aduanas?
neh-seh-SEE-toh oon fohr-moo-LAH-ree-oh deh ah-DWAH-nahs

Do you sell insurance for packages?

¿Vende seguros para paquetes?
VEHN-deh seh-GOO-rohs PAH-rah pah-KEH-tehs

Please, mark it fragile.

Por favor, márquelo como frágil.
pohr fah-VOHR MAHR-keh-loh koh-moh FRAH-heel

Please, handle with care.

Por favor, manéjelo con cuidado.
pohr fah-VOHR mah-NEH-heh-loh kohn koo-ee-DAH-doh

Do you have twine?

¿Tiene cuerda?
TYEH-neh KWEHR-dah

Where is a DHL office?

¿Dónde hay una oficina de DHL?
DOHN-deh aye oo-nah oh-fee-SEE-nah deh deh AH-cheh EH-leh

Do you sell stamps?

¿Vende sellos?
VEHN-deh SEH-yohs

Do you sell postcards?

¿Vende postales?
VEHN-deh pohs-TAH-lehs

May I send that first class?

¿Puedo enviar esto por primera clase?
PWEH-doh ehn-VEE-ahr EHS-toh pohr pree-MEH-rah KLAH-seh

Listen Up: Postal Lingo

¡Próximo! *PROHK-see-moh*	Next!
Por favor, póngalo aquí. *pohr fah-VOHR POHNG- gah-loh ah-KEE*	Please, set it here.
¿Qué clase? *KEH KLAH-seh*	Which class?
¿Qué tipo de servicio quiere? *KEH TEE-poh deh sehr- VEE-syoh KYEH-reh*	What kind of service would you like?
¿En qué puedo servirle? *ehn KEH PWEH-doh sehr- VEER-leh*	How can I help you?
ventanilla de entregas *vehn-tah-NEE-yah deh ehn- TREH-gahs*	dropoff window
ventanilla de retiros *vehn-tah-NEE-yah deh reh-TEE-rohs*	pickup window

How much to send that express / air mail?

¿Cuánto cuesta enviar esto por correo urgente / correo aéreo?
KWAHN-toh KWEHS-tah ehn-VEE- ahr EHS-toh pohr koh-RREH-oh oor-HEHN-teh / koh-RREH-oh ah- EH-reh-oh

Do you offer overnight delivery?

¿Ofrece entrega de un día para otro?
oh-FREH-seh ehn-TREH-gah deh oon DEE-ah PAH-rah OH-troh

How long will it take to reach the United States?	**¿Cuánto tardará en llegar a los Estados Unidos?** *KWAHN-toh tahr-dah-RAH ehn yeh-GAHR ah lohs ehs-TAH-dohs oo-NEE-dohs*
I'd like to buy an envelope.	**Quisiera comprar un sobre.** *kee-SYEH-rah kohm-PRAHR oon SOH-breh*
May I send it airmail?	**¿Puedo enviarlo por correo aéreo?** *PWEH-doh ehn-VYAHR-loh pohr koh-RREH-oh ah-EH-reh-oh*
I'd like to send it certified / registered mail.	**Quisiera enviarlo por correo certificado.** *kee-SYEH-rah ehn-VYAHR-loh pohr koh-RREH-oh sehr-tee-fee-KAH-doh*

CHAPTER SEVEN

CULTURE

CINEMA

Is there a movie theater nearby?	**¿Hay un cine cerca?** *aye oon SEE-neh SEHR-kah*
What's playing tonight?	**¿Qué están dando esta noche?** *KEH ehs-TAHN DAHN-doh ehs-TAH NOH-cheh*
Is that in English or Spanish?	**¿Es en inglés o español?** *ehs ehn eeng-GLEHS oh ehs-pah-NYOHL*
Are there English subtitles?	**¿Hay subtítulos en inglés?** *aye soob-TEE-too-lohs ehn eeng-GLEHS*
Is the theater air conditioned?	**¿El teatro tiene aire acondicionado?** *ehl teh-AH-troh TYEH-neh AYE-reh ah-kohn-dee-syoh-NAH-doh*
How much is a ticket?	**¿Cuánto cuesta un boleto / una entrada?** *KWAHN-toh KWEH-stah oon boh-LEH-toh / OOH-na ehn-TRAH-dah*
Do you have a _____ discount?	**¿Ofrecen descuento para _____** *oh-FREH-sehn dehs-KWEHN-toh PAH-rah*
senior	**personas mayores de edad?** *pehr-SOH-nahs mah-YOH-rehs deh eh-DAD?*
student	**estudiantes?** *ehs-too-DYAHN-tehs*
children's	**niños?** *NEE-nyohs*

What time is the movie showing?	**¿A qué hora muestran la película?** *ah KEH OH-rah MWEHS-trahn lah peh-LEE-koo-lah*
How long is the movie?	**¿Cuán larga es la película?** *kwahn LAHR-gah ehs lah peh-LEE-koo-lah*
May I buy tickets in advance?	**¿Puedo comprar los boletos por adelantado?** *PWEH-doh kohm-PRAHR lohs boh-LEH-tohs pohr ah-deh-lahn-TAH-doh*
Is it sold out?	**¿Está todo vendido?** *ehs-TAH TOH-doh vehn-DEE-doh*
When does it begin?	**¿A qué hora comienza?** *ah KEH OH-rah koh-MYEHN-sah*

PERFORMANCES

Are there any plays showing right now?	**¿Hay alguna obra en escena ahora mismo?** *aye ahl-GOO-nah OH-brah ehn ehs-SEH-nah ah-OH-rah MEES-moh*
Is there a dinner theater?	**¿Hay algún espectáculo para ver durante la cena?** *aye ahl-GOON ehs-spehk-TAHK-oo-loh PAH-rah vehr doo-RAHN-teh lah SEH-nah*
Where can I buy tickets?	**¿Dónde puedo comprar boletos?** *DOHN-deh PWEH-doh kohm-PRAHR boh-LEH-tohs*
Are there student discounts?	**¿Ofrecen descuentos para estudiantes?** *oh-FREH-sehn dehs-KWEHN-tohs PAH-rah ehs-too-DYAHN-tehs*
I need _____ seats.	**Quisiera _____ asientos.** *kee-SYEH-rah _____ ah-SYEHN-tohs*

Listen Up: Box Office Lingo

¿Qué le gustaría ver?
KEH leh goos-tah-REE-ah vehr

What would you like to see?

¿Cuántos?
KWAHN-tohs

How many?

¿Para dos adultos?
PAH-rah dohs ah-DOOL-tohs

For two adults?

¿Palomitas?
pah-loh-ME-tahs

Popcorn?

¿Con mantequilla? ¿Sal?
kohn mahn-teh-KEE-yah sahl

With butter? Salt?

¿Algo más?
AHL-goh MAHS

Would you like anything else?

For a full list of numbers, see p7.

An aisle seat.	**Un asiento de pasillo.** *oon ah-SYEHN-toh deh pah-SEE-yoh*
Orchestra seat, please.	**Un asiento a nivel de orquesta, por favor.** *oon ah-SYEHN-toh ah nee-VEHL deh ohr-KEHS-tah pohr fah-VOHR*
What time does the play start?	**¿A qué hora comienza la obra?** *ah KEH OH-rah koh-MYEHN-sah lah OH-brah*
Is there an intermission?	**¿Hay un intervalo?** *aye oon een-tehr-VAH-loh*
Do you have an opera house?	**¿Tienen un teatro de ópera?** *TYEH-nehn oon teh-AH-troh deh OH-peh-rah*
Is there a local symphony?	**¿Hay orquesta sinfónica local?** *aye ohr-KEHS-tah seen-FOH-nee-kah loh-KAHL*

May I purchase tickets over the phone / online?	**¿Puedo comprar boletos por teléfono / por Internet?** *PWEH-doh kohm-PRAHR boh-LEH-tohs pohr teh-LEH-foh-noh / pohr EEN-tehr-net*
What time is the box office open?	**¿A qué hora abre la boletería?** *ah KEH OH-rah AH-breh lah boh-leh-teh-REE-ah*
I need space for a wheelchair, please.	**Necesito espacio para una silla de ruedas, por favor.** *neh-seh-SEE-toh ehs-PAH-syoh PAH-rah oo-nah SEE-yah deh RWEH-dahs pohr fah-VOHR*
Do you have private boxes available?	**¿Tiene asientos de palco privados disponibles?** *TYEH-neh ah-SYEHN-tohs deh PAHL-koh pree-VAH-dohs dees-poh-NEE-blehs*
Is there a church that gives concerts?	**¿Hay una iglesia que ofrece conciertos?** *aye oo-nah ee-GLEH-syah keh oh-FREH-seh kohn-SYEHR-tohs*
A program, please.	**Un programa, por favor.** *oon proh-GRAH-mah pohr fah-VOHR*
Please show us to our seats.	**Por favor llévenos a nuestros asientos.** *pohr fah-VOHR YEH-veh-nohs ah NWEHS-trohs ah-SYEHN-tohs*

CULTURE

MUSEUMS, GALLERIES, AND SIGHTS

Do you have a museum guide?	**¿Tiene una guía del museo?** *TYEH-neh oo-nah GEE-ah dehl moo-SEH-oh*
Do you have guided tours?	**¿Ofrecen una excursión guiada?** *oh-FREH-sehn oo-nah ehs-koor-SYOHN gee-AH-dah*
What are the museum hours?	**¿Cuál es el horario del museo?** *KWAHL ehs ehl oh-RAH-ryoh dehl moo-SEH-oh*
Do I need an appointment?	**¿Necesito una cita?** *neh-seh-SEE-toh oo-nah SEE-tah*
What is the admission fee?	**¿Cuánto es la tarifa de admisión?** *KWAHN-toh ehs lah tah-REE-fah deh ahd-mee-SYOHN*
Do you have _____	**¿Ofrecen _____** *oh-FREH-sehn*
student discounts?	**descuentos para estudiantes?** *dehs-KWEHN-tohs PAH-rah ehs-too-DYAHN-tehs*
senior discounts?	**descuentos para personas mayores / ancianos?** *dehs-KWEHN-tohs PAH-rah pehr-SOH-nahs mah-YOH-rehs / ahn-SYAH-nohs*
Do you have services for the hearing impaired?	**¿Tienen servicios para personas con impedimentos auditivos?** *TYEH-nehn sehr-VEE-syohs PAH-rah pehr-SOH-nahs kohn eem-peh-dee-MEHN-tohs ow-dee-TEE-vohs*
Do you have audio tours in English?	**¿Ofrecen excursiones con audio en inglés?** *oh-FREH-sehn ehs-koor-SYOH-nehs kohn OW-dyoh ehn een-GLEHS*

CHAPTER EIGHT
SHOPPING

This chapter covers the phrases you'll need to shop in a variety of settings, from the mall to the town square artisan market. We also threw in the terminology you'll need to visit the barber or hairdresser.

For coverage of food and grocery shopping, see p100.

GENERAL SHOPPING TERMS

Can you tell me ____	**¿Me puede decir ____**
	meh PWEH-deh deh-SEER
how to get to a mall?	**cómo llego a un centro comercial?**
	KOH-moh YEH-goh ah oon SEHN-troh koh-mehr-SYAHL
the best place for shopping?	**el mejor lugar para ir de compras?**
	ehl meh-HOHR loo-GAHR pah-rah EER deh KOHM-prahs
how to get downtown?	**cómo llego al centro de la ciudad?**
	KOH-moh YEH-goh ahl SEHN-troh deh lah see-oo-DAD

Contrabandistas

Beware of unscrupulous vendors who attempt to sell you illegal, contraband, or fake goods. Most Latin American countries do not allow exportation of pre-Columbian artifacts. (In other words, the ones sold by street vendors aren't real.)

Where can I find a _____	¿Dónde puedo encontrar una _____
	DOHN-deh PWEH-doh ehn-kohn-
	TRAHR oo-nah
shoe store?	**tienda de zapatos?**
	TYEHN-dah deh sah-PAH-tohs
men's / women's / children's clothing store?	**tienda de ropa para hombres / mujeres / niños?**
	TYEHN-dah deh RROH-pah PAH-rah HOM-brehs / moo-HEH-rehs / NEE-nyohs
designer fashion shop?	**tienda de moda de diseñador?**
	TYEHN-dah deh MOH-dah deh dee-seh-nyah-DOHR
vintage clothing store?	**tienda de ropa antigua?**
	TYEHN-dah deh RROH-pah ahn-TEE-wah
jewelry store?	**joyería?**
	hoh-yeh-REE-yah
bookstore?	**librería?**
	lee-breh-REE-ah
toy store?	**juguetería?**
	hoo-geh-teh-REE-ah
flea market?	**mercadillo (de pulgas)**
	mehr-kah-DEE-yoh (deh POOL-gas)

Cuban Cigars

In Latin America, many shops purport to carry Cuban cigars, but it's just a line. Real Cuban cigars are sold only at stores certified by the Cuban government. Certification will be posted, with an anticounterfeiting hologram on the box. When in doubt: if it's cheap, it's fake. That said, most of the "Cubans" on the market, though they're actually from Honduras or the Dominican Republic, are excellent for the price.

antique shop?	**tienda de antigüedades?**
	TYEHN-dah deh ahn-tee-gweh-DAH-dehs
cigar shop?	**tienda de cigarros?**
	TYEHN-dah deh see-GAH-rrohs
souvenir shop?	**tienda de recuerdos?**
	TYEHN-dah deh reh-KWEHR-dohs

CLOTHES SHOPPING

I'd like to buy _____	**Quisiera comprar _____**
	kee-SYEH-rah kohm-PRAHR
men's shirts.	**camisas para hombres.**
	kah-MEE-sahs PAH-rah OHM-brehs
women's shoes.	**zapatos para mujeres.**
	sah-PAH-tohs PAH-rah moo-HEH-rehs
children's clothes.	**ropa para niños.**
	RROH-pah PAH-rah NEE-nyohs
For a full list of numbers, see p7.	
I'm looking for a size _____	**Busco una talla _____**
	BOOS-koh oo-nah TAH-yah
small.	**pequeña.**
	peh-KEH-nyah
medium.	**mediana.**
	meh-DYAH-nah
large.	**grande.**
	GRAHN-deh
extra-large.	**extra grande.**
	EHKS-trah GRAHN-deh
I'm looking for _____	**Busco _____**
	BOOS-koh
a silk blouse.	**una blusa de seda.**
	oo-nah BLOO-sah deh SEH-dah
cotton pants.	**pantalones de algodón.**
	pahn-tah-LOH-nehs deh ahl-goh-DOHN

los aretes
el collar

la camisa
la corbata
la chaqueta

el vestido
el reloj

el cinturón

los pantalones

los zapatos

a hat.	**un sombrero.** *oon sohm-BREH-roh*
sunglasses.	**gafas de sol.** *GAH-fahs deh sohl*
underwear.	**ropa interior.** *RROH-pah een-teh-RYOHR*
cashmere.	**cachemir.** *kah-che-MEER*
socks.	**medias.** *MEH-dyahs*
sweaters.	**suéteres.** *soo-EH-teh-rehs*
a coat.	**un abrigo.** *oon ah-BREE-goh*
a swimsuit.	**un traje de baño.** *oon TRAH-heh deh BAH-nyoh*
May I try it on?	**¿Puedo probármelo?** *PWEH-doh proh-BAR-meh-loh*

las gafas

la camiseta

los jeans

los tenis

Do you have fitting rooms?	**¿Tiene probadores?**
	TYEH-neh proh-bah-DOH-rehs
This is _____	**Esto me queda _____**
	EHS-toh meh KEH-dah
too tight.	**muy apretado.**
	MOO-ee ah-preh-TAH-doh
too loose.	**muy suelto.**
	MOO-ee SWEHL-toh
too long.	**muy largo.**
	MOO-ee LAHR-goh
too short.	**muy corto.**
	MOO-ee KOHR-toh
This fits great!	**¡Esto me queda bien!**
	EHS-toh meh KEH-dah byehn
Thanks, I'll take it.	**Gracias, me lo llevo.**
	GRAH-syahs meh loh YEH-voh
Do you have that in _____	**¿Tiene eso en _____**
	TYEH-neh EH-soh ehn
a smaller / larger size?	**una talla más pequeña / grande?**
	oo-nah TAH-yah mahs peh-KEH-nyah / GRAHN-deh

a different color?	**un color diferente?** *oon koh-LOHR dee-feh-REHN-teh*
How much is it?	**¿Cuánto es?** *KWAHN-toh ehs*

ARTISAN MARKET SHOPPING

Is there a craft / artisan market?	**¿Hay un mercado de artesanías?** *aye oon mehr-KAH-doh deh ahr-teh-SAH-nee-ahs*
That's beautiful. May I look at it?	**¡Eso es hermoso! ¿Puedo verlo?** *EH-soh ehs ehr-MOH-soh PWEH-doh VEHR-loh*
When is the farmers' market open?	**¿Cuándo está abierto el mercado de granjeros?** *KWAHN-doh ehs-TAH ah-BYEHR-toh ehl mehr-KAH-doh deh grahn-HEH-rohs*
Is that open every day of the week?	**¿Eso está abierto todos los días de la semana?** *EH-soh ehs-TAH ah-BYEHR-toh TOH-doh lohs DEE-ahs deh lah seh-MAH-nah*
How much does that cost?	**¿Cuánto cuesta eso?** *KWAHN-toh KWEHS-tah EH-soh*
That's too expensive.	**Eso es muy caro.** *EH-soh ehs MOO-ee KAH-roh*
How much for two?	**¿Cuánto por los / las dos?** *KWAHN-doh pohr lohs / lahs dohs*
Do I get a discount if I buy two or more?	**¿Me da un descuento si compro dos o más?** *meh dah oon dehs-KWEHN-toh see KOHM-proh dohs oh mahs*
Do I get a discount if I pay in cash?	**¿Me da un descuento si pago en efectivo?** *meh DAH oon desh-KWEHN-toh see PAH-goh ehn eh-FEHK-tee-voh*

Listen Up: Market Lingo

Por favor pida que le asistan, antes de tocar la mercadería.
pohr fah-VOHR PEE-dah keh leh ah-sees-TAHN ahn-TEHS deh toh-KAHR lah mehr-kah-deh-REE-ah

Please ask for help before handling goods.

Aquí tengo su cambio.
ah-KEE TEHNG-goh soo KAHM-byoh

Here is your change.

Dos por cuarenta, señor.
dohs pohr kwah-REHN-tah sehn-YOHR

Two for forty, sir.

No thanks, maybe I'll come back.

No gracias, quizás regrese más tarde.
noh GRAH-syahs kee-SAHS reh-GREH-seh mahs TAHR-deh

Would you take $____?

¿Aceptaría $____?
ah-SEHP-tah-REE-ah ____ DOH-lah-rehs

For a full list of numbers, see p7.
That's a deal!

¡Trato hecho!
TRAH-toh EH-choh

Do you have a less expensive one?

¿Tiene uno -a menos caro -a?
TYEH-neh oon / oo-nah MEH-nohs KAH-roh / KAH-rah

Is there tax?

¿Hay un impuesto?
aye oon eem-PWEHS-toh

May I have the VAT forms? (Europe only)

¿Me puede dar los formularios IVA?
meh PWEH-deh dahr lohs fohr-moo-LAHR-yohs ee-veh-AH

BOOKSTORE / NEWSSTAND SHOPPING

Is there a _____ nearby?	**¿Hay _____ cerca?**
	aye _____ SEHR-kah
a bookstore	**una librería**
	oo-nah lee-breh-REE-ah
a newsstand	**un quiosco**
	oon kee-OHS-koh
Do you have _____ in English?	**¿Tiene _____ en inglés?**
	TYEH-neh _____ ehn een-GLEHS
books	**libros**
	LEE-brohs
newspapers	**periódicos**
	pehr-YOH-dee-kohs
magazines	**revistas**
	reh-VEES-tahs
books about local history	**libros acerca de la historia local**
	LEE-brohs ah-SEHR-kah deh lah ees-TOHR-yah loh-KAHL
picture books	**libros de fotos**
	LEE-brohs deh FOH-tohs

SHOPPING FOR ELECTRONICS

With some exceptions, shopping for electronic goods in Latin America or Spain is generally not recommended. Many DVDs, CDs, and other products contain different signal coding from that used in the United States or Canada, to help deter piracy. Note: Electronic formats are the same for the United States and Canada.

Can I play this in the United States?

¿Funciona en Estados Unidos?
foon-see-OH-nah ehn ehs-TAH-dohs ooh-NEE-dohs

Will this game work on my game console in the United States?

¿Este juego funcionará en mi consola de juegos en Estados Unidos?
EHS-teh HWEH-goh foon-syoh-nah-RAH ehn mee kohn-SOH-lah deh HWEH-gohs ehn ehs-TAH-dohs oo-NEE-dohs

Do you have this in a U.S. market format?

¿Tiene esto en un formato para el mercado de Estados Unidos?
TYEH-neh EHS-toh ehn oon fohr-MAH-toh PAH-rah ehl mehr-KAH-doh deh ehs-TAH-dohs oo-NEE-dohs

Can you convert this to a U.S. market format?

¿Puede convertir esto a un formato para el mercado de Estados Unidos?
PWEH-deh kohn-vehr-TEER EHS-toh ah oon fohr-MAH-toh PAH-rah ehl mehr-KAH-doh deh ehs-TAH-dohs oo-NEE-dohs

Will this work with a 110 VAC adapter?

¿Esto funcionará con un adaptador de 110 VAC?
EHS-toh foon-syoh-nah-RAH kohn oon ah-dahp-tah-DOHR deh SYEHN-toh-ee-dyehs VOHL-tyohs deh koh-rree-EHN-teh ahl-TEHR-nah

Do you have an adapter plug for 110 to 220?

¿Tiene un enchufe adaptador de 110 a 220?
TYEH-neh oon ehn-CHOO-feh ah-dahp-tah-DOHR deh SYEHN-toh-ee-dyehs ah doh-SYEHN-tohs-ee-VEH-een-teh

Do you sell electronics adapters here?	**¿Vende adaptadores electrónicos aquí?** *VEHN-deh ah-dahp-tah-DOH-rehs eh-lehk-TROH-nee-kohs ah-KEE*
Is it safe to use my laptop with this adapter?	**¿Es seguro usar mi computadora portátil con este adaptador?** *ehs seh-GOO-roh oo-SAHR mee kohm-poo-tah-DOH-rah pohr-TAH-teel kohn EHS-teh ah-dahp-tah-DOHR*
If it doesn't work, may I return it?	**¿Si no funciona, puedo devolverlo?** *see noh foon-SYOH-nah PWEH-doh deh-vohl-VEHR-loh*
May I try it here in the store?	**¿Puedo probarlo aquí en la tienda?** *PWEH-doh proh-BAHR-loh ah-KEE ehn lah TYEHN-dah*

AT THE BARBER / HAIRDRESSER

Do you have a style guide?	**¿Tiene una guía de estilo?** *TYEH-neh oo-nah GEE-ah deh eh-STEE-loh*
A trim, please.	**Un recorte, por favor.** *oon rreh-KOHR-teh pohr fah-VOHR*
I'd like it bleached.	**Me gustaría el pelo descolorado.** *meh goos-tah-REE-ah ehl PEH-loh dehs-koh-loh-RAH-doh*
Would you change the color _____	**¿Usted le cambiaría el color _____** *oos-TED leh kahm-byah-REE-ah ehl koh-LOHR*
darker?	**más oscuro?** *mahs ohs-KOO-roh*
lighter?	**más claro?** *mahs KLAH-roh*

Would you just touch it up a little?	**¿Lo puede retocar un poco?** *loh PWEH-deh reh-toh-KAHR oon POH-koh*
I'd like it curled.	**Me gustaría rizado.** *meh goos-tah-REE-ah ree-SAH-doh*
Do I need an appointment?	**¿Necesito una cita?** *neh-seh-SEE-toh oo-nah SEE-tah*
Do you do permanents?	**¿Hacen permanentes?** *AH-sehn pehr-mah-NEHN-tehs*
May I make an appointment?	**¿Puedo hacer una cita?** *PWEH-doh ah-SEHR oo-nah SEE-tah*
Please use low heat.	**Por favor use poco calor.** *pohr fah-VOHR OO-seh POH-koh kah-LOHR*
Please don't blow dry it.	**Por favor no lo seque con secadora.** *pohr fah-VOHR noh loh SEH-keh kohn seh-kah-DOH-rah*
Please dry it curly / straight.	**Por favor séquelo rizado / lacio.** *pohr fah-VOHR SEH-keh-loh ree-SAH-doh / LAH-syoh*
Would you fix my highlights?	**¿Puede arreglar mis destellos?** *PWEH-deh ah-rreh-GLAHR mees dehs-TEH-yohs*
Do you wax?	**¿Hacen depilación con cera?** *AH-sehn deh-pee-lah-SYOHN kohn SEH-rah*
I'd like a Brazilian wax.	**Quiero hacerme la cera brasileña.** *kee-EH-roh ah-SEHR-meh lah SEH-rah bra-see-LEH-nya*

Please wax my _____	**Por favor, depile mis _____** *pohr fah-VOHR deh-PEE-leh mees*
legs.	**piernas.** *PYEHR-nahs*
bikini line.	**área del bikini.** *AH-reh-ah dehl bee-KEE-nee*
eyebrows.	**cejas.** *SEH-hahs*
under my nose.	**debajo de mi nariz.** *deh-BAH-hoh deh mee nah-REES*
Please trim my beard.	**Por favor recorte mi barba.** *pohr fah-VOHR reh-KOHR-teh mee* *BAHR-bah*
A shave, please.	**Una afeitada, por favor.** *oo-nah ah-feh-ee-TAH-dah pohr* *fah-VOHR*
Use a fresh blade please.	**Use una navaja nueva por favor.** *OOH-seh oo-nah nah-VAH-hah* *NWEH-vah pohr fah-VOHR*
Sure, cut it all off.	**Seguro, córtelo todo.** *seh-GOO-roh KOHR-teh-loh* *TOH-doh*

CHAPTER NINE

SPORTS & FITNESS

GETTING FIT

Is there a gym nearby?	**¿Hay un gimnasio cerca?** *aye oon heem-NAH-syoh SEHR-kah*
Does the hotel have a gym?	**¿Tiene gimnasio el hotel?** *TYEH-neh him-NAH-syo ehl oh-TEHL*
Do you have free weights?	**¿Tienen pesas de mano?** *TYEH-nehn PEH-sahs deh MAH-noh*
Is there a pool?	**¿Hay piscina?** *aye pees-SEE-nah*
Do I have to be a member?	**¿Tengo que ser miembro?** *TEHNG-goh keh sehr MYEHM-broh*
May I come here for one day?	**¿Puedo venir por un día, nada más?** *PWEH-doh veh-NEER pohr oon DEE-ah NAH-dah mahs*
How much does a membership cost?	**¿Cuánto cuesta ser socio?** *KWAHN-toh KWEHS-tah sehr SOH-see-oh*
I need a locker.	**Necesito un casillero.** *neh-seh-SEE-toh oon kah-see-YEH-roh*

Do you have a lock?	**¿Tiene un candado?** *TYEH-neh oon kahn-DAH-doh*
Do you have a treadmill?	**¿Tiene una caminadora?** *TYEH-neh oo-nah kah-mee-nah-DOH-rah*
Do you have a stationary bike?	**¿Tiene una bicicleta fija?** *TYEH-neh oo-nah bee-see-KLEH-tah FEE-hah*
Do you have handball / squash courts?	**¿Tiene canchas de balonmano / squash?** *TYEH-neh KAHN-chahs deh bah-lohn-MAH-noh / skwahsh?*
Are they indoors?	**¿Son bajo techo?** *sohn BAH-hoh TEH-cho*
I'd like to play tennis.	**Me gustaría jugar tenis.** *meh goos-tah-REE-ah hoo-GAHR TEH-nees*
Would you like to play?	**¿Le gustaría jugar?** *leh goos-tah-REE-ah hoo-GAHR*
I'd like to rent a racquet.	**Quisiera alquilar una raqueta.** *kee-SYEH-rah ahl-kee-LAHR oo-nah rrah-KEH-tah*
I need to buy some _____	**Necesito comprar _____** *neh-seh-SEE-toh kohm-PRAHR*
new balls.	**pelotas nuevas.** *peh-LOH-tahs NWEH-vahs*
safety glasses.	**gafas de protección.** *GAH-fahs deh proh-tehk-SYOHN*
May I rent a court for tomorrow?	**¿Puedo alquilar una cancha para mañana?** *PWEH-doh ahl-kee-LAHR oo-nah KAHN-chah PAH-rah mah-NYAH-nah*
May I have clean towels?	**¿Me puede dar toallas limpias?** *meh PWEH-deh dahr toh-AH-yahs LEEM-pyahs*

Where are the showers / locker-rooms?	**¿Dónde están las duchas / los vestuarios?** *DOHN-deh ehs-TAHN lahs DOO-chas / lohs vehs-TWAHR-yohs*
Do you have a workout room for women only?	**¿Tienen un cuarto de entrenamiento para mujeres solamente?** *TYEH-nehn oon KWAHR-toh deh ehn-treh-nah-MYEHN-toh PAH-rah moo-HEH-rehs soh-lah-MEHN-teh*
Do you have aerobics classes?	**¿Tienen clases de aeróbicos?** *TYEH-nehn KLAH-sehs deh ah-eh-ROH-bee-kohs*
Are there yoga / pilates classes?	**¿Hay clases de yoga / pilates?** *aye KLAH-sehs deh-YOH-gah / pee-LAH-tehs*
Do you have a women's pool?	**¿Tienen una piscina para mujeres?** *TYEH-nehn oo-nah pees-SEE-nah PAH-rah moo-HEH-rehs*
Let's go for a jog.	**Vamos a trotar.** *VAH-mohs ah troh-TAHR*
That was a great workout.	**Fue un tremendo entrenamiento.** *fweh oon treh-MEHN-doh ehn-treh-nah-MYEHN-toh*

CATCHING A GAME

Who's playing?	**¿Quién juega?** *kee-EHN hooh-EH-gah*
Where is the stadium?	**¿Dónde es el estadio?** *DOHN-deh ehs ehl ehs-TAH-dyoh*
Is there a bullfight?	**¿Hay una corrida de toros?** *aye oo-nah koh-RREE-dah deh TOH-rohs*
Who is your favorite toreador / matador?	**¿Quién es su toreador / matador favorito?** *kyehn ehs soo toh-reh-ah-DOHR / mah-tah-DOHR fah-voh-REE-toh*
Who is the best goalie?	**¿Quién es el mejor portero?** *kyehn ehs ehl meh-HOHR pohr-TEH-roh*
Do you have any amateur / professional teams?	**¿Tienen algún equipo aficionado / profesional?** *TYEH-nehn ahl-GOON eh-KEE-poh ah-fee-syoh-NAH-doh / proh-feh-syoh-NAHL*
Is there a game I could play in?	**¿Hay algún juego en el que yo pueda jugar?** *aye ahl-GOON HWEH-goh ehn ehl keh yoh PWEH-dah hoo-GAHR*
Which is the best team?	**¿Cuál es el mejor equipo?** *KWAHL ehs ehl meh-HOHR eh-KEE-poh*
Will the game be on television?	**¿El juego será televisado?** *ehl HWEH-goh seh-RAH teh-leh-vee-SAH-doh*
Where can I buy tickets?	**¿Dónde puedo comprar boletos/entradas?** *DOHN-deh PWEH-doh kohm-PRAHR boh-LEH-tohs / ehn-TRAH-dahs*

The best seats, please.	**Los mejores asientos, por favor.**
	lohs meh-HOH-rehs ah-SYEHN-tohs
	pohr fah-VOHR
The cheapest seats, please.	**Los asientos más baratos, por favor.**
	lohs ah-SYEHN-tohs mahs bah-
	RAH-tohs pohr fah-VOHR
Where are these seats?	**¿Dónde están estos asientos?**
	DOHN-deh ehs-TAN EHS-tohs
	ah-SYEHN-tohs
How close are these seats?	**¿Cuán cerca están estos asientos?**
	kwahn SEHR-kah ehs-TAHN EHS-
	tohs ah-SYEHN-tohs
May I have box seats?	**¿Me puede dar asientos de palco?**
	meh PWEH-deh dahr ah-SYEHN-
	tohs deh PAHL-koh
Wow! What a game!	**¡Caray! ¡Que juego!**
	kah-RAH-ee keh HWEH-goh
Go Go Go!	**¡Dale, dale, dale!**
	DAH-leh, DAH-leh, DAH-leh
Go for it!	**¡Ve por él!**
	Veh pohr ehl
Score!	**¡Anota!**
	ah-NOH-tah
What's the score?	**¿Cómo van?**
	KOH-moh van
Who's winning?	**¿Quién está ganando?**
	kyehn ehs-TAH gah-NAHN-doh

HIKING

Is there a trail map?	**¿Hay un mapa de senderos?**
	aye oon MAH-pah deh sehn-
	DEH-rohs
Do we need to hire a guide?	**¿Necesitamos contratar a un guía?**
	neh-seh-see-TAH-mohs kohn-trah-
	TAHR ah oon GEE-ah

Where can I rent equipment?	**¿Dónde puedo alquilar equipo?** *DOHN-deh PWEH-doh ahl-kee-LAHR eh-KEE-poh*
Do they have rock climbing there?	**¿Tienen escalada de rocas ahí?** *TYEH-nehn ehs-kah-LAH-dah deh RROH-kahs ah-EE*
We need more ropes and carabiners.	**Necesitamos más cuerda y carabineros.** *neh-seh-see-TAH-mohs mahs KWEHR-dah ee kah-rah-bee-NEH-rohs*
Where can we go mountain climbing?	**¿Dónde podemos ir de alpinismo?** *DOHN-deh poh-DEH-mohs eer deh ahl-pee-NEES-moh*
Are the routes _____	**¿Todas las rutas están _____** *TOH-dahs lahs RROO-tahs ehs-TAHN*
well marked?	**bien marcadas?** *byehn mahr-KAH-dahs*
in good condition?	**en buenas condiciones?** *ehn BWEH-nahs kohn-dee-SYOH-nehs*
What is the altitude there?	**¿Cuál es la altitud allí?** *KWAHL ehs lah ahl-tee-TOOD ah-YEE*

How long will it take?	**¿Cuánto tomará?** *KWAHN-toh toh-mah-RAH*
Is it very difficult?	**¿Es muy difícil?** *ehs MOO-ee dee-FEE-seel*
I'd like a challenging climb but I don't want to take oxygen.	**Me gustaría un ascenso desafiante, pero no quiero tener que llevar oxígeno.** *meh goos-tah-REE-ah oon ahs-SEHN-soh deh-sah-fee-AHN-teh peh-roh noh KYEH-roh teh-NEHR keh yeh-VAHR ohk-SEE-heh-noh*
I need to hire a porter.	**Necesito contratar a un porteador.** *neh-seh-SEE-toh kohn-trah-TAR ah oon pohr-teh-AH-dohr*
We don't have time for a long route.	**No tenemos tiempo para una ruta larga.** *noh teh-NEH-mohs TYEHM-poh PAH-rah oo-nah RROO-tah LAHR-gah*
I don't think it's safe to proceed.	**No creo que sea seguro continuar.** *noh KREH-oh keh SEH-ah seh-GOO-roh kohn-tee-NWAHR*
Do we have a backup plan?	**¿Tenemos un plan de respaldo?** *teh-NEH-mohs oon plahn deh rrehs-PAHL-doh*
If we're not back by tomorrow, send a search party.	**Si no volvemos mañana, manden rescate.** *see noh vohl-VEH-mohs ma-NYAN-na, MAHN-dehn rehs-KAH-teh*
Are the campsites marked?	**¿Los campamentos están marcados?** *lohs kahm-pah-MEHN-tohs ehs-TAHN mahr-KAH-dohs*

Can we camp off the trail?	**¿Podemos acampar lejos del sendero?** *poh-DEH-mohs ah-kahm-PAHR LEH-hohs dehl sehn-DEH-roh*
Is it okay to build fires here?	**¿Está bien hacer fogatas aquí?** *ehs-TAH byehn ah-SEHR foh-GAH-tahs ah-KEE*
Do we need permits?	**¿Necesitamos permisos?** *neh-seh-see-TAH-mohs pehr-MEE-sohs*

For more camping terms, see p79.

BOATING OR FISHING

I'd like to go fishing.	**Quisiera ir a pescar.** *kee-SYEH-rah ihr ah pehs-CAR*
When do we sail?	**¿Cuándo partimos / salimos?** *KWAHN-doh pahr-TEE-mohs / sah-LEE-mohs*
Where are the life preservers?	**¿Dónde están los salvavidas?** *DOHN-deh ehs-TAHN lohs sahl-vah-VEE-dahs*
Can I purchase bait?	**¿Puedo comprar carnada?** *PWEH-doh kohm-PRAHR kahr-NAH-dah*
Can I rent a rod / pole?	**¿Puedo alquilar una caña de pescar?** *PWEH-doh ahl-kee-LAHR oo-nah KAH-nyah deh pehs-KAHR*

How long is the trip?	**¿Cuánto dura el viaje?**
	KWAN-toh DOOH-rah ehl vee-AH-heh
Are we going up river or down?	**¿Vamos río arriba o río abajo?**
	VAH-mohs RREE-oh ah-RREE-bah oh RREE-oh ah-BAH-hoh
How far are we going?	**¿Qué tan lejos vamos?**
	KEH tahn LEH-hos VAH-mohs
How fast are we going?	**¿Qué tan rápido vamos?**
	KEH tahn RRAH-pee-doh VAH-mohs
How deep is the water here?	**¿Qué profundidad tiene el agua (aquí)?**
	KEH proh-foon-dee-DAD TYEH-neh ehl AH-wah (ah-KEE)
I got one!	**¡Pesqué uno!**
	pehs-KEH OO-noh
I can't swim.	**No sé nadar.**
	noh seh nah-DAHR
Help! Lifeguard!	**¡Socorro! ¡Salvavidas!**
	soh-KOH-rroh sahl-vah-VEE-dahs
Can we go ashore?	**¿Podemos ir a la orilla?**
	poh-DEH-mohs eer ah lah oh-REE-yah

For more boating terms, see p62.

DIVING

I'd like to go snorkeling.	**Quisiera hacer snorkeling/snorkel**
	kee-SYEH-rah ah-SEHR snork-ehl-ling / snork-ehl
I'd like to go scuba diving.	**Quisiera ir de buceo con tanques de oxígeno.**
	kee-SYEH-rah eer deh boo-SEH-oh kohn TAHN-kehs deh ohk-SEE-heh-noh

I have a NAUI / PADI certification.	**Tengo certificación NAUI / PADI.** *TEHNG-goh sehr-tee-fee-kah-SYOHN EH-neh ah oo ee / peh ah deh ee*
I need to rent gear.	**Necesito alquilar equipo.** *neh-seh-SEE-toh ahl-kee-LAHR eh-KEE-poh*
We'd like to see some shipwrecks if we can.	**Quisiéramos ver algunos restos de barcos que hayan naufragado si podemos.** *kee-SYEH-rah-mohs vehr ahl-GOO-nohs PREHS-tohs deh BAR-kohs keh AYE-ahn now-frah-GAH-doh see poh-DEH-mohs*
Are there any good reef dives?	**¿Hay buenos lugares para buceo en arrecifes?** *aye BWEH-nohs loo-GAH-rehs PAH-rah boo-SEH-oh ehn ah-rreh-SEE-fehs*
I'd like to see a lot of sea-life.	**Quisiera ver mucha vida marina.** *kee-SYEH-rah vehr MOO-chah VEE-dah mah-REE-nah*
Are the currents strong?	**¿Las corrientes son fuertes?** *lahs koh-RREE-EHN-tehs sohn FWEHR-tehs*
How clear is the water?	**¿Qué tan clara es el agua?** *KEH tahn KLAH-rah ehs ehl AH-wah*
I want / don't want to go with a group	**Quiero / No quiero ir con un grupo.** *KYEH-roh / NOH kyeh-roh eer kohn oon GROO-poh*
Can we charter our own boat?	**¿Podemos fletar nuestro propio bote?** *poh-DEH-mohs fleh-TAHR NWEHS-troh PROH-pyoh BOH-teh*

SURFING

I'd like to go surfing.

Quisiera hacer surfing.
kee-SYEH-rah ah-SEHR soor-FEENG

Are there any good beaches?

¿Hay buenas playas?
aye BWEH-nahs PLAH-yahs

Can I rent a board?

¿Puedo alquilar una tabla?
PWEH-doh ahl-kee-LAHR oo-nah TAH-blah

How are the currents?

¿Cómo son las corrientes?
KOH-moh sohn lahs koh-RREE-EHN-tehs

How high are the waves?

¿Cuán altas son las olas?
KWAHN AHL-tahs sohn lahs OH-lahs

Is it usually crowded?

¿Generalmente está llena de personas?
heh-neh-rahl-MEHN-teh ehs-TAH YEH-nah deh pehr-SOH-nahs

Are there facilities on that beach?

¿Hay facilidades en esa playa?
aye fah-see-lee-DAH-dehs ehn EH-sah PLAH-yah

Is there wind surfing there also?

¿Hay windsurfing allí también?
aye weend-SOOR-feeng ah-YEE tahm-BYEHN

GOLFING

I'd like to reserve a
tee-time, please.

**Quisiera reservar tiempo para
jugar golf, por favor.**
*kee-SYEH-rah rreh-sehr-VAHR
TYEHM-poh PAH-rah hoo-GAHR
golf, pohr fah-VOHR*

Do we need to be
members to play?

**¿Tenemos que ser miembros para
jugar?**
*teh-NEH-mohs keh sehr MYEHM-
brohs PAH-rah hoo-GAHR*

How many holes is your
course?

¿De cuántos hoyos es el campo?
*deh KWAHN-tohs OH-yohs ehs ehl
KAHM-poh*

What is par for the course?

¿Cuál es el par para el campo?
*KWAHL ehs ehl PAHR PAH-rah ehl
KAHM-poh*

What is the dress code for players?

**¿Hay código de vestimenta para
los jugadores?**
*aye KOH-dee-goh deh vehs-tee-
MEN-tah PAH-rah lohs hooh-gah-
DOH-rehs*

I need to rent clubs.

Necesito alquilar los palos.
*neh-seh-SEE-toh ahl-kee-LAHR
lohs PAH-lohs*

I need to purchase a
sleeve of balls.

**Necesito alquilar una bolsa de
pelotas.**
*neh-seh-SEE-toh ahl-kee-LAHR oo-
nah BOHL-sah deh peh-LOH-tahs*

I need a glove.

Necesito un guante.
neh-seh-SEE-toh oon GWAHN-teh

Do you require soft spikes?	**¿Ustedes requieren zapatos con púas blandas?** *oos-TEH-dehs rreh-KYEH-rehn sah-PAH-tohs kohn POO-ahs BLAHN-dahs*
Do you have carts?	**¿Tienen carritos?** *TYEH-nehn kah-RREE-tohs*
I'd like to hire a caddy.	**Quisiera contratar a alguien que cargue mis palos.** *kee-SYEH-rah kohn-trah-TAHR ah AHL-gee-ehn keh KAHR-geh mees PAH-lohs*
Do you have a driving range?	**¿Tienen un campo de práctica?** *TYEH-nehn oon KAHM-poh deh PRAHK-tee-kah*
How much are the greens fees?	**¿Cuánto es la cuota para jugar?** *KWAHN-toh ehs lah KWOH-tah PAH-rah hoo-GAHR*
Can I book a lesson with the pro?	**¿Puedo reservar una lección con el profesional?** *PWEH-doh rreh-sehr-VAHR oo-nah lehk-SYOHN kohn ehl proh-feh-syoh-NAHL*
I need to have a club repaired.	**Necesito reparar un palo de golf.** *neh-seh-SEE-toh rreh-pah-RAHR oon PAH-loh deh golf*
Is the course dry?	**¿El campo está seco?** *ehl KAHM-poh ehs-TAH SEH-koh*
Are there any wildlife hazards?	**¿Hay peligros de vida silvestre?** *aye peh-LEEG-rohs deh VEE-dah seel-VEHS-treh*
How many meters is the course?	**¿De cuántos metros es el campo?** *deh KWAHN-tohs MEH-trohs ehs ehl KAHM-poh*
Is it very hilly?	**¿Tiene muchas colinas pequeñas?** *TYEH-neh moo-chahs koh-LEE-nahs peh-KEH-nyahs*

CHAPTER TEN

NIGHTLIFE

For coverage of movies and cultural events, see p144, Chapter Seven, "Culture."

NIGHTCLUBBING

Where can I find _____	¿Dónde puedo encontrar _____ *DOHN-deh PWEH-doh ehn-kohn-TRAHR*
a good nightclub?	**un buen club nocturno?** *oon bwehn kloob nohk-TOOR-noh*
a club with a live band?	**un club con banda en vivo?** *oon kloob kohn BAHN-dah ehn VEE-voh*
a reggae club?	**un club con reggae?** *oon kloob kohn RREH-geh*
a hip hop club?	**un club con música hip-hop?** *oon kloob kohn MOO-see-kah EEP-ohp / HEEP-hohp*
a techno club?	**un club con música techno?** *oon kloob kohn MOO-see-kah TEHK-noh*
a jazz club?	**un club con música jazz?** *oon kloob kohn MOO-see-kah jahs*
a country-western club?	**un club con música country?** *oon kloob kohn MOO-see-kah KOHN-tree*
a gay / lesbian club?	**un club de gays?** *oon kloob deh geh-ees*
a club where I can dance?	**un club dónde pueda bailar?** *oon kloob DOHN-deh PWEH-dah bah-ee-LAHR*

a club with Latin music?	**un club con música latina?** *oon kloob kohn MOO-see-kah lah-TEE-nah*
the most popular club in town?	**el club más popular en el pueblo?** *ehl kloob mahs poh-poo-LAHR ehn ehl PWEH-bloh*
a singles bar?	**una cantina para solteros?** *oo-nah kahn-TEE-nah PAH-rah sohl-TEH-rohs*
a piano / jazz bar?	**un bar de jazz / con piano?** *oon bar deh jazz / kohn pee-AH-no*
the most upscale club?	**el club de élite?** *ehl kloob de EH-lee-teh*
What's the hottest bar these days?	**¿Cuál es la cantina más popular de estos días?** *KWAHL ehs lah kahn-TEE-nah mahs poh-poo-LAHR deh EHS-tohs DEE-ahs*
What's the cover charge?	**¿Cuánto es el cover / la entrada?** *KWAN-toh ehs ehl KOH-vehr / lah ehn-TRAH-dah*
Do they have a dress code?	**¿Tienen un código de vestimenta?** *TYEH-nehn oon KOH-dee-goh deh vehs-tee-MEHN-tah*

NIGHTLIFE

Cover Your Culo

Be careful with the verb culear. *Culear* is "to shake one's bottom" or "dance," but in Colombia it means "to have sex." Because *el culo* is a vulgar term for derriere, *culear* may mean "to have anal sex" in many Latin American countries.

Is it expensive?	**¿Es caro?** *ehs KAH-roh*
What's the best time to go?	**¿Cuál es la mejor hora para ir?** *KWAHL ehs lah meh-HOHR OH-rah PAH-rah eer*
What kind of music do they play there?	**¿Qué tipo de música tocan ahí?** *KEH TEE-poh deh MOO-see-kah TOH-kahn ah-EE*
Is it smoking?	**¿Permiten fumar?** *pehr-MEE-tehn foo-MAHR*
Is it nonsmoking?	**¿Se prohíbe fumar?** *seh proh-EE-beh foo-MAHR*
I'm looking for _____	**Estoy buscando _____** *ehs-TOY boos-KAHN-doh*
a good cigar shop.	**una buena tienda de cigarros.** *oo-nah BWEH-nah TYEHN-dah deh see-GAH-rrohs*
a pack of cigarettes.	**un paquete de cigarrillos.** *oon pah-KEH-teh deh see-gah-RREE-yohs*

Do You Mind If I Smoke?

¿Tiene un cigarrillo? *TYEH-neh oon see-gah-RREE-yoh*	Do you have a cigarette?
¿Tiene lumbre? *TYEH-neh LOOM-breh*	Do you have a light?
¿Le puedo ofrecer lumbre / encender su cigarrillo? *leh PWEH-doh oh-freh-SEHR LOOM-breh / ehn-sehn-DEHR soo see-gah-RREE-yoh*	May I offer you a light?
Prohibido fumar. *proh-ee-BEE-doh foo-MAHR*	Smoking not permitted.

I'd like ____

Quisiera ____
kee-SYEH-rah

a drink, please.

    una bebida, por favor.
    oo-nah beh-BEE-dah pohr fah-VOHR

a bottle of beer, please.

    una botella de cerveza, por favor.
    oo-nah boh-TEH-yah deh sehr-VEH-sah pohr fah-VOHR

A beer on tap, please.

    una cerveza de barril, por favor.
    oo-nah sehr-VEH-sah deh bah-RREEL pohr fah-VOHR

a shot of ____, please.

    un trago de ____, por favor.
    oon TRAH-goh deh ____ pohr fah-VOHR

For a full list of drinks, see p88.
Make it a double, please!

¡Hazlo doble, por favor!
AHS-loh DOH-bleh pohr fah-VOHR

With ice, please.

Con hielo, por favor.
kohn YEH-loh pohr fah-VOHR

And one for the lady / the gentleman!

¡Y uno para la dama / el caballero!
ee oo-noh PAH-rah lah DAH-mah / ehl kah-bah-YEH-roh

How much for a bottle / glass of beer?

¿Cuánto por una botella / un copa de cerveza?
KWAHN-toh pohr oo-nah boh-TEH-yah / oon KOH-pah deh sehr-VEH-sah

I'd like to buy a drink for that girl / guy over there.

Quisiera comprarle una bebida a aquella chica / aquel chico allá.
kee-SYEH-rah kohm-PRAHR-leh oo-nah beh-BEE-dah ah ah-KEH-yah CHEE-kah / ah-KEHL CHEE-koh ah-YAH

A pack of cigarettes, please.

Un paquete de cigarrillos, por favor.
oon pah-KEH-teh deh see-gah-RREE-yohs pohr fah-VOHR

Do you have a lighter or matches?	**¿Tiene un encendedor o fósforos?** *TYEH-neh oon ehn-sehn-deh-DOHR oh FOHS-foh-rohs*
Do you smoke?	**¿Usted fuma?** *oos-TED FOO-mah*
Would you like a cigarette?	**¿Le gustaría un cigarrillo?** *leh goos-tah-REE-ah oon see-gah-RREE-yoh*
May I run a tab?	**¿Puedo mantener una cuenta abierta?** *PWEH-doh man-teh-NEHR oo-nah KWEN-tah ah-bee-EHR-tah*
What's the cover?	**¿Cuánto es el cargo de entrada?** *KWAHN-toh ehs ehl KAHR-goh deh ehn-TRAH-dah*

ACROSS A CROWDED ROOM

I wanted to meet you.	**Quería conocerte.** *keh-REE-ah koh-noh-SEHR-teh*
You look great.	**Te ves muy bien / Estás muy guapa / guapo** *teh vehs MOO-ee bee-EHN / ehs-TAHS MOO-ee WA-pah/ WA-poh*
Are you single?	**¿Es soltero/soltera?** *EHS sohl-TEH-roh / sohl-TEH-rah*

You look like the most interesting person in the room.	**Usted se ve como la persona más interesante aquí.** *oos-TED seh veh koh-moh lah pehr-SOH-nah mahs een-teh-reh-SAHN-teh ah-KEE*
Would you like to dance?	**¿Le gustaría bailar?** *leh goos-tah-REE-ah bah-ee-LAHR*
Do you like to dance fast or slow?	**¿Le gusta bailar rápido o lento?** *leh GOOS-tah bah-ee-LAHR RRAH-pee-doh oh LEHN-toh*
Give me your hand.	**Déme su mano.** *DEH-meh soo MAH-noh*
What would you like to drink?	**¿Qué le gustaría tomar?** *KEH leh goos-tah-REE-ah toh-MAHR*
You're a great dancer.	**Usted es un gran bailador / una gran bailadora.** *oos-TED ehs oon grahn bah-ee-lah-DOHR / oo-nah grahn bah-ee-lah-DOH-rah*
Do you like this song?	**¿Le gusta esta canción?** *leh GOOS-tah EHS-tah kahn-SYOHN*
You have nice eyes!	**¡Usted tiene / Tú tienes ojos lindos!** *oos-TED TYEH-neh / too TYEH-nehs OH-hohs LEEN-dohs*

For a full list of features, see p118.

May I have your phone number?	**¿Me puede dar su número de teléfono?** *meh PWEH-deh dahr soo NOO-meh-roh deh teh-LEH-foh-noh*
Would you like to go out (with me)?	**¿Le gustaría salir (conmigo)?** *leh goos-tah-REE-ah sa-LEER kohn-MEE-goh*
I'd love to.	**Me encantaría.** *me ehn-kahn-tah-REE-ah*

NIGHTLIFE

GETTING CLOSER

You're very attractive.

Tú eres muy atractivo -a.
too EH-rehs MOO-ee ah-trahk-TEE-voh -vah

I like being with you.

Me gusta estar contigo.
meh GOOS-tah ehs-TAHR kohn-TEE-goh

I like you.

Me gustas.
meh GOOS-tahs

I want to hold you.

Quiero abrazarte.
KYEH-roh ah-brah-SAHR-teh

Kiss me.

Bésame.
BEH-sah-meh

May I give you _____

¿Te puedo dar _____
teh PWEH-doh dahr

  a hug?

  un abrazo?
  oon ah-BRAH-soh

  a kiss?

  un beso?
  oon BEH-soh

Would you like _____

¿Te gustaría _____
teh goos-tah-REE-ah

  a back rub?

  un masaje en la espalda?
  oon mah-SAH-heh ehn lah ehs-PAHL-dah

  a massage?

  un masaje?
  oon mah-SAH-heh

GETTING INTIMATE

Would you like to come inside?	**¿Te gustaría entrar?** *teh goos-tah-REE-ah ehn-TRAHR*
May I come inside?	**¿Puedo entrar?** *PWEH-doh ehn-TRAHR*
Let me help you out of that.	**Déjame ayudarte a quitarte eso.** *DEH-hah-meh ah-yoo-DAHR-teh ah kee-TAHR-teh EH-soh*
Would you help me out of this?	**¿Me puedes ayudar a quitarme esto?** *meh PWEH-dehs ah-yoo-DAHR ah kee-TAHR-meh EHS-toh*
You smell so good.	**Hueles tan bien.** *WEH-lehs tahn byehn*
You're beautiful / handsome.	**Eres bella / guapo.** *EH-rehs BEH-yah / GWAH-poh*
May I?	**¿Puedo?** *PWEH-doh*
OK?	**¿Está bien?** *ehs-TAH byehn*
Like this?	**¿Así?** *ah-SEE*
How?	**¿Cómo?** *KOH-moh*

NIGHTLIFE

HOLD ON A SECOND

Please don't do that.	**Por favor no hagas eso.** *pohr fah-VOHR noh AH-gahs EH-soh*
Stop, please.	**Para por favor.** *PAH-rah pohr fah-VOHR*
Do you want me to stop?	**¿Quieres que pare?** *KYEH-rehs keh PAH-reh*
Let's just be friends.	**Seamos sólo amigos.** *seh-AH-mohs SOH-loh ah-MEE-gohs*

Don't Mix the Message

Te deseo. *teh deh-SEH-oh*	I desire you. This is pretty much a physical expression.
Te quiero. *teh KEE-EH-roh*	While this literally means "I want you," in Spanish, it implies "I love you" in the romantic and erotic sense.
Te amo. *teh AH-moh*	This is used very seriously. If you're not the person's parent or grandparent, you'd better not be saying this without a ring in your pocket.

Do you have a condom?	**¿Tienes un condón?** *TYEH-nehs oon kohn-DOHN*
Are you on birth control?	**¿Estás usando anticonceptivos?** *ehs-TAHS oo-SAHN-doh ahn-tee-kohn-sehp-TEE-vohs*
I have a condom.	**Tengo un condón.** *TEHNG-goh oon kohn-DOHN*
Do you have anything you should tell me first?	**¿Tienes que decirme algo primero?** *TYEH-nehs keh deh-SEER-meh AHL-goh pree-MEH-roh*

BACK TO IT

That's it.	**Eso es.** *EH-soh ehs*
That's not it.	**Eso no es.** *EH-soh noh ehs*
Here.	**Ahí.** *ah-EE*
There.	**Allá.** *ah-YAH*

For a full list of features, see p118.
For a full list of body parts, see p190.

More.	**Más.**
	MAHS
Harder.	**Más duro.**
	mahs DOO-roh
Faster.	**Más rápido.**
	mahs RRAH-pee-doh
Deeper.	**Más profundo.**
	mahs proh-FOON-doh
Slower.	**Más lento.**
	mahs LEHN-toh
Easier.	**Más suave.**
	mahs SWAH-veh

COOLDOWN

You're great.	**Eres fántastico -a.**
	EH-rehs FAHN-tahs-tee-koh -kah
That was great.	**Eso estuvo fabuloso.**
	EH-soh ehs-TOO-voh fah-boo-LOH-soh
Would you like ____	**¿Te gustaría ____**
	teh goos-tah-REE-ah
a drink?	**un trago?**
	oon TRAH-goh
a snack?	**un bocadillo?**
	oon boh-kah-DEE-yoh
a shower?	**una ducha?**
	oo-nah DOO-cha
May I stay here?	**¿Puedo quedarme aquí?**
	PWEH-doh keh-DAHR-meh ah-KEE
Would you like to stay here?	**¿Te gustaría quedarte aquí?**
	teh goos-tah-REE-ah keh-DAHR-teh ah-KEE
I'm sorry. I have to go now.	**Lo siento. Me tengo que ir ahora.**
	loh SYEHN-toh meh TEHN-goh keh eer ah-OH-rah
Where are you going?	**¿Adónde vas?**
	ah-DOHN-deh vahs

I have to work early.	**Tengo que trabajar temprano.** *TEHNG-goh keh trah-bah-HAHR tehm-PRAH-noh*
I'm flying home in the morning.	**Regreso a casa en la mañana.** *rreh-GREH-soh ah KAH-sah ehn lah mah-NYAH-nah*
I have an early flight.	**Tengo un vuelo temprano.** *TEHNG-goh oon VWEH-loh tehm- PRAH-noh*
I think this was a mistake.	**Creo que esto fue un error.** *KREH-oh keh EHS-toh fweh oon eh-RROHR*
Will you make me breakfast?	**¿Puedes prepararme el desayuno?** *PWEH-dehs preh-pah-RAHR-meh ehl deh-sah-YOOH-noh*
Stay. I'll make you breakfast.	**Quédate. Te haré el desayuno.** *KEH-dah-teh teh ah-REH ehl deh- sah-YOO-noh*

IN THE CASINO

How much is this table?	**¿Cuánto cuesta esta mesa?** *KWAHN-toh KWEHS-tah EHS-tah MEH-sah*
Deal me in.	**Repártame las cartas.** *reh-PAHR-tah-meh lahs KAHR-tahs*
Put it on red!	**¡Ponlo en rojo!** *POHN-loh ehn ROH-hoh*
Put it on black!	**¡Ponlo en negro!** *POHN-loh ehn NEH-groh*
Let it ride!	**¡Déjalo ir!** *DEH-hah-loh eer*
21!	**¡21!** *veh-een-TEE-OO-noh*
Snake-eyes!	**¡Ojos de serpiente!** *OH-hohs deh sehr-PEE-EHN-teh*

Seven.	**Siete.** *SYEH-teh*
For a full list of numbers, see p7. Damn, eleven.	**Maldición, once.** *mahl-dees-SYOHN OHN-seh*
I'll pass.	**Paso.** *PAH-soh*
Hit me!	**¡Dame!** *DAH-meh*
Split.	**Divida.** *dee-VEE-dah*
Are the drinks complimentary?	**¿Las bebidas son complementarias?** *lahs beh-BEE-dahs sohn kohm-pleh-mehn-TAH-ryahs*
May I bill it to my room?	**¿Puedo facturarlo a mi habitación?** *PWEH-doh fahk-too-RAHR-loh ah mee ah-bee-tah-SYOHN*
I'd like to cash out.	**Quisiera llevarme el dinero.** *kee-SYEH-rah yeh-VAHR-meh ehl dee-NEH-roh*
I'll hold.	**Me quedo.** *meh KEH-doh*
I'll see your bet.	**Veo tu apuesta.** *VEH-oh too ah-PWEHS-tah*
I call.	**Igualo tu apuesta.** *ee-GWAH-loh too ah-PWEHS-tah*
Full house!	**¡Full!** *fool*
Royal flush.	**Escalera real.** *ehs-kah-LEH-rah reh-AHL*
Straight.	**Escalera.** *ehs-kah-LEH-rah*

CHAPTER ELEVEN

HEALTH & SAFETY

This chapter covers the terms you'll need to maintain your health and safety—including the most useful phrases for the pharmacy, the doctor's office, and the police station.

AT THE PHARMACY

Please fill this prescription.	**Por favor, despache esta receta.** *pohr fah-VOHR dehs-PAH-cheh EHS-tah rreh-SEH-tah*
Do you have something for ____	**¿Tiene algo para ____** *TYEH-neh AHL-goh PAH-rah*
a cold?	**un resfriado?** *oon rrehs-FRYAH-doh*
a cough?	**la tos?** *lah TOHS*
I need something ____	**Necesito algo para ____** *neh-seh-SEE-toh AHL-goh PAH-rah*
to help me sleep.	**ayudarme a dormir.** *ah-yoo-DAHR-meh ah dohr-MEER*
to help me relax.	**ayudarme a relajarme.** *ah-yoo-DAHR-meh ah rreh-lah-HAHR-meh*
I want to buy ____	**Quiero comprar ____** *KYEH-roh kohm-PRAHR*
condoms.	**condones.** *kohn-DOH-nehs*
an antihistamine.	**un antihistamínico.** *oon ahn-tee-ees-tah-MEE-nee-koh*
antibiotic cream.	**una crema antibiótica.** *oo-nah KREH-mah ahn-tee-BYOH-tee-kah*

aspirin.	**aspirina.**
	ahs-pee-REE-nah
non-aspirin pain reliever.	**un analgésico sin aspirina.**
	oon ah-nahl-HEH-see-koh seen
	ahs-pee-REE-nah
medicine with codeine.	**medicina con codeína.**
	meh-dee-SEE-nah kohn koh-deh-EE-nah
insect repellant.	**repelente contra insectos.**
	rreh-peh-LEHN-teh KOHN-trah
	een-SEHK-tohs
I need something for ____	**Necesito algo para ____.**
	neh-seh-SEE-toh AHL-goh PAH-rah
corns.	**los callos.**
	lohs KAH-yohs
congestion.	**la congestión.**
	lah kohn-hehs-TYOHN
warts.	**las verrugas.**
	lahs veh-RROO-gahs
constipation.	**el estreñimiento.**
	ehl ehs-treh-nyee-MYEHN-toh
diarrhea.	**la diarrea.**
	lah dyah-RREH-ah
indigestion.	**la indigestión.**
	lah een-dee-hehs-TYOHN
nausea.	**la náusea.**
	lah NOW-seh-ah
motion sickness.	**el mareo.**
	ehl mah-REH-oh
altitude sickness.	**mal de altura.**
	mahl deh ahl-TOO-rah
seasickness.	**el mareo.**
	ehl mah-REH-oh
acne.	**el acné.**
	ehl ahk-NEH

HEALTH & SAFETY

AT THE DOCTOR'S OFFICE

I would like to see _____	**Quisiera ver a _____.**
	kee-SYEH-rah vehr ah
a doctor.	**un doctor.**
	oon dohk-TOHR
a chiropractor.	**un quiropráctico.**
	oon kee-roh-PRAHK-tee-koh
a gynecologist.	**un ginecólogo.**
	oon hee-neh-KOH-loh-goh
an eye / ears / nose / throat specialist.	**un especialista en ojos / oídos / nariz / garganta.**
	oon ehs-peh-syah-LEES-tah ehn OH-hohs / oh-EE-dohs / nah-REES / gahr-GAHN-tah
a dentist.	**un dentista.**
	oon dehn-TEES-tah
an optometrist.	**un optometrista.**
	oon ohp-TOH-meh-treehs-tah
Do I need an appointment?	**¿Necesito una cita?**
	neh-seh-SEE-toh oo-nah SEE-tah
Do I have to pay upfront?	**¿Tengo que pagar por adelantado?**
	TEHNG-goh keh pah-GAHR pohr ah-deh-lan-TAH-doh
I have an emergency.	**Tengo una emergencia.**
	TEHNG-goh oo-nah eh-mehr-HEHN-syah
I need an emergency prescription refill.	**Necesito un reabastecimiento de emergencia de mi receta.**
	neh-seh-SEE-toh oon rreh-ah-bahs-teh-see-MYEHN-toh deh eh-mehr-HEHN-syah deh mee rreh-SEH-tah
Please call a doctor.	**Por favor llame a un doctor.**
	pohr fah-VOHR YAH-meh ah oon dohk-TOHR
I need an ambulance.	**Necesito una ambulancia.**
	neh-seh-SEE-toh oo-nah ahm-boo-LAHN-syah

SYMPTOMS

For a full list of body parts, see p190.

My _____ hurts.

Me duele la/el _____.
meh DWEH-leh lah/ ehl

My _____ is stiff.

Mi _____ está tenso.
mee _____ ehs-TAH TEHN-soh

I think I'm having a heart attack.

Creo que estoy teniendo un ataque cardiaco.
KREH-oh keh ehs-TOY teh-NYEHN-doh oon ah-TAH-keh kahr-DYAH-koh

I can't move.

No me puedo mover.
noh meh PWEH-doh moh-VEHR

I fell.

Me caí.
meh kah-EE

I fainted.

Me desmayé.
meh dehs-mah-YEH

I have a cut on my _____.

Tengo un corte en mi _____.
TEHNG-goh oon KOHR-teh ehn mee

I have a headache.

Tengo dolor de cabeza.
TEHNG-goh doh-LOHR deh kah-BEH-sah

My vision is blurry

Mi visión está borrosa.
mee vee-SYOHN ehs-TAH boh-RROH-sah

I feel dizzy.

Estoy mareado.
ehs-TOY mah-reh-AH-doh

I think I'm pregnant.

Creo que estoy embarazada.
KREH-oh keh ehs-TOY ehm-bah-rah-SAH-dah

I don't think I'm pregnant.

No creo estar embarazada.
noh KREH-oh ehs-TAHR ehm-bah-rah-SAH-dah

I'm having trouble walking.

Tengo dificultad al caminar.
TEHNG-goh dee-fee-kool-TAHD ahl kah-mee-NAHR

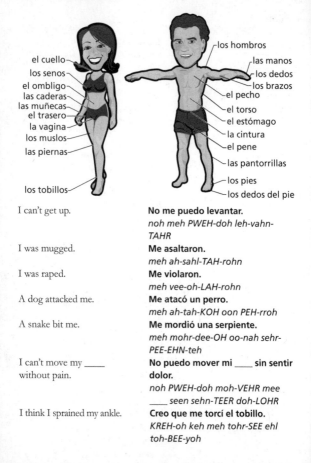

el cuello
los senos
el ombligo
las caderas
las muñecas
el trasero
la vagina
los muslos
las piernas
los tobillos

los hombros
las manos
los dedos
los brazos
el pecho
el torso
el estómago
la cintura
el pene
las pantorrillas
los pies
los dedos del pie

I can't get up.	**No me puedo levantar.** *noh meh PWEH-doh leh-vahn-TAHR*
I was mugged.	**Me asaltaron.** *meh ah-sahl-TAH-rohn*
I was raped.	**Me violaron.** *meh vee-oh-LAH-rohn*
A dog attacked me.	**Me atacó un perro.** *meh ah-tah-KOH oon PEH-rroh*
A snake bit me.	**Me mordió una serpiente.** *meh mohr-dee-OH oo-nah sehr-PEE-EHN-teh*
I can't move my ____ without pain.	**No puedo mover mi ____ sin sentir dolor.** *noh PWEH-doh moh-VEHR mee ____ seen sehn-TEER doh-LOHR*
I think I sprained my ankle.	**Creo que me torcí el tobillo.** *KREH-oh keh meh tohr-SEE ehl toh-BEE-yoh*

MEDICATIONS

I need morning-after pills.
Necesito píldoras del día después.
neh-seh-SEE-toh PEEL-doh-rahs dehl DEE-ah dehs-PWEHS

I need birth control pills.
Necesito píldoras anticonceptivas.
neh-seh-SEE-toh PEEL-doh-rahs ahn-tee-kohn-sehp-TEE-vahs

I lost my eyeglasses and need new ones.
Perdí mis gafas y necesito unas nuevas.
pehr-DEE mees GAH-fahs ee neh-seh-SEE-toh oo-nahs NWEH-vahs

I need new contact lenses.
Necesito lentes de contacto nuevos.
neh-seh-SEE-toh LEHN-tehs deh kohn-TAHK-toh NWEH-vohs

I need erectile dysfunction pills.
Necesito píldoras para la disfunción eréctil.
neh-seh-SEE-toh PEEL-doh-rahs PAH-rah lah dees-foon-SYOHN eh-REHK-teel

It's cold in here!
¡Hace frío aquí!
AH-seh FREE-oh ah-KEE

I am allergic to _____
Soy alérgico a _____
soy ah-LEHR-hee-koh ah

  penicillin.
  la penicilina.
  lah peh-nee-see-LEE-nah

  antibiotics.
  los antibióticos.
  lohs ahn-tee-BYOH-tee-kohs

  sulfa drugs.
  las sulfonamidas.
  lahs sool-foh-nah-MEE-dahs

  steroids.
  los esteroides.
  lohs ehs-teh-ROH-EE-dehs

I have asthma.
Tengo asma.
TEHNG-goh AHS-mah

DENTAL PROBLEMS

I have a toothache.	**Tengo dolor de dientes.**
	TEHNG-goh doh-LOHR deh
	DYEHN-tehs
I chipped a tooth.	**Se me partió un diente.**
	seh meh pahr-tee-OH oon
	DYEHN-teh
My bridge came loose.	**Mi puente se soltó.**
	mee PWEHN-teh seh sohl-TOH
I lost a crown.	**Perdí una corona.**
	pehr-DEE oo-nah koh-ROH-nah
I lost a denture plate.	**Perdí mi dentadura postiza.**
	pehr-DEE mee dehn-tah-DOO-rah
	pohs-TEE-sah

AT THE POLICE STATION

I'm sorry, did I do something wrong?	**Lo siento, ¿hice algo mal?**
	loh SYEHN-toh EE-seh AHL-goh
	mahl
I am _____	**Soy _____**
	soy
an American.	**estadounidense.**
	ehs-tah-doh-oo-nee-DEHN-seh
British.	**británico.**
	bree-TAH-nee-koh
a Canadian.	**canadiense.**
	kah-nah-DYEHN-seh
Irish.	**irlandés.**
	eer-lahn-DEHS
an Australian.	**australiano.**
	ows-trah-LYAH-noh
a New Zealander.	**de Nueva Zelanda.**
	deh NWEH-vah seh-LAHN-dah
The car is a rental.	**El auto es alquilado.**
	ehl OW-toh ehs ahl-kee-LAH-doh

Listen Up: Police Lingo

Su licencia, registro y seguro por favor. *soo lee-SEHN-syah rreh-HEES-troh ee seh-GOO-roh pohr fah-VOHR*	Your license, registration and insurance, please.
La multa es diez dólares y me la puede pagar directo. *lah MOOL-tah ehs dyehs DOH-lah-rehs ee meh lah PWEH-deh pah-GAHR dee-REHK-toh*	The fine is $10. You can pay me directly.
Su pasaporte, por favor. *soo pah-sah-POHR-teh pohr fah-VOHR*	Your passport please?
¿A dónde va? *ah DOHN-deh vah*	Where are you going?
¿Por qué tiene tanta prisa? *pohr KEH TYEH-neh TAHN-tah PREE-sah*	Why are you in such a hurry?

Do I pay the fine to you?	**¿Le pago la multa a usted?** *leh PAH-goh lah MOOL-tah ah oos-TED*
Do I have to go to court?	**¿Tengo que ir a corte?** *TEHNG-goh keh eer ah KOHR-teh*
When?	**¿Cuándo?** *KWAHN-doh*
I'm sorry, my Spanish isn't very good.	**Lo siento, mi español no es muy bueno.** *loh SYEHN-toh mee ehs-pah-NYOHL noh ehs MOO-ee BWEH-noh*

I need an interpreter.	**Necesito un intérprete.** *neh-seh-SEE-toh oon een-TEHR- preh-teh*
I'm sorry, I don't understand the ticket.	**Lo siento, no entiendo la multa.** *loh SYEHN-toh noh ehn-TYEHN- doh lah MOOL-tah*
May I call my embassy?	**¿Puedo llamar a mi embajada?** *PWEH-doh yah-MAHR ah mee ehm-bah-HA-dah*
I was robbed.	**Me robaron.** *meh rroh-BAH-rohn*
I was mugged.	**Me asaltaron.** *meh ah-sahl-TAH-rohn*
I was raped.	**Me violaron.** *meh vee-oh-LAH-rohn*
Do I need to make a report?	**¿Tengo que hacer un informe?** *TEHNG-goh keh ah-SEHR oon een- FOHR-meh*
Somebody broke into my room.	**Alguien entró en mi habitación.** *AHL-gee-ehn ehn-TROH ehn mee ah-bee-tahs-SYOHN*
Someone stole my_____	**Alguien me robó_____** *AHL-gee-ehn meh rroh-BOH*
telephone.	**el teléfono** *ehl teh-LEH-foh-noh*
passport.	**el pasaporte** *ehl pah-sah-POHR-teh*
computer.	**la computadora / el ordenador** *lah kohm-poo-tah-DOH-rah / ehl ohr-deh-NAH-dohr*
backpack.	**la mochila** *lah moh-CHEE-lah*
camera.	**la cámara** *lah KAH-mah-rah*

DICTIONARY KEY

n	noun	m	masculine
v	verb	f	feminine
adj	adjective	s	singular
prep	preposition	pl	plural
adv	adverb		

All verbs are listed in infinitive (to + verb) form, cross-referenced to the appropriate conjugations page. Adjectives are listed first in masculine singular form, followed by the feminine ending.

For food terms, see the Menu Reader (p91) and Grocery section (p100) in Chapter 4, Dining.

ENGLISH—SPANISH

A

able, to be able to (can) *v* poder **p31**

above *adj* sobre **p78**

accept, to accept *v* aceptar **p22**
Do you accept credit cards? *¿Acepta tarjetas de crédito?* **p38**

accident *n* el accidente *m* **p57**
I've had an accident. *He tenido un accidente.*

account *n* la cuenta *f* **p135**
I'd like to transfer to / from my checking / savings account. *Quisiera transferir a / de mi cuenta de cheques / ahorros.*

acne *n* el acné *m* **p187**

across *prep* a través de, al otro lado de **p5**
across the street *al otro lado de la calle*

actual *adj* verdadero-a **p16**

adapter plug *n* el enchufe adaptador *m*

address *n* la dirección *f*
What's the address? *¿Cuál es la dirección?*

admission fee *n* la tarifa de entrada *m* **p148**

in advance *por adelantado*

African-American *adj* afroamericano -a **p119**

afternoon *n* la tarde *f* **p13**
in the afternoon *en la tarde*

age *n* la edad *f*
What's your age? *¿Cuántos años tiene?*

agency *n* la agencia *f* **p50**
car rental agency *la agencia de alquiler de autos*

agnostic *adj* agnóstico -a

air conditioning n el aire acondicionado m p68

Would you lower / raise the air conditioning? ¿Puede bajar / subir el aire acondicionado?

airport n el aeropuerto m

I need a ride to the airport. Necesito llegar al aeropuerto.

How far is it from the airport? ¿Cuán lejos está del aeropuerto?

airsickness bag n la bolsa para casos de mareos f p48

aisle (in store) n el pasillo m

Which aisle is it in? ¿En qué pasillo está?

alarm clock n el reloj despertador m

alcohol n el alcohol m p88

Do you serve alcohol? ¿Sirven alcohol?

I'd like nonalcoholic beer. Quisiera una cerveza sin alcohol.

all n el todo m p11

all adj todo -a p11

all of the time todo el tiempo

That's all, thank you. Eso es todo, gracias.

allergic adj alérgico -a p75

I'm allergic to ____. Soy alérgico -a a ____. See p87 and 191 for common allergens.

altitude n la altitud f p166

aluminum n el aluminio m

ambulance n la ambulancia f

American adj estadounidense

amount n la cantidad f p63

angry adj enojado -a

animal n el animal m

another adj otro -a p48, 72

answer n la contestación f

answer, to answer (phone call, question) v contestar

Answer me, please. Contéstame por favor.

antibiotic n el antibiótico m

I need an antibiotic. Necesito un antibiótico.

antihistamine n el antihistamínico m p186

anxious adj ansioso -a

any adj cualquier, cualquiera

anything n cualquier cosa

anywhere adv dondequiera, cualquier lugar

April n abril p14

appointment n la cita f p148

Do I need an appointment? ¿Necesito una cita?

are v See be, to be. p27, 28

Argentinian adj argentino -a

arm n el brazo m p16

arrive, to arrive *v llegar* **p22**

arrival(s) *n las llegadas f*

art *n el arte m*

  exhibit of art *exhibición de arte*

art *adj de arte*

art museum *museo de arte*

artist *n el artista m, la artista f*

Asian *adj asiático -a* **p80**

ask for (request) *v pedir* **p32**

ask a question *v preguntar* **p22**

aspirin *n la aspirina f* **p187**

assist *v ayudar* **p23**

assistance *n la ayuda f*

asthma *n el asma f* **p191**

  I have asthma. *Tengo asma.*

atheist *adj ateo -a* **p127**

ATM *n el cajero automático m*

  I'm looking for an ATM. *Estoy buscando un cajero automático.*

attend *v asistir* **p23**

audio *adj audio, auditivo* **p65**

August *n agosto* **p15**

aunt *n la tía f* **p115**

Australia *n Australia*

Australian *adj australiano -a*

autumn *n el otoño m* **p15**

available *adj disponible* **p147**

B

baby *n el / la bebé m / f* **p117**

baby *adj de bebés, para bebés* **p100**

Do you sell baby food? *¿Venden comida para bebés?*

babysitter *n la niñera f*

Do you have babysitters who speak English? *¿Tiene niñeras que hablen inglés?*

back *n la espalda f*

  My back hurts. *Me duele la espalda.*

back rub *n el masaje de espalda m* **p180**

backed up (toilet) *adj tapado -a*

  The toilet is backed up. *El inodoro está tapado.*

bag *n la bolsa f, el bolso m*

  airsickness bag *bolsa para casos de mareos* **p48**

  My bag was stolen. *Mi bolsa fue robada.*

  I lost my bag. *Perdí mi bolsa.*

bag *v empacar*

baggage *n el equipaje m*

baggage *adj de equipaje* **p39**

  baggage claim *reclamo de equipaje*

bait *n la carnada f, el cebo m*

balance (on bank account) *n el balance m* **p135**

balance *v balancear* **p22**

balcony *n el balcón m* **p69**

ball (sport) *n la bola f*

ballroom dancing *n el baile de salón m*

band (musical ensemble) *n la banda f* p174

band-aid *n vendaje m, venda f*

bank *n el banco m* p133

Can you help me find a bank? *¿Puede ayudarme a encontrar un banco?*

bar *n la cantina f, el bar m*

barber *n el barbero m* p158

bass (instrument) *n el contrabajo m*

bath *n el baño m*

bathroom (restroom) *n el baño m* p68

Where is the nearest public bathroom? *¿Dónde está el baño público más cercano?*

bathtub *n la bañera f, la tina de baño f* p68

bathe, to bathe oneself *v bañarse* p22, 35

battery (for flashlight) *n la pila f*

battery (for car) *n la batería f, el acumulador m, la acumuladora f*

bee *n la abeja f*

I was stung by a bee. *Me picó una abeja.*

be, to be (temporary state, condition, mood) *v estar* p27

be, to be (permanent quality) *v ser* p28

beach *n la playa* p130

beach *v varar, encallar* p22

beard *n barba f*

beautiful *adj bello -a* p117

bed *n la cama f* p67, 69

beer *n la cerveza f* p88

beer on tap *cerveza de barril*

begin *v comenzar, empezar* p22

behave *v comportar* p22

behind *adv detrás* p5

below *adv abajo* p78

belt *n el cinturón m*

conveyor belt *correa transportadora*

berth *n el camarote m*

best *mejor*

bet, to bet *v apostar* p22

better *mejor*

big *adj grande* p12

bilingual *adj bilingüe*

bill (currency) *n el billete m*

bill *v facturar* p22

biography *n la biografía f*

biracial *adj birracial* p119

bird *n el pájaro m*

birth control *n los anticonceptivos m* p182, 191

birth control *adj anticonceptivo -a* p182, 191

I'm out of birth control pills. *Se me acabaron las pastillas anticonceptivas.*

I need more birth control pills. *Necesito más pastillas anticonceptivas.*

bit (small amount) *n* un poco *m*

black *adj* negro -a p118

blanket *n* la cobija *f*, la frazada *f* p47

bleach *n* el blanqueador *m*

blind *adj* ciego -a

block *v* bloquear **p22**

blond(e) *adj* rubio -a p117

blouse *n* la blusa *f* p151

blue *adj* azul p119

blurry *adj* borroso -a p189

board *n* tabla *f* p171

board *v* abordar **p22**

on board a bordo

boarding pass *n* la tarjeta de embarque *f* p45

boat *n* el barco *m*

Bolivian *adj* boliviano -a

bomb *n* la bomba *f* p16

book *n* el libro *m* p156

bookstore *n* la librería *f* p38, 150, 156

boss *n* el jefe *m*, la jefa *f*

bottle *n* la botella *f* p177

May I heat this (baby) bottle someplace? *¿Puedo calentar este biberón en algún lugar?*

box (seat) *n* el palco *m* p165

box office *n* la boletería *f*

boy *n* el niño *m*

boyfriend *n* el novio *m* p115

braid *n* la trenza *f*

braille, American *n* el braille estadounidense *m*

brake *n* el freno *m* p55

emergency brake el freno de emergencia

brake *v* frenar **p22**

brandy *n* el brandy *m* p89

bread *n* el pan *m* p100

break *v* romper **p22**

breakfast *n* el desayuno *m*

What time is breakfast? *¿A qué hora es el desayuno?*

bridge (across a river, dental) *n* el puente *m* p192

briefcase *n* el maletín *m* p49

bright *adj* brillante

broadband *n* la banda ancha *f*

bronze *adj* bronce

brother *n* el hermano *m* p115

brown *adj* café, castaño -a, marrón, moreno -a, pardo -a p119

brunette *n* el moreno *m*, la morena *f* p117

Buddhist *n* el budista *m*, la budista *f* p127

budget *n* el presupuesto *m*,

budget *adj* económico -a p81

buffet *n* el bufé *m*

bug n el insecto m, el bicho m

bull n el toro m

bullfight n la corrida de toros f

bullfighter n el torero m, el matador m

burn v quemar p22

Can I burn a CD?
¿Puedo quemar un CD? p139

bus n el autobús m p57

Where is the bus stop?
¿Dónde es la parada de autobuses?

Which bus goes to ____?
¿Cuál autobús va hacia ____? p60

business n el negocio m p44

business adj de negocios p73

business center centro de negocios

busy adj concurrido -a (restaurant), ocupado -a (phone)

butter n la mantequilla f p86

buy, to buy v comprar p22

C

café n el café m p37

Internet café cibercafé

call, to call v llamar (shout) telefonear (phone) p22

camp, to camp v acampar p22

camper n el campista m

camping adj para acampar

Do we need a camping permit? ¿Necesitamos un permiso para acampar?

campsite n el campamento m

can n la lata f

can (able to) v poder p31

Canada n Canadá

Canadian adj canadiense

cancel, to cancel v cancelar p22

My flight was canceled. Mi vuelo fue cancelado.

canvas n el lienzo m (for painting), la lona f p49 (material)

cappuccino n el cappuccino m

car n el auto m

car rental agency agencia de alquiler de autos

I need a rental car. Necesito un auto alquilado.

card n la tarjeta f p122

Do you accept credit cards? ¿Aceptan tarjetas de crédito?

May I have your business card? ¿Me puede dar su tarjeta de presentación?

car seat (child's safety seat) n el asiento para niños m

Do you rent car seats for children? ¿Ustedes alquilan asientos para niños para el auto?

carsickness n mareo por el movimiento del auto m

cash n el efectivo m p133

cash only efectivo solamente p133, 154

cash, to cash v hacer efectivo p30

to cash out (gambling) hacer efectivo p185

cashmere n el cachemir m

casino n el casino m p66

cat n el gato m, la gata f

Catholic adj católico -a p127

cavity (tooth cavity) n la caries f

I think I have a cavity. Creo que tengo una caries.

CD n el CD m, el disco compacto m p139

CD player n el lector de discos compactos m p51

celebrate, to celebrate v celebrar p22

cell phone n el teléfono celular m p134

centimeter n el centímetro m

chamber music n la música de cámara f

change (money) n el cambio m

I'd like change, please. Quisiera obtener cambio, por favor.

This isn't the correct change. Este no es el cambio correcto.

change (to change money, clothes) v cambiar p22

changing room n el vestuario, probador m

charge, to charge (money) v cobrar p22

charge, to charge (a battery) v recargar p22

charmed adj encantado -a

charred (meat) adj achicharrado -a p85

charter, to charter v fletar p22

cheap adj barato -a p51

check n el cheque m p90

check, to check v comprobar, verificar p22

checked (pattern) adj a cuadros

check-in n registro / check-in p36

What time is check-in? ¿A qué hora es el check-in?

check-out n la salida f

check-out time la hora de salida

What time is check-out? ¿A que hora es la salida?

check out, to check out v despedirse

cheese n el queso m p100

chicken n el pollo m p96

child n el niño m, la niña f

children n los niños m p45

Are children allowed? ¿Se permiten niños?

Do you have children's programs? ¿Tienen programas para niños?

Do you have a children's menu? ¿Tienen un menú para niños?

Chinese adj chino -a p120

chiropractor n el quiropráctico m p188

church n la iglesia f p126, 147

cigar n el cigarro m p151

cigarette n el cigarrillo m

a pack of cigarettes un paquete de cigarrillos

cinema n el cine m, el cinema m

city n la ciudad f p36, 69

claim n el reclamo m

I'd like to file a claim. Quisiera presentar un reclamo.

clarinet n el clarinete m

class n la clase f p41

business class clase de negocios

economy class clase económica

first class primera clase

classical (music) adj clásico -a

clean adj limpio -a

clean, to clean v limpiar p22

Please clean the room today. Por favor limpia la habitación hoy.

clear v aclarar p22

clear adj claro -a p170

climbing n la escalada f p166

climb, to climb v escalar, subir p22, 23

to climb a mountain escalar una montaña

to climb stairs subir las escaleras

close, to close v cerrar p22

close (near) cerca, cercano p6, 58, 165

closed adj cerrado -a p56

cloudy adj nublado -a p125

clover n el trébol m

go clubbing, to go clubbing v ir a los clubes nocturnos p25

coat n el abrigo m p152

cockfight n la pelea de gallos f

coffee n el café m p90, 131

iced coffee café helado

cognac n el coñac m p89

coin n la moneda f

cold n el resfriado m p111

I have a cold. Tengo un resfriado.

cold adj frío -a p191

I'm cold. Tengo frío.

It's cold out. Hace frío.

coliseum n el coliseo m

collect adj a cobro revertido
**I'd like to place a collect
call.** Quisiera hacer una
llamada a cobro revertido.
collect, to collect v recolectar
p22
college n la universidad f
Colombian adj colombiano -a
color n el color m
color v colorear p22
computer n la computadora f
concert n el concierto m p130
condition n la condición f
in good / bad condition en
buena / mala condición
condom n el condón m p182
Do you have a condom?
¿Tienes un condón?
not without a condom no
sin un condón
condor n el cóndor m
confirm, to confirm v
confirmar p22
**I'd like to confirm my
reservation.** Quisiera
confirmar mi reservación.
confused adj confundido -a
congested adj congestionado -a
connection speed n la
velocidad de conexión f
p140
constipated adj estreñido -a
I'm constipated. Estoy
estreñido -a.

contact lens n el lente de
contacto m
I lost my contact lens. Perdí
mi lente de contacto.
continue, to continue v
continuar p22
convertible n el convertible m
cook, to cook v cocinar p22
**I'd like a room where I can
cook.** Quisiera una
habitación donde pueda
cocinar.
cookie n la galleta f
copper adj cobre
corner n la esquina f
on the corner en la esquina
correct v corregir p23
correct adj correcto -a p58
Am I on the correct train?
¿Estoy en el tren correcto?
cost, to cost v costar p22
How much does it cost?
¿Cuánto cuesta?
Costa Rican adj costarricense
costume n el disfraz m
cotton n el algodón m p152
cough n la tos f p186
cough v toser p23
counter (in bar) n la barra m
p36
country-and-western n la
música country f p128
court (legal) n la corte f p193

court (sport) n la cancha f
courteous adj cortés p78
cousin n el primo m, la prima f
cover charge (in bar) n el cargo de entrada m p175
cow n la vaca f
crack (in glass object) n la grieta f
craftsperson n el artesano m, la artesana f p122
cream n la crema f p94
credit card n la tarjeta de crédito f p133

> **Do you accept credit cards?** ¿Aceptan tarjetas de crédito?

crib n la cuna f p69
crown (dental) n la corona f
curb n el borde de la acera m
curl n el rizo m
curly adj rizado -a p118
currency exchange n el cambio de moneda m p37, 133

> **Where is the nearest currency exchange?** ¿Dónde está el lugar de cambio de moneda más cercano?

current (water) adj corriente
customs n aduana f p39

cut (wound) n el corte m, la cortadura f p189

> **I have a bad cut.** Tengo una cortadura seria.

cut, to cut v cortar p22
cybercafé n el cibercafé m

> **Where can I find a cybercafé?** ¿Dónde puedo encontrar un cibercafé?

D

damaged adj dañado -a p49
Damn! expletive ¡Maldición!
dance v bailar p22
danger n el peligro m p56
dark n la oscuridad f
dark adj oscuro -a
daughter n la hija f p117
day n el día m

> **the day before yesterday** el día antes de ayer / anteayer p14
> **these last few days** estos últimos días

dawn n la madrugada m p13

> **at dawn** al amanecer

deaf adj sordo -a
deal (bargain) n la ganga f

> **What a great deal!** ¡Que ganga increíble!

deal (cards) v repartir p23

> **Deal me in.** Repárteme.

December n diciembre p15

declined adj rechazado -a

Was my credit card declined? ¿Mi tarjeta de crédito fue rechazada?

declare v declarar **p22**

I have nothing to declare. No tengo nada que declarar.

deep adj profundo -a **p169**

delay n el retraso m **p44**

How long is the delay? ¿Cuán largo es el retraso?

delighted adj deleitado -a

democracy n la democracia f

dent v abollar **p22**

He / She dented the car. Él / Ella abolló el auto.

dentist n el dentista m **p188**

denture n la dentadura f

denture plate dentadura

departure n la salida f

designer n el diseñador m, la diseñadora f **p122**

dessert n el postre m **p88**

dessert menu el menú de postres

destination n el destino m

diabetic adj diabético -a **p85**

dial (a phone) v marcar **p22**

dial direct marcar directo

diaper n el pañal m

Where can I change a diaper? ¿Dónde puedo cambiar un pañal?

diarrhea n la diarrea f **p187**

dictionary n el diccionario m

different (other) adj diferente **p154**

difficult adj difícil **p167**

dinner n la cena f **p130**

directory assistance (phone) n la asistencia telefónica f

disability n la incapacidad f

disappear v desaparecer **p23**

disco n el disco m **p128**

disconnected adj desconectado -a **p138**

Operator, I was disconnected. Operadora, fui desconectado -a.

discount n el descuento m

Do I qualify for a discount? ¿Cumplo los requisitos para recibir un descuento?

dish n el plato m **p85**

dive v bucear **p22**

scuba dive buceo con tanques de oxígeno **p169**

divorced adj divorciado -a

dizzy adj mareado -a **p189**

do, to do v hacer **p30**

doctor n el doctor m, la doctora f **p122, 188**

doctor's office n la oficina del doctor m

dog n el perro m **p21**

service dog perro de servicio **p70**

dollar n el dólar m

door n la puerta f

double adj doble p8

double bed cama doble p67
double vision visión doble

down adj abajo p5

download v descargar p22

downtown n el centro de la ciudad m p149

dozen n la docena f p11

drain n el drenaje m

drama n el drama m

drawing (work of art) n el dibujo m

dress (garment) n el vestido m

dress (general attire) n la vestimenta f p175

What's the dress code? ¿Cuál es el código de vestimenta?

dress v vestirse p23, 35

Should I dress up for that affair. Debería vestirme para ese evento.

dressing (salad) n el aderezo m

dried adj secado -a p109

drink n la bebida f p177

I'd like a drink. Quisiera una bebida.

drink, to drink v beber p23

drip v gotear p22

drive v guiar, manejar p22

driver n el chofer m p57

driving range n el campo para practicar tiros de golf m

drum n el tambor m

dry adj seco -a

This towel isn't dry. Esta toalla no está seca.

dry, to dry v secar p22

I need to dry my clothes. Necesito secar mi ropa.

dry cleaner n la tintorería f

dry cleaning n la limpieza en seco f

duck n el pato m

duty-free adj libre de impuestos p38

duty-free shop n la tienda libre de impuestos f p38

DVD n el DVD m p51

Do the rooms have DVD players? ¿Las habitaciones tienen lectores de DVD?
Where can I rent DVDs? ¿Dónde puedo alquilar DVD?

E

early adj temprano -a p13

It's early. Es temprano.

eat v comer p23

to eat out comer afuera

economy n la economía f

Ecuadorian adj ecuatoriano -a

editor n el editor m, la editora f p122

educator n el educador m, la educadora f p122

eight n el ocho m p7
eighteen n el dieciocho m p7
eighth n el octavo m p9
eighty n el ochenta m p8
election n la elección f p126
electrical hookup n la conexión eléctrica f p79
elevator n el elevador m p69
eleven n el once m p7
e-mail n el e-mail m p124

May I have your e-mail address? ¿Me puede dar su dirección de e-mail?
e-mail message mensaje de e-mail

e-mail, to send e-mail v enviar un e-mail p22
embarrassed adj avergonzado -a p16
embassy n la embajada f
emergency n la emergencia f
emergency brake n el freno de emergencia m
emergency exit n la salida de emergencia f p42
employee n el empleado m, la empleada f p123
employer n el empleador m
engine n el motor m p53
engineer n el ingeniero m, la ingeniera f p122
England n Inglaterra

English n, adj el inglés m, la inglesa f p72

Do you speak English? ¿Habla inglés? p2
enjoy, to enjoy v disfrutar p22
enter, to enter v entrar p22

Do not enter. No entre.
enthusiastic adj entusiasmado -a p121
entrance n la entrada f p39
envelope n el sobre m p143
environment n el ambiente m
escalator n la escalera mecánica f
espresso n el café expreso m
exchange rate n la tasa de cambio f p133

What is the exchange rate for US / Canadian dollars? ¿Cuál es la tasa de cambio para los dólares americanos / canadienses?
excuse (pardon) v excusar, perdonar p22

Excuse me. Perdone.
exhausted adj exhausto -a
exhibit n la exhibición f
exit n la salida f p39

not an exit no es salida
exit v salir p23
expensive adj caro -a p176
explain v explicar p22

express adj exprés p40, 60
  express check-in check-in exprés
extra (additional) adj adicional p74
extra-large adj extra grande
eye n el ojo m p188
eyebrow n la ceja f
eyeglasses n los espejuelos m, las gafas f
eyelash n la pestaña f

F

fabric n la tela f
face n la cara f p119
faint v desmayar p22
fall (season) n el otoño m
fall v caer p23
family n la familia f p115
fan n el abanico m
far lejos p5
  How far is it to _____?
  ¿Cuán lejos es hasta _____?
fare n la tarifa f
fast adj rápido -a p56, 140
fat adj gordo -a p12, 119
father n el padre m p115
faucet n el grifo m
fault n la culpa f p57
  I'm at fault. Es mi culpa.
  It was his fault. Fue su culpa.
fax n el fax m p123
February n febrero p14

fee n el honorario m
female adj hembra
fiancé(e) n el prometido m, la prometida f p115
fifteen adj el quince m p7
fifth adj el quinto -a m p9
fifty adj el cincuenta m p7
find v encontrar, hallar p22
fine (for traffic violation) n la multa f p193
fine bien p1
  I'm fine. Estoy bien.
fire! n el fuego m
first adj primero -a p9
fishing pole n la caña de pescar f
fitness center n el centro de gimnasia m p66
fit (clothes) v entallarse p22, 35
  Does this look like it fits?
  ¿Esto parece que me entalla?
fitting room n el probador m
five adj cinco p8
flight n el vuelo m p39
  Where do domestic flights arrive / depart? ¿Adónde llegan / De dónde salen los vuelos domésticos?
  Where do international flights arrive / depart? ¿Adónde llegan / De dónde salen los vuelos internacionales?

What time does this flight leave? ¿A qué hora sale este vuelo?

flight attendant asistente de vuelo

floor n el piso m p69

ground floor planta baja
second floor primer piso

Note that in Spanish, the second floor is called the first, the third is the second, etc.

flower n la flor f

flush (gambling) n la escalera f

flush, to flush v tirar la cadena del inodoro **p22**

This toilet won't flush. No se puede tirar la cadena del inodoro.

flute n la flauta f

food n la comida f p87

foot (body part, measurement) n el pie m

forehead n la frente f

formula n la fórmula f

Do you sell infants' formula? ¿Venden fórmula para infantes?

forty adj cuarenta p8

forward adj delante p6

four adj cuatro p7

fourteen adj catorce p7

fourth adj cuarto -a p9

one-fourth un cuarto

fragile adj frágil p141

freckle n la peca f

French adj francés p120

fresh adj fresco -a p101

Friday n viernes m p14

friend n el amigo m la amiga f p115

front adj delantero p42

front desk la recepción p73

front door la puerta principal / puerta del frente

fruit n la fruta f p100

fruit juice n el jugo de fruta m

full, to be full (after a meal) adj lleno -a p90

Full house! n ¡Full!

fuse n el fusible m

G

gallon n el galón m p11

garlic n el ajo m p108

gas n el combustible m, la gasolina f p53

gas gauge indicador de combustible

out of gas sin combustible

gate (at airport) n la puerta de salida f p36

German adj alemán, alemana

gift n el regalo m

gin n la ginebra f p89

girl n la chica f, la muchacha f

girlfriend n la novia f p115

give, to give v dar **p22**

glass n la copa f p84

Do you have it by the glass? ¿Se vende por copa?

I'd like a glass please. Quisiera una copa por favor.

glasses (eye) n las gafas f

I need new glasses. Necesito gafas nuevas.

glove n el guante m p172

go, to go v ir p25

goal (sport) n el gol m

goalie n el portero m p164

gold adj oro

golf n el golf m p49

golf, to go golfing v jugar golf p22

good adj bueno -a p111

goodbye n el adiós m p112

grade (school) n el grado m

gram n el gramo m

grandfather n el abuelo m

grandmother n la abuela f

grandparent n el abuelo m, la abuela f

grape n la uva f

gray adj gris

great adj grandioso -a

Greek adj griego -a p81

Greek Orthodox adj ortodoxo griego p127

green adj verde p119

groceries n los comestibles m

group n el grupo m p44

grow, to grow (get larger) v crecer p23

Where did you grow up? ¿Dónde creciste?

guard n el guardia m p37

security guard guardia de seguridad

Guatemalan adj guatemalteco -a p120

guest n el invitado m, la invitada f

guide (of tours) n el / la guía m f p148

guide (publication) n la guía f

guide, to guide v guiar p22

guided tour n la excursión guiada f

guitar n la guitarra f p129

gym n el gimnasio m p161

gynecologist n el ginecólogo m

H

hair n el pelo m, el cabello m

haircut n el recorte de pelo m

I need a haircut. Necesito un corte de pelo.

How much is a haircut? ¿Cuánto cuesta un corte de pelo?

hairdresser n el peluquero m, la peluquera f

ENGLISH—SPANISH

hair dryer n la secadora de pelo f p75

half n la mitad f

one-half medio p8

hallway n el pasillo m

hand n la mano f p179

handicapped-accessible adj accesible para personas con impedimentos

handle, to handle v manejar p22

handsome adj guapo -a, bien parecido -a p117

hangout (hot spot) n el lugar de reunión m

hang out (to relax) v pasar el rato p22

hang up (to end a phone call) v colgar p22

hanger n la percha f

happy adj alegre p121

hard adj difícil (difficult), duro -a (firm) p49

hat n el sombrero m, el gorro m

have v tener p29

hazel adj color café p119

headache n el dolor de cabeza m p111

headlight n el foco delantero m

headphones n los audífonos m

hear v escuchar p22

hearing-impaired adj con impedimentos auditivos

heart n el corazón m p189

heart attack n el ataque cardiaco m, el ataque al corazón m p189

hectare n la hectárea f p10

hello n hola p1

Help! n ¡Ayuda!, ¡Socorro!

help, to help v ayudar p22

hen n la gallina f

her adj de ella p3

herb n la hierba f

here n aquí p5

high adj alto -a p171

highlights (hair) n los destellos m p159

highway n la autopista f

hike, to hike v excursionar p22

him pron él p3

Hindu adj hindú p120

hip-hop n hip-hop p174

his adj de él

historical adj histórico -a

history n la historia f p131

hobby n el pasatiempo m

hold, to hold v sujetar p22

to hold hands sujetar las manos

Would you hold this for me? ¿Sujetas esto por mí?

hold, to hold (to pause) *v* esperar p22

Hold on a minute! *¡Espera un minuto!*
I'll hold. *Espero.*

hold, to hold (gambling) *v* quedar **p22**

holiday *n* el día de fiesta *m*

home *n* el hogar *m*, la residencia *f*

homemaker *n* la ama de casa *f*

Honduran *adj* hondureño -a

horn *n* la bocina *f*

horse *n* el caballo *m*

hostel *n* la hospedería *f* p66

hot *adj* caliente p89

hot chocolate *n* el chocolate caliente *m* p89

hotel *n* el hotel *m* p66

Do you have a list of local hotels? *¿Tiene una lista de hoteles locales?*

hour *n* la hora *f* p139

hours (at museum) *n* el horario *m*

how *adv* cómo, cuánto (how much), cuántos (how many) p3, 12

humid *adj* húmedo -a p125

hundred *n* cien *m*, cientos *m*

hurry *v* apresurar **p35**

I'm in a hurry. *Tengo prisa.*
Hurry, please! *¡Apresúrate por favor!*

hurt, to hurt *v* herir **p23**

Ouch! That hurts! *¡Ay! ¡Eso duele!*

husband *n* el esposo *m* p114

I

I *pron* yo p3

ice *n* el hielo *m* p87

identification *n* la identificación *f* p46

inch *n* la pulgada *f* p10

indigestion *n* la indigestión *f*

inexpensive *adj* económico -a, barato -a p38

infant *n* el infante *m*

Are infants allowed? *¿Se permiten infantes?*

information *n* la información *f*

information booth *n* el puesto de información *m*

injury *n* la lesión *f* p16

insect repellant *n* el repelente para insectos *m* p187

inside adentro p84

insult *v* insultar **p22**

insurance *n* el seguro *m* p193

intercourse (sexual) *n* el coito *m*

interest rate *n* la tasa de interés *f*

intermission *n* el intervalo *m*

Internet *n Internet m* **p68**
  High-speed Internet
  Internet de alta velocidad
  Do you have Internet
  access? *¿Tienen acceso a*
  Internet?
  Where can I find an Internet
  café? *¿Dónde puedo*
  encontrar un cibercafé?
interpreter *n el / la intérprete*
  m f **p194**
  I need an interpreter.
  Necesito un intérprete.
introduce, to introduce *v*
  presentar **p23**
  I'd like to introduce you to
  _____. *Quisiera presentarle*
  a _____.
Ireland *n Irlanda*
Irish *adj irlandés, irlandesa*
is *v See* be (to be). **p27, 28**
Italian *adj italiano -a* **p120**

J

jacket *n la chaqueta f* **p46**
January *n enero* **p14**
Japanese *adj japonés /*
  japonesa **p120**
jazz *n el jazz m* **p128**
Jewish *adj judío -a* **p127**
jog, to run *v trotar* **p22**
juice *n el jugo m* **p100**

June *n junio* **p14**
July *n julio* **p14**

K

keep, to keep *v guardar* **p22**
kid *n el niño m*
  Are kids allowed?
  ¿Se permiten niños?
  Do you have kids'
  programs? *¿Tienen*
  programas para niños?
  Do you have a kids' menu?
  ¿Tienen un menú para
  niños?
kilo *n el kilo m* **p11**
kilometer *n el kilómetro m*
kind *n el tipo m, la clase F*
  (type)
  What kind is it? *¿Qué clase es?*
kiss *n el beso m* **p180**
kitchen *n la cocina f* **p73**
know, to know (something)
  v saber **p33**
know, to know (someone) *v*
  conocer **p33**
kosher *adj kósher* **p85**

L

lactose-intolerant *adj*
  intolerante a la lactosa
  p86
land, to land *v aterrizar* **p22**
landscape *n el paisaje m*

language *n* el idioma *m*

laptop *n* la computadora portátil *f* p158

large *adj* grande p16

last, to last *v* durar **p22**

last *adv* último -a p10

late *adj* tarde p13

 Please don't be late. *Por favor no llegues tarde.*

later *adv* luego, más tarde

 See you later. *Te veo luego.*

laundry *n* la lavandería *f* p74

lavender *adj* lavanda

law *n* la ley *f*

lawyer *n* el abogado / la abogada *m/f* p122

least *n* al menos *f*

least *adj* mínimo

leather *n* el cuero *m* p50

leave, to leave (depart) *v* salir **p23**

left *adj* izquierdo -a p5

 on the left *a la izquierda*

leg *n* la pierna *f*

lemonade *n* la limonada *f*

less *adj* menos p155

lesson *n* la lección *f* p173

license *n* la licencia *f* p193

 driver's license *licencia de conducir*

life preserver *n* el salvavidas *m*

light *n* (lamp) la luz *f* p55

light (for cigarette) *n* la lumbre *f* p176

 May I offer you a light? *¿Puedo ofrecerle lumbre?*

lighter (cigarette) *n* el encendedor *m* p178

like, desire *v* gustar **(to please)** p34

 I would like _____. *Me gustaría _____.*

like, to like *v* gustar **(to please)** p34

 I like this place. *Me gusta este lugar.*

limo *n* la limusina *f* p57

liquor *n* el licor *m* p45

liter *n* el litro *m* p10

little *adj* pequeño -a (size), poco -a (amount)

live, to live *v* vivir **p23**

 Where do you live? *¿Dónde vives?*

living *n* la vida *f* p122

 What do you do for a living? *¿Qué haces para ganarte la vida?*

local *adj* local p60

lock *n* el candado *m* p162

lock, to lock *v* cerrar con llave **p22**

 I can't lock the door. *No puedo cerrar la puerta con llave.*

I'm locked out. *Me quedé fuera sin llave.*

locker *n el casillero m* p161

storage locker *casillero de almacén*

locker room *vestuario* p163

long *adv mucho tiempo, bastante* p12

For how long? *¿Por cuánto tiempo?*

long *adj largo -a* p72

look, to look *v (to observe) mirar* p22

I'm just looking. *Sólo estoy mirando.*

Look here! *¡Mira aquí!*

look, to look *v (to appear) ver* p33

How does this look? *¿Cómo se ve esto?*

look for, to look for *(to search) v buscar* p22

I'm looking for a porter. *Estoy buscando un porteador.*

loose *adj suelto -a* p153

lose, to lose *v perder* p23

I lost my passport. *Perdí mi pasaporte.*

I lost my wallet. *Perdí mi cartera.*

I'm lost. *Estoy perdido -a.*

lost. *See* **lose** *perdido -a* p45

loud *adj ruidoso -a* p78

loudly *adv ruidosamente*

lounge *n el salón público m*

lounge, to lounge *v relajarse* p35

love *n el amor m*

love, to love *v amar* p22

to love (family) *amar*

to love (a friend) *amar, querer*

to love (a lover) *amar*

to make love *hacer el amor*

low *adj bajo -a* p85

lunch *n el almuerzo m* p82

luggage *n el equipaje m* p37

Where do I report lost luggage? *¿Dónde reporto el equipaje perdido?*

Where is the lost luggage claim? *¿Dónde está el reclamo de equipaje?*

M

machine *n la máquina f* p75

made of *adj hecho de*

magazine *n la revista f*

maid (hotel) *n la mucama f*

maiden *adj soltera*

That's my maiden name. *Ese es mi apellido de soltera.*

mail *n* el correo *m*

 air mail *correo aéreo*
 registered mail *correo certificado*

mail *v* enviar **p22**

make, to make *v* hacer **p30**

makeup *n* el maquillaje *m*

make up, to make up (apologize) *v* hacer las paces **p30**

make up, to make up (apply cosmetics) *v* maquillar **p22**

male *n* el varón *m* **p45**

male *adj* masculino

mall *n* el centro comercial *m*

man *n* el hombre *m*

manager *n* el / la gerente *m f*

manual (instruction booklet) *n* el manual *m* **p52**

many *adj* muchos -as **p11**

map *n* el mapa *m* **p55**

March (month) *n* marzo **p14**

market *n* el mercado *m* **p154**

 flea market *mercado de pulgas / pulguero* **p150**
 open-air market *mercado al aire libre*

married *adj* casado -a **p116**

marry, to marry *v* casarse **p22, 35**

massage, to massage *v* dar masaje **p22 p180**

match (sport) *n* el partido *m*

match *n* el fósforo *m*

 book of matches *libro de fósforos*
 Does this ____ match my outfit? *¿Este ____ hace juego con mi vestido?*

match, to match *v* igualar, hacer juego **p22, 30**

May (month) *n* mayo **p14**

may *v aux* poder **p31**

 May I ____? *¿Puedo?*

meal *n* la comida *f* **p42**

meat *n* la carne *f* **p87**

meatball *n* la albóndiga *f*

medication *n* el medicamento *m*

medium (size) *adj* mediano -a

medium rare (meat) *adj* antes del punto **p84**

medium well (meat) *adj* a punto bien cocido **p85**

member *n* el miembro *m*

menu *n* el menú *m* **p82**

 May I see a menu? *¿Puedo ver un menú?*
 children's menu *menú para niños*
 diabetic menu *menú para diabéticos*
 kosher menu *menú kósher*

metal detector *n* el detector de metales *m*

meter *n* el metro *m* **p10**

Mexican *adj* mexicano -a

middle *adj* de en medio p42

midnight *n* la medianoche *f*

mile *n* la milla *f* p10

military *n* el ejército *m*,
la milicia *f*

milk *n* la leche *f* p90

milk shake *batido de leche*

milliliter *n* el mililitro *m*

millimeter *n* el milímetro *m*

minute *n* el minuto *m* p4

in a minute *en un minuto*

miss, to miss (a flight) *v*
perder p23

missing *adj* perdido -a,
ausente

mistake *n* el error *m* p78

moderately priced *adj* de
precio moderado p66

mole (facial feature) *n*
el lunar *m*

Monday *n* lunes *m* p13

money *n* el dinero *m* p132

money transfer
transferencia de dinero

month *n* el mes *m* p4

morning *n* la mañana *f* p13

in the morning *en la
mañana*

mosque *n* la mezquita *f*

mother *n* la madre *f* p115

mother, to mother *v* cuidar
p22

motorcycle *n* la motocicleta *f*

mountain *n* la montaña *f*

mountain climbing
escalar montañas p166

mouse *n* el ratón *m*

mouth *n* la boca *f*

move, to move *v* mover p23

movie *n* la película *f* p145

much *n* mucho *m*, p11

mug, to mug (someone) *v*
asaltar p22

mugged *adj* asaltado -a

museum *n* el museo *m* p130

music *n* la música *f* p128

live music *música en vivo*

musician *n* el músico *m*, la
musica *f* p123

muslim *adj* musulmán p127

mustache *n* el bigote *m*

mystery (novel) *n* la novela
de misterio *f*

N

name *n* el nombre *m* p114

My name is ___. *Me llamo
___.* p1

What's your name? *¿Cómo
se llama? / ¿Cuál es su
nombre?*

napkin *n* la servilleta *f*

narrow *adj* angosto -a p12

nationality *n* la nacionalidad *f*

nausea *n* la náusea *f* p187

near *adj* cercano -a p5

nearby *adj* cercano -a p81

neat (tidy) *adj* limpio -a

need, to need v necesitar p22

neighbor n el vecino m, la vecina f p115

nephew n el sobrino m p115

network n la red f

new adj nuevo -a p162

newspaper n el periódico m

newsstand n el puesto de periódicos m p38

New Zealand n Nueva Zelanda

New Zealander adj neozelandés, neozelandesa

next prep próximo, al lado

next to al lado de

the next station la próxima estación

Nicaraguan adj nicaragüense p121

nice adj agradable

niece n la sobrina f p115

night n la noche f p13

at night en la noche

per night por noche p70

nightclub n el club nocturno m

nine adj nueve p7

nineteen adj diecinueve p7

ninety adj noventa p8

ninth adj noveno -a p10

no adv no p1

noisy adj ruidoso -a p77

none adj ninguno -a p11

nonsmoking adj de no fumar

nonsmoking area
área de no fumar

nonsmoking room
habitación de no fumar

noon n el mediodía m p13

nose n la nariz f p188

novel n la novela f

November n noviembre p15

now adv ahora p4

number n el número m p124

Which room number?
¿Cuál es el número de la habitación?

May I have your phone number? ¿Me puede dar su número de teléfono?

nurse n la enfermera f p122

nurse v amamantar p22

Do you have a place where I can nurse? ¿Tienen un lugar dónde pueda amamantar?

nursery n la guardería infantil f

Do you have a nursery?
¿Tienen una guardería infantil?

nut n la nuez f

O

o'clock adv en punto p4

two o'clock dos en punto

October n octubre p15

offer, to offer v ofrecer p33

ENGLISH—SPANISH

officer n el oficial m, la oficial f p45

oil n el aceite m p53, 86

okay adv OK, de acuerdo

old adj viejo -a p26

olive n la aceituna f

one adj uno -a p7

one way (traffic sign) adj en una sola dirección

open (business) adj abierto -a p154

Are you open? ¿Están abierto?

opera n la ópera f p128

operator (phone) n el operador m, la operadora f

optometrist n el optometrista m, la optometrista f

orange (color) adj anaranjado -a

orange juice n el jugo de naranja m p47

order, to order (demand) v pedir p32

order, to order (request) v ordenar p22

organic adj orgánico -a

Ouch! interj ¡ay!

outside n afuera p84

overcooked adj sobrecocido -a

overheat, to overheat v sobrecalentar p22, 35

The car overheated. El auto se sobrecalentó.

overflow v desbordar

oxygen tank n el tanque de oxígeno m

P

package n el paquete m p110

pacifier n el chupete m

page, to page (someone) v llamar por altavoz (a alguien) p22

paint, to paint v pintar p22

painting n la pintura f

pale adj pálido -a p118

Panamanian adj panameño -a

paper n el papel p100

parade n la desfile f

Paraguayan adj paraguayo -a

parent n el padre m

park n el parque m p130

park, to park v estacionar p22

no parking no estacionar

parking fee tarifa de estacionamiento

parking garage estacionamiento

partner n el compañero m, la compañera f

party n el partido m p126

party n la fiesta f

political party partido político

pass, to pass v pasar p22

I'll pass. Voy a pasar.

passenger n el pasajero m, la pasajera f

passport n el pasaporte m

I've lost my passport.
Perdí mi pasaporte.

pay, to pay v pagar p22

peanut n el cacahuate m

pedestrian n el peatón m,
la peatón f

pediatrician n el pediatra m,
la pediatra f

**Can you recommend a
pediatrician?** *¿Puede
recomendar un pediatra?*

permit n el permiso m

Do we need a permit?
¿Necesitamos un permiso?

permit, to permit v permitir
p23

Peruvian adj peruano -a

phone n el teléfono m p179

**May I have your phone
number?** *¿Me puede dar
su número de teléfono?*

**Where can I find a public
phone?** *¿Dónde puedo
encontrar un teléfono
público?*

phone operator operadora

**Do you sell prepaid
phones?** *¿Venden
teléfonos prepagados?*

phone adj telefónico -a

**Do you have a phone
directory?** *¿Tiene un
directorio telefónico?*

phone call n la llamada
telefónica f

**I need to make a collect
phone call.** *Necesito hacer
una llamada telefónica
con cobro revertido.*

an international phone call
una llamada internacional

photocopy, to photocopy v
fotocopiar p22

piano n el piano m p129

pillow n la almohada f p47

down pillow almohada de
plumas

pink adj rosado -a

pint n la pinta f p11

pizza n la pizza f p80

place, to place v colocar p22

plastic n el plástico m p50

play n la obra de teatro f

play, to play (a game) v jugar
p22

play, to play (an instrument)
v tocar p22

playground n el patio de
juegos m

Do you have a playground?
¿Tienen un patio de recreo?

please (polite entreaty) adv
por favor

please, to be pleasing to v
agradar p22

pleasure n el placer m p1

It's a pleasure. *Es un placer.*

plug n el enchufe m p157

plug, to plug v enchufar **p22**

point, to point v señalar, apuntar **p22**

> Would you point me in the direction of____? ¿Me puede señalar la dirección de____?

police n la policía f p37

police station n la estación de policía f p37

pool n la piscina f p66

pool (the game) n el billar m

pop music n la música pop f

popular adj popular p175

port (beverage) n el oporto m

port (for ship) n el puerto

porter n el portero m, la portera f p36

portion n la porción f

portrait n el retrato m

postcard n la postal f

post office n el correo m

> Where is the post office? ¿Dónde está el correo?

poultry n las aves de corral f pl

pound n la libra f p110

prefer, to prefer v preferir **p23**

pregnant adj embarazada

prepared adj preparado -a

prescription n la receta f p45

price n el precio m

print, to print v imprimir **p23**

private berth / cabin n el camarote privado m p62

problem n el problema m p2

process, to process v procesar **p22**

product n el producto m

professional adj profesional

program n el programa m

> May I have a program? ¿Me puede dar un programa?

Protestant n protestante m

publisher n el editor m

Puerto Rican adj puertorriqueño -a m / f

pull, to pull v halar, tirar, jalar **p22**

pump n la bomba f p16

purple adj morado -a

purse n la cartera f, el bolso m

push, to push v empujar **p22**

put, to put v poner **p29** (conjugate like tener)

Q

quarter adj un cuarto p8

one-quarter un cuarto

quiet adj tranquilo -a p82

R

rabbit n el conejo m p91

radio n la radio f

satellite radio radio por satélite

rain, to rain v llover **p31** (conjugate like poder)

Is it supposed to rain? ¿Se supone que llueva?

rainy adj lluvioso -a p125
  It's rainy. Está lluvioso.
ramp, wheelchair n la rampa para sillas de ruedas f p65
rare (meat) adj vuelta y vuelta p84
rate (for car rental, hotel) n la tarifa f p52
  What's the rate per day? ¿Cuál es la tarifa por día?
  What's the rate per week? ¿Cuál es la tarifa por semana?
rate plan (cell phone) n el plan de tarifa m
rather adv preferiblemente
read, to read v leer p23
really adv verdaderamente
receipt n el recibo m p133
receive, to receive v recibir p23
recommend, to recommend v recomendar p22
red adj rojo -a p184
redhead n el pelirrojo m, la pelirroja f p117
reef n el arrecife m p170
refill (of beverage) v volver a llenar (el vaso)
refill (of prescription) n el reabastecimiento m p188
reggae adj reggae p128
relative (family) n el pariente m
remove, to remove v remover p23

rent, to rent v alquilar p22
  I'd like to rent a car. Quisiera alquilar un auto.
repeat, to repeat v repetir p32 (conjugate like pedir)
  Would you please repeat that? ¿Puede repetir eso por favor? p2
reservation n la reservación m
  I'd like to make a reservation for ____. Quisiera hacer una reservación para ____. p70 See p7 for numbers.
restaurant n el restaurante? m
  Where can I find a good restaurant? ¿Dónde puedo encontrar un buen restaurante. p80
restroom n el baño m p37
  Do you have a public restroom? ¿Tienen un baño público?
return, to return (to a place) v regresar p22
return, to return (something to a store) v devolver (p31, conjugate like poder)
ride, to ride v andar p23
right adj derecho -a p55
  It is on the right. Está a mano derecha.
  Turn right at the corner. Vire a la derecha en la esquina.

rights *n pl los derechos m*
  civil rights *derechos civiles*

river *n el río m* p169

road *n la carretera f* p56

road closed sign *n el letrero de carretera cerrada m* p56

rob, to rob *v robar* **p22**
  I've been robbed. *Me han robado.*

rock and roll *n rock and roll*

rock climbing *n la escalada de rocas f*

rocks (ice) *n el hielo m* p88
  I'd like it on the rocks. *Lo quisiera con hielo.*

romance (novel) *n la novela de romance f*

romantic *adj romántico -a*

room (hotel) *n la habitación f*
  room for one / two *habitación para uno / dos*
  room service *servicio de habitaciones*

rope *n la cuerda f* p16

rose *n la rosa f*

royal flush *n la escalera real f*

rum *n el ron m* p89

run, to run *v correr* **p23**

S

sad *adj triste* p121

safe (for storing valuables) *n la caja fuerte f* p75
  Do the rooms have safes? *¿Las habitaciones tienen caja fuertes?*

safe (secure) *adj seguro -a*
  Is this area safe? *¿Esta área es segura?*

sail *n la vela f*

sail, to sail *v zarpar* **p22**
  When do we sail? *¿Cuándo zarpamos?* p28

salad *n la ensalada f* p109

salesperson *n el vendedor m, la vendedora f* p122

salt *n la sal f* p108
  Is that low-salt? *¿Eso es bajo en sal?*

Salvadorian *adj salvadoreño -a* p121

satellite *n el satélite m* p68
  satellite radio *radio satélite*
  satellite tracking *rastreo por satélite*

Saturday *n sábado m* p14

sauce *n la salsa f*

say, to say *v decir* (**p32**, conjugate like *pedir*)

scan, to scan *v* (document) *escanear* **p22**

schedule *n el itinerario m, el programa m*

school *n la escuela f*

scooter *n la motoneta f* p51

score *n la puntuación f* p165

Scottish *adj escocés*

scratched *adj rayado -a* p53
  scratched surface *superficie rayada*

scuba dive, to scuba dive v
  bucear con tanques de
  oxígeno **p22**
sculpture n *la escultura* f
seafood n *los mariscos* m **p87**
search n *la búsqueda* f
  hand search *búsqueda*
  manual
search, to search v *buscar*
  p22
seasick adj *mareado -a* **p62**
  I am seasick. *Estoy*
  mareado -a.
seasickness pill n *la píldora*
  para el mareo f
seat n *el asiento* m **p41, 146**
  child seat *asiento de niño*
second adj *segundo -a* **p9**
security n *la seguridad* f **p36**
  security checkpoint *punto*
  de control de seguridad
  security guard *guardia de*
  seguridad
sedan n *el sedán* m
see, to see v *ver* **p23**
  (conjugate like *ser*)
  May I see it? *¿Puedo verlo?*
self-serve adj *autoservicio*
sell, to sell v *vender* **p23**
seltzer n *el seltzer* m **p88**
send, to send v *enviar* **p22**
separated (marital status)
  adj *separado -a* **p116**
September n *septiembre* m **p15**
serve, to serve v *servir* **p32**

service n *el servicio* m **p43**
  out of service *fuera de*
  servicio **p136**
services (religious) n
  el servicio m **p127**
service charge n *el cargo por*
  servicio m **p72**
seven adj *siete* **p7**
seventy adj *setenta* **p7**
seventeen adj *diecisiete* **p7**
seventh adj *séptimo -a* **p9**
sew, to sew v *coser* **p23**
sex (gender) n *el sexo* m
sex, to have (intercourse) v
  tener relaciones
shallow adj *poco profundo -a*
sheet (bed linen) n *la sábana* f
shellfish n *el crustáceo* m **p87**
ship n *el barco* m **p62**
ship, to ship v *enviar* **p22**
  How much to ship this to
  ____? *¿Cuánto cuesta*
  enviar esto ____?
shipwreck n *el naufragio* m
shirt n *la camisa* f
shoe n *el zapato* m **p150**
shop n *la tienda* f **p150**
shop v *comprar, ir de*
  compras **p23**
  I'm shopping for mens'
  clothes. *Estoy comprando*
  ropa de hombres.
  I'm shopping for womens'
  clothes. *Estoy comprando*
  ropa de mujer.

I'm shopping for childrens' clothes. *Estoy comprando ropa para niños.*

short *adj corto -a* **p10**

shorts *n los pantalones cortos m* **p83**

shot (liquor) *n el trago m*

shout *v gritar* **p22**

show (performance) *n el espectáculo m, la función f*

What time is the show? *¿A qué hora es el espectáculo?*

show, to show *v mostrar* **p31** (conjugate like *poder*)

Would you show me? *¿Puede mostrarme?*

shower *n la ducha f* **p68**

Does it have a shower? *¿Tiene una ducha?*

shower, to shower *v ducharse* **p22, 35**

shrimp *n el camarón m* **p102**

shuttle bus *n el autobús de transbordo m*

sick *adj enfermo -a* **p48**

I feel sick. *Me siento enfermo -a.*

side *n el lado m* **p86**

on the side (e.g., salad dressing) *por el lado*

sidewalk *n la acera f*

sightsee *v salir a conocer* **p23**

sightseeing bus *n el autobús de excursión m*

sign, to sign *v firmar* **p22**

Where do I sign? *¿Dónde firmo?*

silk *n la seda f* **p151**

silver *adj plato -a*

sing, to sing *v cantar* **p22**

single (unmarried) *adj soltero -a* **p116**

Are you single? *¿Eres soltero -a?*

single (one) *adj sencillo -a, individual*

single bed *cama individual*

sink *n el fregadero m*

sister *n la hermana f* **p115**

sit, to sit *v sentar*

six *adj seis* **p7**

sixteen *adj dieciséis* **p7**

sixty *adj sesenta* **p8**

size (clothing, shoes) *n la talla f* **p151**

skin *n la piel f*

sleeping berth *n el camarote para dormir m*

slow *adj lento -a* **p179**

slow, to slow down *v reducir la velocidad* **p33**

Slow down! *¡Reduzca la velocidad!* **p58**

slow(ly) *adv lentamente*

Speak more slowly. *Hable más lentamente.* **p112**

slum n el suburbio m p16

small adj pequeño -a p11

smell, to smell v oler

smoke, to smoke v fumar p22

smoking n el fumar m p37

smoking area área de fumar

No Smoking No fumar p39

snack n el bocadillo m p183

Snake eyes! n ¡Ojos de serpiente!, ¡Par de ases! p184

snorkel n snorkel m

soap n el jabón m p16

sock n la media f

soda n la soda f, el refresco m, la gaseosa f p47

diet soda refresco dietético

soft adj suave

software n el software m

sold out adj vendido -a

some adj algún, alguno -a

someone n alguien p38

something n algo m p48

son n el hijo m p117

song n la canción f p179

sorry adj apenado -a

I'm sorry. Lo siento.

soup n la sopa f p16

spa n el balneario m p67

Spain n España

Spanish adj español p2

spare tire n la llanta de respuesto f

speak, to speak v hablar p22

Do you speak English? ¿Habla inglés?

Would you speak louder, please? ¿Podría hablar más alto, por favor?

Would you speak slower, please? ¿Podría hablar más lento, por favor?

special (featured meal) n el especial m

specify, to specify v especificar p22

speed limit n el límite de velocidad m p56

What's the speed limit? ¿Cuál es el límite de velocidad?

speedometer n el velocímetro m

spell, to spell v deletrear p22

How do you spell that? ¿Cómo se deletrea eso?

spice n la especia f

spill, to spill v derramar p22

split (gambling) n la división f

sports n los deportes m p130

spring (season) n la primavera f p15

stadium n el estadio m p164

staff (employees) n el personal m p78

stamp (postage) n la estampilla f

stair n la escalera f

Where are the stairs? ¿Dónde están las escaleras?

ENGLISH—SPANISH

Are there many stairs?
¿Hay muchas escaleras?

stand, to stand v *pararse*
p22, 35

start, to start (commence) v
comenzar

start, to start (a car) v
encender p31
(conjugate like *querer*)

state n *el estado* m

station n *la estación* f p58

Where is the nearest_____?
*¿Dónde está ____ más
cercana?*

gas station
la gasolinera

bus station
la estación de autobuses

subway station
la estación del metro

train station
la estación del tren

stay, to stay v *quedarse* p22, 35

**We'll be staying for ____
nights.** *Me quedaré por
____ noches.* Numbers, p7.

steakhouse n *el restaurante
de parrilla* m p80

steal, to steal v *robar* p22

stolen adj *robado -a* p49

stop n *la parada* f p59

Is this my stop? *¿Esta es mi
parada?*

I missed my stop. *Perdí mi
parada.*

stop, to stop v *detener* p29

Please stop. *Por favor deténgase.*

STOP (traffic sign) *PARE*

Stop, thief! *¡Alto, ladrón!*

store n *la tienda* f p150

straight adj *recto -a, derecho
-a, lacio -a* (hair) p118

straight ahead *derecho,
hacia adelante* p5

straight (drink) *sencillo*

**Go straight. (giving
directions)** *Siga derecho.*
p55

straight (gambling) n *la
escalera* f p185

street n *la calle* f p6

across the street *al cruzar la
calle*

down the street *calle abajo*

Which street? *¿En cuál calle?*

How many more streets?
¿Cuántas calles más?

stressed adj *estresado -a*

striped adj *a rayas*

stroller n *el cochecito para
niños / bebés* m

Do you rent baby strollers?
*¿Alquilan cochecitos para
bebés?*

substitution n *la sustitución* f

suburb n *el barrio* m p16

subway n *el metro* m p63

subway line *línea del metro*

subway station *estación del
metro*

**Which subway do I take for
_____?** *¿Cuál metro tomo
para _____?*

subtitle *n* el subtítulo *m*

suitcase *n* la maleta *f* p49

suite *n* la suite *f* p69

summer *n* el verano *m* p15

sun *n* el sol *m*

sunburn *n* la quemadura
de sol *f*

I have a bad sunburn.
*Me quemé demasiado
con el sol.*

Sunday *n* domingo *m* p13

sunglasses *n* las gafas de sol *f*

sunny *adj* soleado -a p125

It's sunny out. *Está soleado
afuera.*

sunroof *n* el techo corredizo *m*

sunscreen *n* el protector
solar *m*

**Do you have sunscreen SPF
_____?** *¿Tienen bloqueador
de sol SPF _____?* See
numbers p7.

supermarket *n* el
supermercado *m*

surf *v* surfear p22

surfboard *n* la tabla de
surfear *f*

suspiciously *adv*
sospechosamente p48

swallow, to swallow *v*
tragar p22

sweater *n* el suéter *m* p46

swim, to swim *v* nadar p22

Can one swim here?
¿Puedo nadar aquí?

swimsuit *n* el traje de baño *m*

swim trunks *n* el pantalón de
traje de baño *m*

symphony *n* la orquesta
sinfónica *f*

T

table *n* la mesa *f* p21

table for two *mesa para dos*

tailor *n* el sastre *m* p74

**Can you recommend a good
tailor?** *¿Puede recomendar
un buen sastre?*

take, to take *v* tomar, llevar
p22

Take me to the station.
Lléveme a la estación.

**How much to take me to
_____?** *¿Cuánto cuesta
llevarme a _____?*

takeout menu *n* el menú de
comidas para llevar *m*

talk, to talk *v* hablar p22

tall *adj* alto -a p119

tanned *adj* bronceado -a

taste (flavor) *n* el sabor *m*

taste n (discernment) el gusto m

taste, to taste v probar p22

tax n el impuesto m p155

value-added tax (VAT) impuesto al valor agregado (IVA)

taxi n el taxi m p57

Taxi! ¡Taxi!

Would you call me a taxi? ¿Me puede llamar un taxi?

tea n el té m p90

team n el equipo m p164

Techno n el techno m p128

television n la televisión f

temple n el templo m p126

ten adj diez p7

tennis n el tenis m p67

tennis court cancha de tenis

tent n la carpa f

tenth adj décimo -a p8

terminal n (airport) la terminal f p39

Thank you. Gracias. p1

that (near) adj ese / eso / esa

that (far away) adj aquel / aquello / aquella

theater n el teatro m p145

them (m/f) ellos / ellas p3

there (demonstrative) adv ahí (nearby), allí (far)

Is / Are there ? ¿Hay ?

over there allí

these adj estos -as p6

thick adj grueso -a, espeso -a

thin adj delgado -a, flaco -a, fino -a p119

third adj tercero -a p9

thirteen adj trece p7

thirty adj treinta p8

this adj este, esto, esta p6

those adj aquellos -as, esos -as

thousand mil p8

three tres p7

Thursday n jueves m p14

ticket n el boleto m p36

ticket counter mostrador de venta de boletos

one-way ticket boleto de ida p38

round-trip ticket boleto de ida y vuelta p38

tight adj apretado -a p153

time n el tiempo m p167

Is it on time? ¿Está a tiempo?

At what time? ¿A qué hora?

What time is it? ¿Qué hora es?

timetable n (train) el horario m p59

tip (gratuity) la propina f p90

tire n la llanta f p53

I have a flat tire. Tengo una llanta vacía.

tired adj cansado -a p121

today n *hoy*

toilet n *el inodoro m* p76

The toilet is overflowing.
El inodoro se está desbordando.

The toilet is backed up.
El inodoro está tapado.

toilet paper n *el papel higiénico m*

You're out of toilet paper.
Se le acabó el papel higiénico.

toiletries n *los artículos de tocador m* p100

toll n *el peaje m* p56

tomorrow n *mañana* p4

ton n *la tonelada f*

too (excessively) adv *demasiado -a*

too (also) adv *también* p171

tooth n *el diente m* p192

I lost my tooth. *Perdí mi diente.*

toothache n *el dolor de dientes m*

I have a toothache. *Tengo dolor de dientes.*

total n *el total m*

What is the total? *¿Cuál es el total?*

tour n *la excursión f*

Are guided tours available?
¿Hay excursiones guiadas disponibles?

Are audio tours available?
¿Hay excursiones con audio disponibles?

towel n *la toalla f*

May we have more towels? *¿Me puede dar más toallas?*

toy n *el juguete m*

toy store n *la juguetería f*

Do you have any toys for the children? *¿Tiene juguetes para niños?*

traffic n *el tráfico m, el tránsito m* p52

How's traffic? *¿Cómo está el tráfico?*

traffic rules *reglas de tránsito*

trail n *el sendero m* p168

Are there trails? *¿Hay senderos?*

train n *el tren m* p59

express train *tren expreso*

local train *tren local*

Does the train go to ____?
¿El tren va a _____?

May I have a train schedule? *¿Me puede dar el horario de los trenes?*

Where is the train station?
¿Dónde está la estación del tren?

train, to train v *entrenar* **p22**

transfer, to transfer v *transferir* **p29**

I need to transfer funds. *Necesito transferir fondos.*

transmission n *la transmisión* f

automatic transmission *transmisión automática*

standard transmission *transmisión manual*

travel, to travel v *viajar* **p22**

trim, to trim (hair) v *recortar, cortar* **p22**

trip n *el viaje* m **p111**

triple adj *triple* **p8**

trumpet n *la trompeta* f

trunk n *el baúl* m **p49**

try, to try (attempt) v *intentar* **p22**, *tratar* **p22**

try, to try on (clothing) v *medir* **p32**

try, to try (food) v *probar*

Tuesday n *martes* m **p13**

turkey n *el pavo* m **p96**

turn, to turn v *virar, girar* **p22**

to turn left / right *vire a la izquierda / derecha*

to turn off / on *encender / apagar* **p22**

twelve adj *doce* **p7**

twenty adj *veinte* **p7**

twine n *la cuerda* f **p141**

two adj *dos* **p7**

U

umbrella n *la sombrilla* f, *el paraguas* m

uncle n *el tío* m **p115**

undercooked adj *crudo* -a

understand, to understand v *entender* **p29**

I don't understand. *No entiendo.*

Do you understand? *¿Entiende?*

underwear n *la ropa interior* f

university n *la universidad* f

up adv *arriba* **p5**

update, to update v *actualizar* **p22**

upgrade n *la mejora de categoría* f **p52**

upload, to upload v *cargar* **p22**

upscale adj *de más clase* **p175**

Uruguayan adj *uruguayo* -a **p121**

us pron *nosotros* -as **p3**

USB port n *el puerto USB* m

use, to use v *usar* **p22**

V

vacation n *la vacación* m **p44**

on vacation *de vacaciones*

to go on vacation *ir de vacaciones*

vacancy n *el vacante* m

van n *la furgoneta* f, *la van* f

vegetable n *el vegetal* m

vegetarian n *el vegetariano*
m, *la vegetariana* f p42

vending machine n *la*
máquina expendedora f

Venezuelan adj *venezolano -a*
p121

version n *la versión* f

very muy p78

view n *la vista* f p68

  beach view *vista a la playa*

  city view *vista a la ciudad*

vineyard n *el viñedo* m

vinyl n *el vinilo* m p50

violin n *el violín* m

visa n *la visa* f

  Do I need a visa? ¿*Necesito*
  una visa?

vision n *la visión* f p189

visit, to visit v *visitar* p22

visually-impaired adj *con*
impedimentos visuales f

vodka n *el vodka* m p89

voucher n *el vale* m p44

W

wait, to wait v *esperar* p22

  Please wait. *Por favor*
  espere.

  How long is the wait?
  ¿*Cuán larga es la espera?*

waiter n *el camarero* f

waiting area n *el área de*
espera f p37

wake up call n *la llamada de*
despertar f p75

wallet n *la cartera* f,
la billetera f p46

  I lost my wallet.
  Perdí mi cartera.

  Someone stole my wallet.
  Alguien me robó mi
  billetera.

walk, to walk v *caminar* p22

walker (ambulatory device)
n *el andador* m p43

walkway n *la pasarela* f

  moving walkway *pasarela*
  mecánica

want, to want v *querer* p31

war n *la guerra* f p126

warm adj *caliente* p77, 125

watch, to watch v *observar*
p22

water n *el agua* m p46

  Is the water potable?
  ¿*El agua es potable?*

  Is there running water?
  ¿*Hay agua corriente?* p79

wave, to wave v *agitar las*
manos p22

waxing n *la depilación con*
cera f

weapon n *el arma* f p16

wear, to wear *v usar* p22
weather forecast *n el pronóstico del tiempo m*
Wednesday *n miércoles m*
week *n la semana f* p4, 14
  this week *esta semana*
  last week *la semana pasada*
  next week *la próxima semana*
weigh *v pesar* p22
  I weigh ____. *Yo peso ____.*
  It weighs ____. *Pesa ____.*
  See p7 for numbers.
weights *n las pesas f* p161
welcome *adv bienvenido*
  You're welcome. *Es bienvenido.*
well *adv bien*
  well done (meat) *bien cocido* p85
  well done (task) *bien hecho*
  I don't feel well. *No me siento bien.*
western *adj occidental, de vaqueros*
whale *n la ballena f*
what *adv qué* p3
  What sort of ____? *¿Qué clase de ____?*
  What time is ____? *¿A qué hora es ____?* p12
  See p112 for questions.

wheelchair *n la silla de ruedas f* p43
  wheelchair access *acceso para sillas de ruedas* p70
  wheelchair ramp *rampa para sillas de ruedas*
  power wheelchair *silla de ruedas eléctricas*
wheeled (luggage) *adj con ruedas*
when *adv cuándo* p3
  See p3 for questions.
where *adv dónde* p3
  Where is it? *¿Dónde está?*
  See p3 for questions.
which *adv cuál* p3
  Which one? *¿Cuál?*
  See p3 for questions.
white *adj blanco -a*
who *adv quién* p3
whose *adj de quién*
wide *adj ancho -a* p12
widow, widower *n la viuda f, el viudo m* p116
wife *n la esposa f* p114
wi-fi *n la red inalámbrica f*
window *n la ventana f, la ventanilla f* p41, 142
  drop-off window *ventanilla de entregas*
  pickup window *ventanilla de retiros*

windshield n el parabrisas m
windshield wiper n el limpiaparabrisas m
windy adj ventoso -a p125
wine n el vino m p47, 84
winter n el invierno m p15
wiper n el limpiaparabrisas m
with prep con p87
withdraw v retirar p22
  I need to withdraw money. Necesito retirar dinero.
without prep sin p87
woman n la mujer f
work, to work v trabajar, funcionar p22
  This doesn't work. Esto no funciona.
workout n el ejercicio m
worse peor
worst lo peor
write, to write v escribir p23
  Would you write that down for me? ¿Podría escribir eso para mí?
writer n el escritor m p122

X

x-ray machine n la máquina de rayos X f

Y

yellow adj amarillo -a
Yes. adv Sí.
yesterday n ayer m p4

the day before yesterday anteayer p14
yield sign n la señal para ceder el paso f
you pron usted, tú, ustedes, vosotros -as p3
  you (singular, informal) tú
  you (singular, formal) usted
  you (plural informal) vosotros -as **(rare)**
  you (plural formal AND informal) ustedes
your, yours adj suyo -a, tuyo -a
young adj joven p116

Z

zoo n el zoológico m p130

A

abajo *down adv* p5

abajo *below adj* p78

el abanico *m fan (hand-held) n*

la abeja *f bee n*

abierto -a *open (business) adj*

el abogado *m /* **la abogado** *f lawyer n* p122

la abolladura *f dent n*

abordar *to board v* **p22**

el abrigo *m coat n* p152

el abril *m April n* p14

la abuela *f grandmother n*

el abuelo *m grandfather n*

acampar *to camp v* **p22**

el accidente *m accident n*

el aceite *m oil n* p55, 86

la aceituna *f olive n*

aceptar *to accept v* **p22**

Se aceptan tarjetas de crédito. *Credit cards accepted.*

la acera *f sidewalk n*

achicharrado -a *charred (meat) adj* p85

aclarar *to clear v* **p22**

el acné *m acne n* p187

actual *current adj* p16

actualizar *to update v* **p22**

de acuerdo *Okay adj adv*

el acumulador *m,* **la batería** *f battery (for car) n*

adelante *forward adj* p5

el adelanto *m advance n*

adentro *inside adj* p84

el aderezo *m dressing (salad) n*

adicional *extra adj* p75

el adiós *m goodbye n* p112

la aduana *f customs n* p39

el aeropuerto *m airport n*

afroamericano -a *African American adj* p119

afro, africano *afro adj*

afuera *outside adv* p84

¡Agarren al ladrón! *Stop, thief!*

la agencia *f agency n* p50

la agencia de alquiler de autos *f car rental agency*

la agencia de crédito *f credit bureau n* p133

el agnóstico *m,* **la agnóstica** *f agnostic n adj* p127

agosto *m August n* p15

agotado -a *exhausted (person) adj, sold out (thing) adj*

agradable *nice adj*

agradar *to please v, to be pleasing to v* **p22**

el agua *f water n* p46

el agua caliente *hot water*
el agua fría *cold water*

el águila *f eagle n*

ahí *there (nearby) adv (demonstrative)* p182

ahora *now adv* p4

el aire acondicionado *m air conditioning n* p68

el ajo *m garlic n* p108

la albóndiga *f meatball n*

el alcohol *m alcohol n* p88

alegre *happy adj* p121

el alemán *m*, **la alemana** *f German n adj* p80

la alergia *f allergy n*

alérgico -a *allergic adj* p75, 86

Soy alérgico / alérgica a ____. *I'm allergic to ____.*

algo *m something n* p48

el algodón *m cotton n* p151

alguien *someone n* p38

algún, alguno -a *some adj*

allá *over there adv*

allí *there (far) adv (demonstrative)* p5

la almohada *f pillow n* p47

la almohada de plumas *down pillow*

el almuerzo *m lunch n* p82

alquilar *to rent v*

el alpinismo *m mountain climbing n*

alto -a *high adj, tall adj* p119

alto *high adj* p119
más alto *higher*
lo más alto *highest*

la altitud *f altitude n* p166

el aluminio *m aluminum n*

amable *kind (nice) adj*

la ama de casa *f homemaker n*

amamantar *to breastfeed v* p22

al amanecer *at dawn*

amar *to love v* **p22**

amarillo -a *yellow adj*

el ambiente *m environment n*

la ambulancia *f ambulance n*

el amigo *m* / **la amiga** *f friend n* p115

el amor *m love n*

anaranjado -a *orange adj*

ancho -a *wide adj* p12

el andador *m walker (ambulatory device) n* p43

andar *to ride v / to run v* **p23**

el animal *m animal n*

ansioso -a *anxious adj* p121

el antibiótico *m antibiotic n*

Necesito un antibiótico. *I need an antibiotic.*

los anticonceptivos *m pl birth control n* p182, 191

Estoy usando anticonceptivos. *I'm on birth control.*

anticonceptivo -a *birth control adj*

Se me acabaron las pastillas anticonceptivas. *I'm out of birth control pills.*

el antihistamínico *m antihistamine n* p186

el año m year n
¿Cuántos años tiene?
What's your age?
apagar to turn off (lights) v **p22**
el apellido m last name
Me quedé con mi apellido
de soltera. I kept my
maiden name.
apenado -a sorry adj
Lo siento. I'm sorry.
apostar to bet v **p22**
apresurarse to hurry v **p22, 35**
¡Apresúrate por favor!
Hurry, please!
apretado -a tight adj **p153**
la apuesta f bet n **p185**
Igualo tu apuesta. I'll see
your bet. **p185**
apuntar to point v **p22**
aquel / aquello that (far
away) adj **p6**
aquellos / aquellas those adj pl
aquí here adv **p5**
argentino -a Argentinian adj
p120
el área de espera f waiting
area n **p37**
el arma f weapon n **p16**
el arrecife m reef n **p170**
arriba up adv **p5**
arriba above adj **p78**
el arte m art n
la exhibición de arte exhibit
of art

de arte art adj
el museo de arte art
museum
el artesano m, **la artesana** f
craftsperson / artisan n
los artículos de tocador m
toiletries n **p100**
el / la artista m f artist n
asaltar to mug (assault) v **p22**
asaltado to get mugged
asiático -a Asian adj **p80**
el asiento m seat n **p41**
el asiento a nivel de
orquesta orchestra seat
la asistencia f attendance n
la asistencia telefónica f
directory assistance
asistir to attend v / to assist v
p23
el asma f asthma n **p191**
Yo tengo asma. I have
asthma.
la aspirina f aspirin n **p187**
el asunto m matter, affair
No te metas en mis asuntos.
Mind your own business.
el ataque cardiaco m, **el**
ataque al corazón m heart
attack n
ateo -a atheist adj
aterrizar to land v **p22**
los audífonos m headphones n
el audio m audio n **p148**

audio -a, auditivo -a *audio adj* p65

ausente *missing adj*

Australia *m Australia n*

australiano -a *Australian adj*

el auto *m,* **el automóvil** *m,* **el carro** *m car n*

la agencia de alquiler de autos *car rental agency*

el autobús *m bus n* p57

la parada de autobuses *bus stop*

el autobús de transbordo *shuttle bus*

el autobús de excursión *sightseeing bus*

la autopista *f highway n*

de autoservicio *self-serve adj*

el avance *m advance n*

avergonzado -a *embarrassed adj* p16

las aves de corral *f pl poultry n*

¡Ay! *Ouch! interj*

ayer *yesterday adv* p4

el día antes de ayer / anteayer *the day before yesterday adv* p14

la ayuda *f help n* p56

¡Ayuda! *Help! n*

ayudar *to help v* **p22**

azul *blue adj* p119

B

el baile de salón *m ballroom dancing n*

bajo -a *low adj* p85

bajo *low adj* p85

más bajo *lower*

lo más bajo *lowest*

el balance *m balance (on bank account) n* p135

balancear *to balance v* **p22**

el balcón *m balcony n* p69

el balneario *m spa n*

bancario -a *bank adj*

la cuenta bancaria *bank account*

la tarjeta bancaria *bank card*

el banco *m bank n* p133

la banda *f band n*

la banda ancha *f broadband n*

bañarse *to bathe v* **p22, 35**

la bañera *f,* **la tina de baño** *f bathtub n* p68

el baño *m bathroom, restroom n, bath n* p37

¿Tienen un baño público? *Do you have a public restroom?*

el baño de caballeros *men's restroom*

el baño de damas *women's restroom*

barato -a *cheap adj* p51

barato *cheap* p51
más barato *cheaper* p51
lo más barato *cheapest*
el barbero *m barber n* p158
el barco *m boat n, ship n* p63
el barrio *m suburb n* p16
la batería *f battery (for car) n*
el baúl *m trunk n*
el / la bebé *m f baby n* p117
de bebés, para bebés *for babies adj*
coches para bebés *baby strollers?*
comida para bebés *baby food*
beber *to drink v* **p23**
la bebida *f drink n* p177
la bebida complementaria *complimentary drink*
Quisiera una bebida. *I'd like a drink.*
bello -a *beautiful adj* p117
el beso *m kiss n* p180
bien *okay adv*
¿Está bien? *Are you okay?*
bien *well adv*
bien *fine adj* p1
Estoy bien. *I'm fine.*
bien parecido *m handsome adj*
bienvenido -a *welcome adj*
Está bienvenido. *You're welcome.*

bilingüe *bilingual adj*
el billar *m pool (the game) n*
el billete *m bill (currency) n*
la billetera *f wallet n*
birracial *biracial adj*
blanco -a *white, off-white adj*
el blanqueador *m bleach n*
el bloque *m block n*
bloquear *to block v* **p22**
la blusa *f blouse n* p151
la boca *f mouth n*
el bocadillo *m snack n* p183
la bocina *f horn n*
la bola *f ball (sport) n*
la boletería *f box office n*
el boleto *m ticket n* p38
el mostrador de venta de boletos *ticket counter* p36
el boleto de ida *one-way ticket* p38
el boleto de ida y vuelta *round-trip ticket* p38
boliviano -a *Bolivian adj, n* p120
la bolsa *f /* **el bolso** *m bag n*
el bolso *m purse n* p46
la bomba *f bomb n* p16
la bomba *f pump n*
el borde de la acera *m curb n*
bordo *m board n*
a bordo *on board*
borroso -a *blurry adj* p189

la **botella** f bottle n p177

el **braille americano** m braille (American) n

el **brandy** m brandy n p89

el **brazo** m arm n p16

brillante bright adj

bronceado -a tanned adj

bronce (color) bronze (color) adj

bucear to dive v **p22**

bucear con tanques de oxígeno to scuba dive v

Buceo con tanques de oxígeno. I scuba dive. **snorkel** to snorkel v.

el **budista** m, la **budista** f Buddhist n p127

bueno -a good adj p111

buenos días good morning

buenas noches good evening p111

buenas noches good night

buenas tardes good afternoon p111

el **bufé** m buffet n

de tipo bufé buffet-style adj

el **burro** m donkey n

buscar to look for (to search) v p22

la **búsqueda** f search n

búsqueda manual hand search

C

el **caballo** m horse n

el **cabello** m hair n

la **cabra** f goat n p101

el **cacahuate** m peanut n

el **cachemir** m cashmere n

caer to fall v **p23**

café (color) hazel adj p119

el **café** m café n, coffee n

el **café helado** iced coffee

el **café expreso** m espresso n

el **cibercafé** Internet café

la **caja fuerte** f safe (for storing valuables) n p75

el **cajero automático** m ATM n

caliente hot adj, warm adj

el **calipso** m calypso (music) n

callado -a quiet adj

la **calle** f street n p6

calle abajo down the street

al cruzar la calle across the street

la **cama** f bed n

el **camarero** m waiter n

el **camarón** m shrimp n p102

el **camarote** m berth n

cambiar to change (money) v / to change (clothes) v **p22**

el **cambio** m change (money) n

el **cambio de moneda** m currency exchange n p37, 133

la **caminadora** f treadmill n

caminar *to walk* v **p22**
la caminata f *walk* n
la camisa f *shirt* n
el campamento m *campsite* n
el campista m *camper* n
el campo para practicar tiros de golf m *driving range* n
Canadá m *Canada* n
canadiense *Canadian* adj p192
cancelar *to cancel* v **p22**
la cancha f *court (sport)* n
la canción f *song* n p179
el candado m *lock* n p162
cansado -a *tired* adj p121
cantar *to sing* v **p22**
la cantidad f *amount* n p63
la cantina f *bar* n p59
  bar con piano *piano bar*
  la cantina para solteros *singles bar* p175
la caña de pescar f *fishing pole* n
el cappuccino m *cappuccino* n
la cara f *face* n p119
cargar *to upload* v **p22**
el cargo de entrada m *cover charge (in bar)* n p178
el cargo por servicio m *service charge* n p72
la caries f *cavity (tooth cavity)* n
la carnada f *bait* n p168
la carne f *meat* n p87
caro -a *expensive* adj p176
la carpa f *tent* n

la carretera f *road* n p56
el carro para dormir m *sleeping car* n
la cartera f *purse n, wallet* n
  Perdí mi cartera. *I lost my wallet.*
  Alguien me robó mi cartera. *Someone stole my wallet.*
casado -a *married* adj p116
casarse *to marry* v **p22, 35**
el casillero m *locker* n p161
  casillero del gimnasio *gym locker*
  casillero de almacén *storage locker*
el casino m *casino* n p66
el católico m, **la católica** f *Catholic* n adj p127
catorce *fourteen* n adj p7
el CD m, **el disco compacto** m *CD* n p139
el cebo m *bait* n
la ceja f *eyebrow* n
celebrar *to celebrate* v **p22**
la cena f *dinner* n
el centímetro m *centimeter* n
el centro comercial m *mall* n
el centro de la ciudad m *downtown* n p149
el centro de gimnasia m *fitness center* n p66
cerca *close, near* adj p5
  cerca *close* p5
  más cerca *closer* p5
  lo más cerca *closest* p5

cercano -a *near, nearby adj*

cercano *near adj*

más cercano *nearer (comparative)*

lo más cercano *nearest (superlative)*

el cerdo *m pig n*

cerrado -a *closed adj* p56

la cerradura *f lock n*

cerrar *to close v* **p22**

cerrar con llave *to lock v* **p22**

la cerveza *f beer n* p88

cerveza de barril *beer on tap, draft beer* p177

la chaqueta *f jacket n* p46

el check-in *check-in n* p36

el check-in electrónico *electronic check-in* p41

el check-in exprés *express check-in* p40

el cheque *m check n*

la chica *f girl n* p177

chino -a *Chinese adj* p120

el chocolate caliente *m hot chocolate n* p89

el chupete *m pacifier n*

el cibercafé *m cybercafé n*

ciego -a *blind adj*

cien *m*, **cientos** *m hundred n adj* p8

el cigarrillo *m cigarette n*

el paquete de cigarrillos *pack of cigarettes*

el cigarro *m cigar n*

cinco *five n adj* p7

el cincuenta *m fifty n adj* p8

el cine *m*, **el cinema** *m cinema n*

la cinta transportadora *conveyor belt* p46

el cinturón *m belt n* p54, 152

el cisne *m swan n*

la cita *f appointment n* p148

la ciudad *f city n* p69

el clarinete *m clarinet n*

claro -a *clear adj* p170

la clase *f kind (type) n*

¿Qué clase es? *What kind is it?*

la clase *f class n* p41

la clase de negocios *business class* p41

la clase económica *economy class* p41

la primera clase *first class* p41

clásico -a *classical (music) adj*

el club nocturno *m nightclub n*

la cobija *f blanket n*

cobrar *to charge (money) v* **p22**

cobre (color) *copper adj*

a cobro revertido *collect adj*

el cochecito para niños / bebés *m stroller n*

la cocina *f kitchen n* p73

la cocina pequeña *f kitchenette n* p69

cocinar to cook v **p22**

el coito m intercourse (sexual) n

el colegio m college n, high school n

colgar hang up (to end a phone call) v **p22**

el coliseo m coliseum n

colocar to place v **p22**

colombiano -a Colombian adj

el color m color n p154

colorear to color v **p22**

el combustible m gas n p54

el indicador de combustible gas gauge

sin combustible out of gas

comenzar to begin v, to start (commence) v **p22**

comer to eat v **p23**

comer afuera to eat out

los comestibles m groceries n

la comida f food n p87

la comida f meal n p42

la comida para diabéticos diabetic meal p42

la comida kósher kosher meal p42

la comida vegetariana vegetarian meal p42

cómo how adv p3

el compañero m, **la compañera** f partner n

compensar to make up (compensate) v **p22**

comportar to behave v **p22**

comprar to shop v **p22**

comprobar, verificar to check v **p22**

la computadora f computer n

la computadora portátil f laptop n p123

con with prep p87

el concierto m concert n p130

concurrido -a busy (restaurant) adj

la condición f condition n

en buena / mala condición in good / bad condition

el condón m condom n p182

¿Tienes un condón? Do you have a condom? p182

no sin un condón not without a condom

el conductor m driver n p57

el conejo m rabbit n p91

la conexión eléctrica f electrical hookup n p79

la confirmación f confirmation n

confirmar to confirm v **p22**

confundido -a confused adj

la congestión f congestion (sinus) n p187

congestionado -a congested adj p16

la congestión de tránsito f congestion (traffic) n

conocer to know (someone) v **p33**

la consola de juegos f game console n p157

el contacto de emergencia m emergency contact n

la contestación f answer n

Necesito una contestación. I need an answer.

contestar to answer (phone call) v, to answer (respond to a question) v **p22**

Contésteme por favor. Answer me, please.

continuar to continue v **p22**

el contrabajo m bass (instrument) n

la contraseña f password n

el convertible m convertible n

el coñac m cognac n p89

la copa f glass (drinking) n

¿Lo tienen por la copa? Do you have it by the glass?

Quisiera una copa por favor. I'd like a glass please.

el corazón m heart n p189

la corona f crown (dental) n

la correa f belt n

correcto -a correct adj p58

corregir to correct v **p23**

el correo m mail n / post office n p141

el correo aéreo air mail

el correo certificado certified mail

el correo expreso express mail

el correo de primera clase first class mail

el correo certificado registered mail

¿Dónde está el correo? Where is the post office?

la corrida de toros f bullfight n

corriente current (water) n

la cortadura f cut (wound) n

cortar to cut v **p22**

la corte f court (legal) n p193

tribunal de faltas traffic court

cortés courteous adj p78

corto -a short adj p10

coser to sew v **p23**

costarricense Costa Rican n adj p120

costear to cost v **p22**

cuánto how (much) adv p3

¿Cuánto? How much? p3

¿Por cuánto tiempo? For how long?

cuántos how (many) adv

country (música) f country-and-western adj

crecer to grow (get larger) v **p23**

¿Dónde creciste? Where did you grow up?

la crema f cream n p94

cremoso -a off-white adj

crudo -a rare (meat) adj, undercooked adj p87

el crustáceo *m shellfish n* p87

a cuadros *checked (pattern) adj*

cuál *which adv* p3

cualquier -a *any adj*

cualquier cosa *anything n*

cuándo *when adv* p3

cuarenta *forty n adj*

cuarto *fourth n adj* p9

  un cuarto *one quarter, one fourth*

un cuarto de galón *m quart n*

cuatro *four n adj* p7

el cubismo *m Cubism n*

cuenta *f account n* p135

la cuerda *f rope n, twine n*

el cuero *m leather n* p50

cuidar *to mother v* **p22**

la culpa *f fault n* p57

  Es mi culpa. *I'm at fault.* p57

  Fue su culpa. *It was his / her fault.*

la cuna *f crib n* p69

D

dañado -a *damaged adj* p49

dar *to give v* **p25** (conjugate like *ir*)

dar masaje *to massage v* **p22**

décimo -a *tenth adj* p8

decir *to say v* **p32**

declarar *to declare v* **p22**

delantero -a *front adj*

deleitado -a *delighted adj*

deletrear *to spell v* **p22**

  ¿Cómo se deletrea eso? *How do you spell that?*

delgado -a *thin (slender) adj*

demasiado -a *too (excessively) adv*

la democracia *f democracy n*

la dentadura *f dentures, denture plate n* p192

el dentista *m dentist n* p188

la depilación con cera *f waxing n*

los deportes *m pl sports n*

derecho -a *right adj, straight adv* p55

  Está a mano derecha. *It is on the right.* p55

  Vira a la derecha en la esquina. *Turn right at the corner.*

  Siga derecho. *Go straight. (giving directions)*

los derechos *m pl rights n pl*

  los derechos civiles *civil rights*

derramar *to spill v* **p22**

desacelerar *to slow v* **p22**

desaparecer *to disappear v* **p33** (conjugate like *conocer*)

el desayuno *m breakfast n*

la descarga *f download n*

descargar *to download v* **p22**

desconectar *to disconnect v* **p22**

el descuento *m discount n*

el descuento para niños *children's discount*

el descuento para personas mayores de edad *senior discount*

el descuento para estudiantes *student discount*

el desfile *m parade n*

desmayar *to faint v* **p22**

despedirse *to check out (of hotel) v* **p23, 25**

los destellos *m pl highlights (hair) n* **p159**

el destino *m destination n*

el detector de metales *m metal detector n*

detener *to stop v* **p29**

Deténgase por favor. *Please stop.*

detrás *behind adv*

devolver *to return (something) v* **p31** *(conjugate like poder)*

el día *m day n* **p161**

el día antes de ayer / anteayer *the day before yesterday* **p14**

estos últimos días *these last few days*

diabético -a *diabetic adj* **p85**

el día de fiesta *m holiday n*

la diarrea *f diarrhea n* **p187**

dibujar *m drawing (activity) v* **p22**

el dibujo *m drawing (work of art) n*

el diccionario *m dictionary n*

diciembre *m December n*

diecinueve *nineteen n adj* **p7**

dieciocho *eighteen n adj* **p7**

dieciséis *sixteen n adj* **p7**

diecisiete *seventeen n adj* **p7**

el diente *m tooth n* **p192**

diez *ten n adj* **p7**

diferente *different (other) adj* **p154**

difícil *difficult adj* **p167**

el dinero *m money n* **p132**

la transferencia de dinero *money transfer* **p132**

la dirección *f direction*

en una sola dirección *one way (traffic sign)*

la dirección *f address n* **p124**

¿Cuál es la dirección? *What's the address?*

el disco *m disco n* **p128**

el diseñador *m,* **la diseñadora** *f designer n* **p122**

el disfraz *m costume n*

disfrutar *to enjoy v* **p22**

disponible *available adj* **p147**

la división *f split (gambling) n*

divorciado -a *divorced adj*

doble *double adj* p8

doce *twelve n adj* p7

la docena *f dozen n* p11

el doctor *m* / **la doctora** *f doctor n* p122, 188

el dólar *m dollar n*

doler *to hurt (to feel painful) v* p23

¡Ay! ¡Eso duele! *Ouch! That hurts!*

el dolor de cabeza *m headache n* p111

el dolor de dientes *m toothache n*

Tengo dolor de dientes. *I have a toothache.*

domingo *m Sunday n* p13

dónde *where adv* p3

¿Dónde está? *Where is it?*

dondequiera, cualquier lugar *anywhere adv*

dorado -a *golden adj*

dos *two n adj* p7

el drama *m drama n*

el drenaje *m drain n*

la ducha *f shower n* p68

ducharse *to shower v* p22, 35

durar *to last v* p22

duro *hard (firm) adj* p50

el DVD *m DVD n* p51

E

la economía *f economy n*

económico -a, barato -a *inexpensive adj* p38

ecuatoriano -a *Ecuadorian adj*

la edad *f age n* p116

¿Qué edad tienes? *What's your age?*

el editor *m,* **la editora** *f editor, publisher n* p122

el educador *m,* **la educadora** *f educator n* p122

el efectivo *m cash n* p133

efectivo solamente *cash only* p134

el ejercicio *m workout n*

el ejército *m military n*

él *him pron* p3

de él *his adj*

la elección *f election n* p126

el elefante *m elephant n*

el elevador *m elevator n* p69

élite *upscale adj* p175

ella *f she pron* p3

de ella *hers adj* p3

ellos / ellas *them pron pl* p3

el e-mail *m e-mail n* p124

¿Me puede dar su dirección de e-mail? *May I have your e-mail address?* p124

el mensaje de e-mail *e-mail message* p124

la embajada *f embassy n*

embarazada *pregnant adj n*

embarcar to ship v **p22**

la emergencia f emergency n

empacar to bag v **p22**

el empleado m, **la empleada** f employee n

el empleador m employer n

empujar to push v **p22**

encallar to beach v **p22**

encantado -a charmed adj

el encendedor m lighter (cigarette) n **p178**

encender to start (a car) v, to turn on v **p31** (conjugate like querer)

enchufar to plug v **p22**

el enchufe m plug n **p158**

el enchufe adaptador m adapter plug n

encontrar, hallar to find v **p22**

el enero m January n **p14**

la enfermera f nurse n **p122**

enfermo -a sick adj **p48**

enojado -a angry adj **p121**

la ensalada f salad n **p110**

entallar to fit (clothes) v **p22**

entender to understand v **p23**

No entiendo. I don't understand.

¿Entiende? Do you understand?

la entrada f entrance n **p39**

entrar to enter v **p22**

No entrar. Do not enter.

Prohibida la entrada. Entry forbidden.

entrenar to train v **p22**

entusiasmado -a enthusiastic adj **p121**

enviar to send v **p22**

enviar un e-mail to send e-mail v **p22**

el equipaje m baggage, luggage n **p39**

el equipaje perdido lost baggage

de equipaje baggage adj **p39**

reclamo de equipaje baggage claim **p39**

el equipo m team n / equipment n **p166**

el error m mistake n **p78**

la escalada f climbing n **p166**

la escalada de rocas rock climbing **p166**

para escalar climbing adj

el equipo para escalar climbing gear

escalar, subir to climb v **p22, 23**

escalar una montaña to climb a mountain

subir las escaleras to climb stairs

la escalera f stair n / flush, straight (gambling) n **p185**

la escalera real royal flush

la escalera mecánica f escalator n

escanear to scan (document) v
p22

escocés Scottish adj

escribir to write v **p23**

**¿Podría escribir eso para
mí?** Would you write that
down for me?

el escritor m writer n **p122**

escuchar to listen v **p22**

la escuela f school n

la escuela intermedia junior
high / middle school

la facultad de leyes law
school

la facultad de medicina
medical school

la escuela primaria primary
school

**la escuela superior /
secundaria** high school

la escultura f sculpture n

ese / eso / esa that (near) adj

esos / esas those (near) adj pl

la espalda f back n **p180**

español Spanish n adj **p2**

el especial m special
(featured meal) n

la especia f spice n

especificar to specify v **p22**

el espectáculo m show
(performance) n

los espejuelos m eyeglasses n

la espera f wait n **p82**

esperar to hold (to pause) v,
to wait v **p22**

espeso -a thick adj

la esposa f wife n **p114**

el esposo m husband n **p114**

la esquina f corner n

en la esquina on the corner

la estación f station n **p58**

**¿Dónde está la gasolinera
más cercanía?** Where is
the nearest gas station?

la estación de policías f
police station n **p37**

estacionamiento parking adj

estacionar to park v **p22**

no estacionar no parking

el estadio m stadium n **p164**

el estado m state n

estadounidense American
adj

la estampilla f stamp
(postage) n

estar to be (temporary state,
condition, mood) v **p27**

éste / ésta this adj **p6**

esto this n

estos / estas these n adj pl **p6**

estrecho -a narrow adj **p12**

estreñido -a constipated adj

estresado -a stressed adj

la excursión f tour n

excursionar to hike v **p22**

la excursión guiada f guided
tour n

excusar, perdonar to excuse (pardon) v **p22**

   Perdone. Excuse me.

exhausto -a exhausted adj

la exhibición f exhibit n

explicar to explain v **p22**

exprés express adj p41, 60

   el check-in exprés express check-in p41

extra grande extra-large adj

F

facturar to bill v **p22**

la familia f family n p115

el fax m fax n p123

el febrero m February n p14

el festival m festival n

fino -a thin (fine) adj

firmar to sign v **p22**

   Firme aquí. Sign here.

flaco -a thin (skinny) adj

la flauta f flute n

fletar to charter (transportation) v **p22**

fleteado charter adj

   vuelo fleteado charter flight

la flor f flower n

el foco delantero m headlight n

el formato m format n p157

la fórmula f formula n

el fósforo m match (fire) n

fotocopiar to photocopy v **p22**

frágil fragile adj p141

francés m, **francesa** f French adj n p120

la frazada f blanket n p47

el fregadero m sink n

frenar to brake v **p22**

el freno m brake n p54

la frente f forehead n

del frente front adj

fresco fresh adj p101

frío -a cold adj p125

la fruta f fruit n p90

el fuego m fire n

las fuerzas armadas f pl armed forces n pl

¡Full! Full house! n

fumar to smoke v **p22**

el fumar m smoking n

   la área de fumar smoking area p37

   no fumar no smoking p39

la función f show (performance) n

funcionar to work v **p22**

la furgoneta f van n p50

el fusible m fuse n

G

las gafas f pl glasses (spectacles) n p162

las gafas de sol f pl sunglasses n p152

la galleta f cookie n p100

el galón *m gallon n* p11
la ganga *f deal (bargain) n*
la gasolina *f gas n*
el gato *m*, **la gata** *f cat n*
el / la gerente *m f manager n*
el gimnasio *m gym n* p161
la ginebra *f gin n* p89
el / la ginecólogo -a
  gynecologist n
girar *to turn v* p22
el gol *m goal (sport) n*
el golf *m golf n* p49

  el campo de golf
  golf course

gordo -a *fat adj* p12, 119
el gorro *m hat n*
gotear *to drip v* p22
gracias *thank you*
el grado *m grade (school) n*
el gramo *m gram n*
la gran cantidad *f a lot n*
grande *big adj, large adj* p12

  grande *big, large* p12, 16
  más grande *bigger, larger*
  p51, 153
  lo más grande *biggest,*
  largest

¡Grandioso! *Great! interj*
griego -a *Greek adj* p81
la grieta *f crack (in glass*
  object) n
el grifo *m faucet n*
gris *gray adj*

gritar *to shout v* p22
grueso -a *thick adj*
el grupo *m group n* p44
el guante *m glove n* p172
guapo *handsome adj* p117
guardar *to keep v* p22
la guardería infantil *f nursery n*
el guardia *m guard n* p37

  el guardia de seguridad
  security guard p37

guatemalteco -a *Guatemalan*
  adj p120
la guerra *f war n* p126
la guía *f guide (publication) n*
el / la guía *m f guide (of tours) n*
guiar *to guide v* p22
guiar, manejar *to drive v* p22
la guitarra *f guitar n* p129
gustar *to like* See p22
  (explanation of gustar)
  to please v p34
el gusto *m taste (discernment) n*

H

la habitación *f room (hotel) n*
hablar *to speak v, to talk v* p22

  Se habla inglés aquí.
  English spoken here.

hacer *to do v, to make v* p30
hacer efectivo *to cash v* p30
hacer juego *to match v* p30
hacer las paces *to make up*
  (apologize) v p30

hacia *toward* prep

halar *to pull* v **p22**

¿Hay ___? *Is / Are there ___?*

hecho de *made of* adj

la hectárea f *hectare* n **p10**

la herida f *injury* n **p16**

la hermana f *sister* n

el hermano m *brother* n **p115**

el hielo m *ice* n **p87**

con hielo *on the rocks*

la máquina de hielo *ice machine*

la hierba f *herb* n

la hija f *daughter* n **p117**

el hijo m *son* n **p117**

el hindú m, la hindú f *Hindu* n

hip-hop *hip-hop* n **p174**

la historia f *history* n **p131**

histórico -a *historical* adj

el hogar m *home* n

la hoja del limpiaparabrisas f *wiper blade* n

hola *hello* n **p1**

el hombre m *man* n

hondureño -a *Honduran* adj

el honorario m *fee (professional)* n

la hora f *hour* n, *time* n **p139**

el horario m *hours, schedule (at museum)* n

el horario m *schedule* n, *timetable (train)* n **p59**

la hospedería de cama y desayuno f *bed-and-breakfast (B & B)* n

la hospedería f *hostel* n **p66**

el hotel m *hotel* n **p66**

hoy *today* adv **p4**

húmedo -a *humid* adj **p125**

I

la identificación f *identification* n **p46**

el idioma m *language* n

la iglesia f *church* n **p126**

igualar *to match* v **p22**

el impedimento m, la persona con impedimento f *handicap* n

con impedimentos auditivos *hearing-impaired* adj

el impresionismo m *Impressionism* n

imprimir *to print* v **p23**

el impuesto m *tax* n **p155**

impuesto al valor agregado (IVA) *value-added tax (VAT)*

la incapacidad f *disability* n

la indigestión f *indigestion* n

el infante m *infant* n

la información f *information* n

el ingeniero m, la ingeniera f *engineer* n **p122**

Inglaterra f *England* n

inglés, inglesa *English* adj **p72**

el inodoro *m* *toilet* n p76
el insecto *m* *bug* n p87
insultar *to insult* v p22
intentar *to try (attempt)* v p22
el / la Internet *m* *Internet* n p68

¿Dónde puedo encontrar un cibercafé? *Where can I find an Internet café?*

el / la intérprete *m f* *interpreter* n p194
el intervalo *m* *intermission* n
intolerante a la lactosa *lactose-intolerant* adj p86
el invierno *m* *winter* n p15
el invitado *m* / la invitada *f* *guest* n
ir *to go* v (See *Future* p25)
ir a los clubes nocturnos *to go clubbing* v (See *Future* p25)
ir de compras *to shop* v (See *Future* p25)
Irlanda *f* *Ireland* n
irlandés, irlandesa *Irish* adj
italiano -a *Italian* adj p120
izquierdo -a *left* adj p5

J

el jabón *m* *soap* n p16
japonés, japonesa *Japanese* adj p120
el jazz *m* *jazz* n p128

el jefe *m*, la jefa *f* *boss* n
joven *young* adj p116
judío -a *Jewish* adj p127
jueves *m* *Thursday* n p14
jugar golf *to go golfing* v p22
jugar *to play (a game)* v p22
el jugo *m* *juice* n p100
el jugo de fruta *m* *fruit juice* n
el jugo de naranja *m* *orange juice* n
el juguete *m* *toy* n
la juguetería *f* *toy store* n
julio *m* *July* n p14
junio *m* *June* n p14

K

kilo *m* *kilo* n p11
kioska *m* *newsstand* n p38
kilómetro *m* *kilometer* n p10
kósher *kosher* adj p85

L

lacio -a *straight (hair)* adj
el lado *m* *side* n p86
al lado *on the side (e.g., salad dressing)* p85
al lado *next* prep p5
del lado *next to*
largo -a *long* adj p10
largo *long* adj p10
más largo *longer*
lo más largo *longest*

SPANISH—ENGLISH

la lata f can n
el lavamanos m sink n
lavanda lavender adj
la lavandería f laundry n p74
la lección f lesson n p173
la leche f milk n p90
el batido de leche milk shake
el lector de discos compactos m CD player n
leer to read v p23
lejos far adj p5
más lejos farther
lo más lejos farthest
lentamente slowly adv
el lente de contacto m contact lens n
lento -a slow adj p179
el letrero de carretera cerrada m road closed sign n
la ley f law n
la libra f pound n
libre de impuestos duty-free adj
la librería f bookstore n p156
el libro m book n p156
la licencia f license n p193
la licencia de conducir driver's license
la placa de matrícula automobile license plate
el licor m liqueur, liquor n
el límite de velocidad m speed limit n p56

la limonada f lemonade n
la limusina f limo n p57
el limpiaparabrisas m windshield wiper n
limpiar to clean v p22
la limpieza en seco f dry cleaning n
limpio -a clean neat (tidy) adj
el litro m liter n p10
la llamada para despertar f wake-up call n p75
la llamada telefónica f phone call n
la llamada con cobro revertido collect phone call
la llamada internacional international phone call
la llamada de larga distancia long-distance phone call
llamar to call (shout) v p22
llamar por altavoces to page (someone) v p22
llamar, telefonear to call (to phone) v p22
la llanta f tire n p53
la llanta de repuesto spare tire n
las llegadas f pl arrivals n
llegar to arrive v p22
lleno -a full adj p90
llevar to take v p22

llevarse el dinero to cash out (gambling) **p30**, p185

llover to rain v **p31** (conjugate like poder)

lluvioso -a rainy adj p125

local local adj p60

la lona f canvas (fabric) n p49

luego, más tarde later adv

Hasta luego. See you later.

el lugar de reunión m hangout (hot spot) n

la lumbre f light (for cigarette) n p176

¿Puedo ofrecerle lumbre? May I offer you a light?

el lunar m mole (facial feature) n

lunes m Monday n p13

la luz f light (lamp) n p48

la luz indicadora light (on car dashboard)

la luz del freno brake light

la luz de examinar el motor check engine light p53

el foco delantero headlight

la luz del aceite oil light p53

M

la madre f mother n p115

la madrugada f dawn n p13

¡Maldición! Damn! expletive

la maleta f suitcase n p49

el maletín m briefcase n p49

la mamá f mom n, mommy n

manejar to handle v **p22**

Manejar con cuidado. Handle with care p141.

la mano f hand n p179

la mantequilla f butter n p86

el manual m manual (instruction booklet) n p52

el mañana m tomorrow n adv

la mañana f morning n p13

en la mañana in the morning p73

el mapa m map n p55

el mapa a bordo onboard map

el maquillaje m makeup n

maquillar to make up (apply cosmetics) v **p22**

la máquina f machine n p75

la máquina de rayos X x-ray machine

la máquina expendedora vending machine

marcar to dial (a phone number) v **p22**

marcar directo to dial direct

mareado -a dizzy adj / seasick adj p62, 189

el mareo por el movimiento del auto m carsickness n

los mariscos m seafood n p81

marrón brown adj p119

martes m Tuesday n p13

marzo *m* March (month)*n*

el masaje en la espalda *m* back rub*n* p180

masculino *male*adj

el matador *m* bullfighter*n*

mayo *m* May (month)*n*

la media *f* sock*n*

media libra half-pound

mediano -a medium*adj* (size) p12

la medianoche *f* midnight adv p13

la medicina *f* / **el medicamento** *m* medicine*n*, medication*n*

medio -a half*adj*, one-half adj p8

en medio middle*adj* p42

medio bien cocido medium well (meat)*adj* p85

a medio cocer medium rare (meat)*adj*

el mediodía noon*n* p13

medir to measure*v* / to try on (clothing)*v* **p32** (conjugate like pedir)

mejor best. See good

mejor better. See good

la mejora de categoría *f* upgrade*n* p52

la membresía *f* membership*n*

menos less*See* poco p155

al menos *f* at least*n*

el menú *m* menu*n* p82

el menú para niños children's menu

el menú para diabéticos diabetic menu

el menú de comidas para llevar takeout menu

el mercado *m* market*n*

el mercado de pulgas / el pulguero flea market*p*150

el mercado al aire libre open-air market

el mes *m* month*n* p4

la mesa *f* table*n* p21

el metro *m* subway*n* / meter*n*

la línea del metro subway line

la estación del metro subway station

¿Cuál metro tomo para _____? Which subway do I take for _____?

mexicano -a Mexican*adj* p120

la mezquita *f* mosque*n* p126

el miembro *m* member*n*

miércoles *m* Wednesday*n*

mil thousand*n* adj p8

el mililitro *m* milliliter*n*

el milímetro *m* millimeter*n*

la milla *f* mile*n* p10

el minibar *m* minibar*n*

el mínimo *m* least. See little

el minuto *m* minute*n* p4

en un minuto in a minute

mirar *to look (observe) v* **p22**
  ¡Mira aquí! *Look here!*
la mitad *f half n*
la moneda *f coin n*
la montaña *f mountain n*
  el escalado de montaña
  mountain climbing
morado -a *purple adj*
el moreno *m,* **la morena** *f*
  brunette n p117
el mostrador *m counter*
  (for check-in or tickets) n
  p36
mostrar *to show v* **p22**
  ¿Puede mostrarme?
  Would you show me?
la motocicleta *f motorcycle n*
la motoneta *f scooter n* p51
el motor *m engine n* p53
mover *to move v* **p2**
  (like poder)
la mucama *f maid (hotel) n*
la muchacha *f girl n*
mucho -a *much adj* p11
muchos -as *many adj* p11
la mujer *f woman n*
la multa *f fine (for traffic*
  violation) n p193
el museo *m museum n* p130
la música *f music n* p128
  la música pop *pop music*
el musical *m musical*
  (music genre) n

músico -a *musical adj*
el músico *m musician n* p123
el musulmán *m,* **la**
  musulmana *f Muslim n adj*
  p127
muy *very* p78

N

la nacionalidad *f nationality n*
nadar *to swim v* **p22**
  Prohibido nadar. *Swimming*
  prohibited.
la naranja *f orange n*
la nariz *f nose n* p188
el naufragio *m shipwreck n*
la náusea *f nausea n* p187
necesitar *to need v* **p22**
el negocio *m business n*
de negocios *business adj* p73
  el centro de negocios
  business center p73
negro -a *black adj* p118
neozelandés, neozelandesa
  New Zealander adj
nicaragüense *Nicaraguan adj*
  p120
ninguno -a *none n* p11
la niña *f little girl n*
la niñera *f babysitter n*
el niño *m boy n, kid n*
los niños *m pl children n pl*
no *no adj adv* p1

la noche *f night n*
  anoche *last night*
  en la noche *at night*
  por noche *per night* p70
de no fumar *nonsmoking adj*
  el área de no fumar
    nonsmoking area
  el carro de no fumar
    nonsmoking car
  la habitación de no fumar
    nonsmoking room
el nombre *m name n* p114
  **Me llamo ____. / Mi nombre
  es ____.** *My name is ____.*
  **¿Cómo se llama? / ¿Cuál es
  su nombre?** *What's your
  name?*
  el primer nombre *first name*
nosotros -as *we, us pron pl*
la novela *f novel n*
  la novela de misterio
    mystery novel
  la novela de romance
    romance novel
noveno -a *ninth n adj* p10
noventa *ninety n adj* p8
la novia *f girlfriend n* p115
noviembre *m November n*
el novio *m boyfriend n* p115
nublado -a *cloudy adj* p125
Nueva Zelanda *f New Zealand n*
nueve *nine n adj* p7
nuevo -a *new adj* p160

la nuez *f nut n*
el número *m number n* p124

O

la obra de teatro *f play n*
observar *to watch v* p22
occidental *western adj*
ochenta *m eighty n adj* p8
ocho *m eight n adj* p7
octavo *m eighth n adj* p9
  tres octavos *three eighths*
octubre *m October n* p15
ocupado -a *busy adj (phone
  line), occupied adj* p61
el oficial *m officer n* p45
la oficina del doctor *m
  doctor's office n*
ofrecer *to offer v* p23
oír *to hear v*
el ojo *m eye n* p184
¡Ojos de serpiente!
  Snake eyes! n
oler *to smell v* p23
once *eleven n adj* p7
la onza *f ounce n*
la ópera *f opera n* p128
el operador *m,* **la operadora**
  f operator (phone) n p72
el oporto *m port (beverage) n*
el optometrista *m optometrist n*
ordenar *to order (request) v* p22
orgánico -a *organic adj*

el órgano *m organ n*

oro (color) *gold (color) adj*

el oro *m gold n*

la orquesta sinfónica *f symphony n*

ortodoxo griego *Greek Orthodox adj* p127

la oscuridad *f darkness n*

oscuro -a *dark adj*

el otoño *m autumn (fall season) n* p15

otro -a *another adj* p48, 72

P

el padre *m father, parent n*

pagar *to pay v* **p22**

el paisaje *m landscape (painting) n*

el pájaro *m bird n*

el pájaro carpintero *m woodpecker n*

el palco *m box (seat) n* p165

pálido -a *pale adj* p118

el pan *m bread n* p100

panameño -a *Panamanian adj* p121

el pantalón *m pair of pants n*

el pantalón de traje de baño *swim trunks n*

los pantalones cortos *shorts*

el pañal *m diaper n*

el pañal de paño *cloth diaper*

el pañal desechable *disposable diaper*

el papel *m paper n* p100

el plato de papel *paper plate* p100

la servilleta de papel *paper napkin* p100

el papel higiénico *m toilet paper n*

el paquete *m package n* p110

el parabrisas *m windshield n*

la parada *f stop n* p57

la parada del autobús *bus stop*

paraguayo -a *Paraguayan adj* p121

pararse *to stand v* **p22**, 35

¡Par de ases! *Snake eyes! n*

PARE *STOP (traffic sign)*

el pariente *m*, la pariente *f relative n*

el parque *m park n* p130

el partido *m match (sport) n*

el partido político *m political party n* p126

el pasajero *m*, la pasajera *f passenger n* p48

el pasaporte *m passport n*

pasar *to pass (gambling) v* **p22**

la pasarela *f walkway n*

la pasarela mecánica *moving walkway*

pasar el rato *to hang out (relax) v* **p22**

el pasatiempo *m hobby n*

el pasillo *m* aisle (in store) *n* / hallway *n* p100

el patio de juegos *m* playground *n*

el pato *m* duck *n*

el pavo *m* turkey *n* p96

el peaje *m* toll *n* p56

peatonal *pedestrian adj*

el distrito de compras peatonal *pedestrian shopping district*

la peca *f* freckle *n*

el / la pediatra *pediatrician n*

pedir *to order, request, ask v* p32

la pelea de gallos *f* cockfight *n*

la película *f* movie *n* p145

el peligro *m* danger *n* p56

el pelirrojo *m*, la pelirroja *f* redhead *n* adj p117

el pelo *m* hair *n* p118

el peluquero *m*, la peluquera *f* hairdresser *n*

el pensamiento *m* thought *n* / pansy *n*

peor *worse. See bad*

lo peor *worst. See bad*

pequeño -a *small adj, short adj, little adj* p11

pequeño *small, little* p11
más pequeño *smaller, littler*
lo mas pequeño *smallest, littlest*

la percha *f* hanger *n*

perder *to lose v* / *to miss (a flight) v* p23, 29 (conjugate like *tener*)

perdido -a *missing adj, lost adj* p56

el periódico *m* newspaper *n*

el permanente *m* permanent (hair) *n*

el permiso *m* permit *n*

permitir *to permit v* p23

el perro *m* dog *n* p43

el perro de servicio *service dog* p70

la persona *f* person *n*

la persona con impedimentos visuales *visually-impaired person*

el personal *m* staff (employees) *n* p78

el peruano *m*, la peruana *f* Peruvian *n* adj p121

pesar *to weigh v* p22

las pesas *f pl* weights *n* p161

la pestaña *f* eyelash *n*

el piano *m* piano *n* p129

el pie *m* foot (body part) *n*, foot (unit of measurement) *n* p10

la piel *f* skin *n*

la pierna *f* leg *n*

la pila *f* battery (for flashlight) *n*

la píldora *f* pill *n*

la píldora para el mareo *f* seasickness pill

la pinta *f* pint *n* p11

pintar *to paint v* p22

la pintura *f* painting *n*

la **piscina** f pool (swimming) n
el **piso** m floor n p71

el primer piso ground floor, first floor p69

la **pizza** f pizza n p80
el **placer** m pleasure n p1

Es un placer. It's a pleasure.

el **plan de tarifa** m rate plan (cell phone) n

¿Tiene un plan de tarifa? Do you have a rate plan?

el **plástico** m plastic n p50
plata silver (color) adj
la **plata** f silver n
plateado -a silver adj
el **plato** m dish n p85
la **playa** f beach n p130
poco -a little adj p11
un **poco** m bit (small amount) n
poco profundo -a shallow adj
poder to be able to (can) v, may v aux p31

¿Puedo _____? May I _____?

la **policía** f police n p37
el **pollo** m chicken n p96
poner to put (gambling) v p23

¡Ponlo en rojo / negro! Put it on red / black! p184

popular popular adj p175
por adelantado in advance adv
la **porción** f portion (of food) n
por favor please (polite entreaty) adv p1

el **portero** m, la **portera** f goalie n, porter n p36, 164
la **postal** f postcard n
el **postre** m dessert n p88

el menú de postres dessert menu p88

el **precio** m price n

de precio moderado moderately priced p66

preferiblemente preferably adj
preferir to prefer v p23
preguntar to ask v p22
preparado -a prepared adj
presentar to introduce v p22

Quisiera presentarle a _____. I'd like to introduce you to _____.

presupuestar to budget v p22
el **presupuesto** m budget n
la **primavera** f spring (season) n p15
primero -a first adj p9
el **primo** m, la **prima** f cousin n
el **probador** m fitting room n
probar to taste v, to try (food) v p22
el **problema** m problem n p2
procesar to process (a transaction) v p22
el **producto** m product n
profesional professional adj
profundo -a deep adj p169

el programa *m program n*

el prometido *m,* la prometida
f fiancé(e) n

el pronóstico del tiempo *m*
weather forecast n

la propina *f tip (gratuity)* p90

propina incluida *tip*
included p90

protector solar *m sunscreen n*

protestante *Protestant n adj*

próximo -a *next prep* p4

la próxima estación *the*
next station

el puente *m bridge (across a*
river) n / *bridge (dental*
structure) n p192

el puerco *m pig n*

la puerta *f door n*

la puerta de salida *gate*
(at airport) p36

el puerto *port (for ship*
mooring) n p62

el puerto USB *m USB port n*

puertorriqueño -a *Puerto*
Rican adj

el puesto de información *m*
information booth n p37

la pulgada *f inch n* p10

en punto *o'clock adv* p4

dos en punto *two o'clock*

la puntuación *f score n*

Q

qué *what adv* p3

¿Qué hubo? *What's up?*

quedar *to hold (gambling) v*
p22

quedarse *to stay v* p22, 35

la quemadura de sol *f*
sunburn n

quemar *to burn v* p22

querer *to want v* p31

el queso *m cheese n* p100

quién *who adv* p3

¿De quién es _____?
Whose is _____?

quince *m fifteen n adj*

el quinto *m fifth n adj*

quiosco *m newsstand* p156

el quiropráctico *m*
chiropractor n p188

R

la radio *m radio n*

la radio por satélite
satellite radio

la rampa para sillas de ruedas
f wheelchair ramp n

rápido -a *fast adj* p56, 179

el rasguño *m scratch n*

el ratón *m mouse n*

rayado -a *scratched adj* p53

rayar *to scratch v* p22

a rayas *striped adj*

el reabastecimiento *m refill*
(of prescription) n p188

recargar *to charge (a battery)* v
p22

la recepción *f front desk* n

la receta *f prescription* n p45

rechazado -a *declined adj*

> Su tarjeta de crédito fue
> rechazada. *Your credit
> card was declined.*

recibir *to receive* v p23

el recibo *m receipt* n p133

el reclamo *m claim* n

recolectar *to collect* v p22

recomendar *to recommend* v
p22

recortar *to trim (hair)* v p22

el recorte de pelo *m haircut* n

recto -a *straight adj*

la red *f network* n

la red inalámbrica *f wi-fi* n

reducir la velocidad *to slow
down* v **p33** (conjugate
like *conocer*)

> ¡Reduzca la velocidad!
> *Slow down!* p58

el refresco *m soda* n p47

> el refresco dietética
> *diet soda* p47

el regalo *m gift* n

el reggae *m reggae* n p128

regresar *to return (to a
place)* v p22

relajarse *to lounge* v p22, 35

el reloj *m clock* n, *watch* n

el reloj despertador *alarm
clock* p75

remover *to remove* v **p23, 31**
(conjugate like *poder*)

repartir *to deal (cards)* v p23

> Repártame las cartas. *Deal
> me in.* p184

el repelente para insectos *m
insect repellent* n p187

repetir *to repeat* v **p23, 32**
(conjugate like *pedir*)

> ¿Puede repetir eso por
> favor? *Would you please
> repeat that?* p2

la reservación *m reservation* n

el resfriado *m cold (illness)* n

residencial *home adj*

> la dirección residencial
> *home address*
> el número de teléfono
> residencial *home
> telephone number*

el restaurante *m restaurant* n

> el restaurante de parrilla
> *steakhouse*

retirar *to withdraw* v **p22**

el retiro *m withdrawal* n

el retraso *m delay* n p44

el retrato *m portrait* n

la revista *f magazine* n

el río *m river* n p169

rizado -a *curly adj* p118

el rizo *m curln*
robado -a *stolenadj* p49
robar *to robv, to stealv* p22
la roca *f rockn*
el rock and roll *m rock and rolln* p128
rojo -a *redadj* p184
romántico -a *romanticadj*
romper *to breakv* p23
el ron *m rumn* p89
la ropa interior *f underwearn*
la rosa *f rosen*
rosado -a *pinkadj*
el rubio *m*, **la rubia** *f blond(e)n adj* p117
con ruedas *wheeled (luggage)adj*
ruidoso -a *loud, noisyadj 77*

S

sábado *m Saturdayn* p14
la sábana *f sheet (bed linen)n*
saber *to know (something)v* p33
el sabor *m taste, flavorn*
el sabor a chocolate *chocolate flavor*
la sal *f saltn* p108
la sala de degustación *m tasting roomn*
bajos en sal *low-salt*
la salida *f check-outn / departuren / exitn* p39

la hora de salida *check-out time*
no es salida *not an exit*
la salida de emergencia *emergency exitp42*
salir *to leave (depart)v* p23
salir de conocer *sightseev*
el salón público *m loungen*
la salsa *f saucen*
salvadoreño -a *Salvadoran adj* p121
el salvavidas *m life preservern*
el sastre *m tailorn* p74
el satélite *m satelliten* p68
la radio satélite *satellite radio*
rastreo por satélite *satellite tracking*
secado -a *driedadj* p159
la secadora de pelo *f hair dryern* p159
secar *to dryv* p22
seco -a *dryadj*
la seda *f silkn* p151
el sedán *m sedann*
segundo -a *secondadj* p9
la seguridad *f securityn* p36
el punto de control de seguridad *security checkpoint*
la guardia de seguridad *security guardp37*
el seguro *m insurancen* p193

el seguro para colisiones
collision insurance

**el seguro de
responsabilidad civil**
liability insurance

seguro -a *safe (secure)adj*

seis *sixn adj* p7

la semana *f weekn* p4, 14

esta semana *this week*

la semana pasada *last week*

la próxima semana *next week*

una semana *one week*p14

dentro de una semana *a
week from now*

sencillo -a *singlen adj / simple
adj*

sencillo *straight up (drink)*

el sendero *m trailn* p168

sentar *to sitv* p22

señalar *to pointv* p22

**la señal para ceder
el paso** *f yield signn*

separado -a *separated
(marital status)adj* p116

septiembre *m Septembern*

séptimo -a *seventhn adj* p9

ser *to be (permanent quality)
v* p28

el servicio *m servicen* p43

fuera de servicio *out of
service*p136

el servicio *m service
(religious)n* p127

la servilleta *f napkinn*

servir *to servev* **p23, 32**
(conjugate like *pedir*)

sesenta *sixtyn adj* p8

setenta *seventyn adj* p7

el sexo *m sex (gender)n*

sí *yesadv* p1

siete *sevenn adj* p7

la silla de ruedas *f
wheelchairn* p70

**el acceso para sillas de
ruedas** *wheelchair access*

rampa para sillas de ruedas
wheelchair ramp

la silla de ruedas eléctrica
power wheelchair

sin *withoutprep* p87

snorkel *m snorkeln*

el sobre *m envelopen* p143

sobrecalentar *to overheatv*
p22

sobrecocido -a *overcooked
adj*

la sobrina *f niecen* p115

el sobrino *m nephewn* p115

el socialismo *m socialismn*

la soda *f sparkling watern*

el software *m softwaren*

el sol *m sunn*

soleado *sunnyadj* p125

soltero -a *single (unmarried)
adj* p116

Eres soltero / soltera?
*Are you single?*p116

el sombrero *m hat n* p152
la sombrilla *f umbrella n*
la sopa *f soup n* p16
sordo -a *deaf adj*
sospechosamente
  suspiciously adv p48
suave *soft adj*
el subtítulo *m subtitle n*
el suburbio *m slum n* p16
suelto -a *loose adj* p153
el suéter *m sweater n* p46
la suite *f suite n* p69
la suite de lujo *f penthouse n*
sujetar *to hold v* p22

  sujetar las manos *to hold hands*

el supermercado *m supermarket n*
surfear *to surf v* p22

  la tabla de surf *surfboard n*

la sustitución *f substitution n*
suyo -a *your, yours adj sing (formal)*

T

la taberna *f bar n*
la talla *f size (clothing, shoes) n*
también *too (also) adv* p171
el tambor *m drum n*
el tanque de oxígeno *m oxygen tank n*
tarde *late adj* p13

  Por favor no llegues tarde.
  Please don't be late.

la tarde *f afternoon n* p13

  en la tarde *in the afternoon*

la tarifa *f fare n / rate n*

  la tarifa de admisión
  admission fee n p148

la tarjeta *f card n* p122

  la tarjeta de crédito
  credit card p133

  ¿Aceptan tarjetas de crédito? *Do you accept credit cards?*

  la tarjeta de embarque *f boarding pass n* p45

  la tarjeta de presentación
  business card

la tasa de cambio *f exchange rate n* p133

la tasa de interés *f interest rate n*

el taxi *m taxi n* p57

  ¡Taxi! *Taxi!*

  la parada de los taxis
  taxi stand

el té *m tea n* p90

  el té con leche y azúcar
  tea with milk and sugar

  el té con limón *tea with lemon*

  el té de hierbas *herbal tea*

el teatro *m theater n* p144

el teatro de ópera *m opera house n* p146

el techno *m techno n (music)*

el techo *m roof n*
  el techo corredizo *sunroof*
la tela *f fabric n*
telefónico *phone adj* p179
  el directorio telefónico
    phone directory
el teléfono *m phone n*
  el teléfono celular
    cell phone p134
  ¿Me puede dar su número de teléfono? *May I have your phone number?* p179
  el operador *m /*
  la operadora *f de teléfono*
    phone operator
  teléfonos prepagados
    prepaid phones
la televisión *f television n*
  la televisión por cable
    cable television p68
  la televisión por satélite
    satellite television p68
el templo *m temple n* p126
temprano *early adj* p13
tener *to have v* p29
  tener relaciones *to have sex (intercourse)*
el tenis *m tennis n* p67
tercero -a *third n adj* p9
el terminal *m terminal (airport) n* p39
la tía *f aunt n* p115
tirar la cadena del inodoro
    to flush v p22

el tiempo *m time n* p167
la tienda *f shop n, store n*
la tintorería *f dry cleaner n*
el tío *m uncle n* p115
el tipo *m kind (sort, type) n*
la toalla *f towel n*
tocar *to touch v / to play (an instrument) v* p22
todo -a *all adj* p11
  todo el tiempo *all the time*
  Eso es todo. *That's all.*
tomar *to take v* p22
  ¿Cuánto tiempo tomará esto? *How long will this take?*
la tonelada *f ton n*
el torero *m bullfighter n*
el toro *m bull n*
la tos *f cough n*
toser *to cough v* p23
el total *m total n*
  ¿Cuál es el total? *What is the total?*
trabajar *to work v* p22
  Yo trabajo para _____.
    I work for _____.
  ¿En qué trabaja usted?
    What do you do for a living? p122
el tráfico *m traffic n* p52
  ¿Cómo está el tráfico?
    How's traffic?
  El tráfico es terrible.
    Traffic is terrible.

tragar to swallow v p22

el trago m shot (liquor) n

el traje de baño m swimsuit n

la transacción f transaction n

la transferencia f transfer n

la transferencia de dinero money transfer, wire transfer p132

transferir to transfer v p31 (conjugate like querer)

el tránsito m traffic n

las reglas de tránsito traffic rules

la transmisión f transmission n

la transmisión automática automatic transmission p51

la transmisión manual standard transmission p52

trece thirteen adj p7

treinta thirty adj p8

el tren m train n p58

el tren expreso express train

el tren local local train

la trenza f braid n

tres three n adj p7

triste sad adj p121

triple triple adj p8

la trompeta f trumpet n

trotar jogging n p22

trotar to run v p22

tú you pron sing (informal)

tuyo -a your, yours adj sing (informal)

U

último -a last adv adj n p10

la universidad f university n

uno one n adj p7

la uva f grape n

el uruguayo m, **la uruguaya** f Uruguayan n p121

usar to use v / to wear v p22

usted you pron sing (formal)

ustedes you pron pl

V

la vaca f cow n

las vacaciones f vacation n p44

de vacaciones on vacation

ir de vacaciones to go on vacation

el vacante m vacancy n

no hay vacantes no vacancy

el vale m voucher n p44

el vale para comida meal voucher p44

el vale para hospedaje room voucher p44

la van f van n

de vaqueros western adj (movie)

varar to beach v p22

el varón m male (person) n

el vecino m, **la vecina** f neighbor n p115

el **vegetal** *m* *vegetable n*
el **vegetariano** *m*, la **vegeta-riana** *f* *vegetarian n adj*
veinte *twenty n adj* **p7**
la **vela** *f* *sail n*
la **velocidad de conexión** *f* *connection speed n*
el **velocímetro** *m* *speedometer n*
el **vendedor** *m*, la **vendedora** *f* *salesperson n* **p122**
el **vendedor callejero** *m*, la **vendedora callejera** *f* *street vendor*
vender *to sell v* **p23**
venezolano -a *Venezuelan adj*
la **ventana** *f* *window n* **p41**
la **ventanilla** *f* *window n*
la **ventanilla de entregas** *drop-off window* **p142**
la **ventanilla de retiros** *pickup window* **p142**
ventoso -a *windy adj* **p125**
ver *to see v* **p23**
¿**Puedo verlo?** *May I see it?*
el **verano** *m* *summer n* **p15**
verdaderamente *really adj*
verde *green adj* **p98**
la **verruga** *f* *wart n*
verse *to look (appear) v* **p23, 35**
la **versión** *f* *version n* **p140**

el **vestido** *m* *dress (garment) n*
la **vestimenta** *f* *clothing (general attire) n* **p175**
vestirse *to dress v* **p32** (conjugate like *pedir*) **p35**
el **vestuario** *m* *changing room n*
viajar *to travel v* **p22**
el **viaje** *m* *trip n* **p111**
la **vida** *f* *life n* **p170**
el **video** *m* *video n*
la **videograbadora** *f* *VCR n*
viejo -a *old adj* **p26**
viernes *m* *Friday n* **p14**
el **vinilo** *m* *vinyl n* **p50**
el **vino** *m* *wine n* **p47**
el **viñedo** *m* *vineyard n*
el **violín** *m* *violin n*
virar *to turn v* **p22**
Vire a la izquierda / derecha. *Turn left / right.*
la **visa** *f* *visa n*
visitar *to visit v* **p22**
la **vista** *f* *view n* / *vision n* **p68**
la **vista a la playa** *beach view* **p68**
la **vista a la ciudad** *city view*
la **viuda** *f* *widow n* **p116**
el **viudo** *m* *widower n* **p116**
vivir *to live v* **p23**
¿**Dónde vives?** *Where do you live?*

el vodka *m vodka n*

vosotros -as *(Spain) you pron*
  pl (informal)

votar *to vote v* **p22**

el vuelo *m flight n* p39
  el / la asistente de vuelo *m*
  f flight attendant

W

windsurf *to windsurf v*

Y

yo *I pron* p3

Z

el zapato *m shoe n*

zarpar *to sail v* **p22**
  ¿Cuándo zarpamos?
  When do we sail?

el zoológico *m zoo n* p130

NOTES (NOTAS)

NOTES (NOTAS)

NOTES (NOTAS)

NOTES (NOTAS)

NOTES (NOTAS)

NOTES (NOTAS)

NOTES (NOTAS)

NOTES (NOTAS)

NOTES (NOTAS)

NOTES (NOTAS)